Why We Need the Huma

Why We Need the Humanities

Life Science, Law and the Common Good

Donald Drakeman

palgrave
macmillan

First published 2016 by
PALGRAVE MACMILLAN

Palgrave Macmillan in the UK is an imprint of Macmillan Publishers Limited, registered in England, company number 785998, of Houndmills, Basingstoke, Hampshire RG21 6XS.

Palgrave Macmillan in the US is a division of St Martin's Press LLC, 175 Fifth Avenue, New York, NY 10010.

Palgrave Macmillan is the global academic imprint of the above companies and has companies and representatives throughout the world.

Palgrave® and Macmillan® are registered trademarks in the United States, the United Kingdom, Europe and other countries.

ISBN 978–1–137–49745–1 hardback
ISBN 978–1–137–49746–8 paperback

This book is printed on paper suitable for recycling and made from fully managed and sustained forest sources. Logging, pulping and manufacturing processes are expected to conform to the environmental regulations of the country of origin.

A catalogue record for this book is available from the British Library.

A catalog record for this book is available from the Library of Congress.

Contents

Preface

A rule of thumb frequently employed in fundraising—whether in the not-for-profit context or the search for investment capital—is to focus the conversation on the interests of the person holding the checkbook. It is easy to see that things will be better for the people who are, in the fundraising vernacular, 'making the ask'. Their university or soup kitchen or start-up will have more funds with which to achieve its goals. The key question for the grant-giver or investor is, 'Why will funding this particular organization, out of all of the many excellent requests I have received, best fulfill *my* mission?' That same question is asked whether the checkbook belongs to the Red Cross or Goldman Sachs, and the mission might be as different as feeding the poor, for one type of check-writer, and helping already wealthy 'accredited investors' become even wealthier, for another. In either case, the fundraiser who successfully closes the deal is the one who best articulates the common interests of both donor and donee. Over the years, numerous humanities scholars have done an excellent job describing why they believe that their discipline should have our support. My goal is to complete the equation by describing why we—the rest of us—should be equally enthusiastic about doing so. We actually need the humanities because of their practical importance in helping policy-makers address issues directly affecting our civil liberties and significant parts of our economies.

My argument here will largely adopt the rhetorical strategy blasted by Cambridge Professor Stefan Collini following the release of a University of Oxford report, 'Humanities Graduates Hidden Impact'. The Oxford report had highlighted the high numbers of humanities graduates with 'successful careers in sectors driving economic growth'.[1] Professor Collini explained, 'This [report] is in effect saying: "Yes, we [the university community] know this is not the real justification for studying these subjects, but there are some people... who can only understand the question in these terms." '[2]

That is, members of the University of Oxford community have—or should have—better reasons for studying the humanities than arguing that they contribute to economic growth. Oxford Professor Helen

Small points out that this 'belief that the humanities, almost by definition, must be at odds with... economic instrumentalism has been a potent strand in English thinking... running through Newman, Mill, and Matthew Arnold in the nineteenth century, and continuing, with what sometimes looks like incremental ferocity, through T.S. Eliot' and others.[3]

Many of these arguments against the economic utility of the humanities emerged from distinguished men of letters who were not primarily academics, but rather drew their income from jobs in government or industry. Mill spent decades with the East India Company, Arnold was a state inspector of schools and Eliot worked in banking and publishing.[4] The increasingly fierce arguments began to arrive later, with twentieth-century university professors such as F.R. Leavis and Geoffrey Hill.[5] These anti-instrumental arguments may resonate differently when funding for humanities scholars is one of the issues being debated. As Professor Small asks, rhetorically, 'Are academics seriously unwilling to concede that activities for which they receive public money should be partly assessed in terms of measurable benefits passed on to society?'[6] Her Oxford colleague, Nigel Biggar adds, 'We shouldn't idealize or overmoralize universities. Right from their medieval beginnings, they have served private purposes and practical public purposes as well as the sheer *amor scientiae*.'[7]

There are certainly a variety of excellent reasons for pursuing the humanities, most of which have nothing to do with economic growth; nevertheless, as the Oxford report pointed out, and as I hope to supplement here, there are places where economic growth and the humanities do actually overlap. Professor Collini would prefer not to bring that subject up because 'those who live by the sword of contributing to economic growth will die by that sword'.[8] He is probably right: hence the periodic shift of interest toward more practical courses of study in economically trying times. But that phenomenon, at least so far, has been more ebbing-and-flowing than living-and-dying,[9] and especially during the low ebbs, it may be useful for supporters of the humanities to remind everyone else that there are, in fact, connections between the humanities and very important aspects of modern life, including significant portions of the economy.

Those favoring non-economic arguments, including non-instrumental arguments, may worry that, once the subject of practical outcomes, and especially of economic growth, arises, metric-loving, impact-measuring policy-makers will subject the humanities to the kinds of quality assurance and productivity analyses normally associated with corporate efficiency experts.[10] In the STEM (that is, Science, Technology, Engineering and Math) fields, there are numerous things to count: grants come in denominations such as dollars, pounds or euros; patent filings are visible signs of potentially practical innovation; and multi-authored papers allow for quantities of peer-reviewed publications that are virtually unimaginable for those outside science and engineering. The fear of inappropriate modes of measurement, combined with invidious comparisons to the STEM disciplines, is a legitimate concern, but not necessarily one that should cause us to ignore or downplay the connections between real world effects and the humanities where they actually exist. Rather, those who see the connections should consider how to make the case in a manner that illustrates why the imposition of arbitrary measurements on 'productivity in the humanities' may be the wrong thing to do. A field of study that is frequently hailed for its ability to foster critical thinking and persuasive communication skills ought not shy away from making complex and nuanced arguments on its own behalf.

Instead, these value-of-the-humanities discussions have a tendency to be marked by a considerable amount of exasperation, and a general sense on all sides along the lines of, 'I can't believe we have to have this conversation.' As Berkeley Professor Judith Butler has written, 'What is, of course, so increasingly difficult is that we [humanities scholars] are now under pressure to ... defend a set of ... beliefs that we have taken to be true, and whose value informs our daily practices and broader sense of vocation.' These matters are 'such basic issues for educators that I find myself stumbling here .... A gap has emerged between this discourse, one that I would have thought was obvious, and a new metrics of value that is making ... a claim on the obvious.'[11] As a result, she writes, 'Sometimes I find myself quite incredulous because I mistakenly thought the public value of these activities is so obvious that they hardly needed to be defended.'[12]

We can see similar feelings on the funding side of the discussion in a review by UK universities and science minister David Willetts of Stefan Collini's, *What Are Universities For?*[13] In a generally laudatory review, Willetts summarizes Collini's book as arguing 'that universities are not...badly run businesses', and says that Collini makes 'a persuasive case for the humanities as a distinct form of intellectual inquiry that is worthwhile in itself'. After praising the book and expressing his agreement 'with all these propositions', Willetts concludes, 'But I simply do not recognize his attempt to apply these wide propositions to higher education policy today.'[14]

For every scholar who follows Jonathan Bate in saying that the value of humanities research is that it is 'the only activity that can establish the meaning of such a question',[15] there are real world analysts ready with a contrary response. 'We have plenty of tools with which to calculate the value', they would argue: 'A market analysis will tell us how many people will pay for a humanities education; we can model that out fifteen or twenty years, take into account the economic contributions of those humanities graduates, subtract the social costs of the unemployed ones, and then do a discounted cash flow analysis to tell you exactly what your department or degree is worth—to the penny.' In fact, just such a set of calculations has likely been involved when investors have considered providing funding for for-profit colleges and universities, from the intensely practical University of Phoenix to London's New College of the Humanities.

I actually stand with Professor Bate on this issue, but those of us who agree with that view need to work harder to show the checkbook-holders that there are, in fact, important issues of the humanities hidden within the assumptions employed in those economic models. Classics Professor and college president Georgia Nugent may be right when she says, 'We have come to rely on the explanatory power of quantification beyond its usefulness,'[16] but it is not enough for the classicists to reach that conclusion. The financial analysts who employ those quantitative tools need to realize that their analyses often rest on a foundation of assumptions that are, at the very least, open to question. Or, put somewhat differently, the lack of more courses on the epistemological foundations of modern statistics and financial modeling—for non-academics, a rough translation is: 'Do these models really tell us what we think they do?'—is a loss for the humanists and the quants alike.

From time to time over the past millennium, some scholars could afford to inhabit an intellectual universe detached from the many complexities of the people and the problems that made up the so-called real world. At some times, religious organizations or political rulers generously supported humanities scholarship for the greater glory of God or country, and, at other times, economic prosperity trickled down to the universities, and thus to humanities scholarship. In other times and places, some of the people who have wanted to study and write about the humanities have dedicated their efforts largely to the intrinsic value of doing so, that is, they did not expect a paycheck for their efforts. James Turner's study of philologists' progress through the ages includes the story of the great brother–sister pair of British scholars Will and Elizabeth Elstob in the early eighteenth century. Thomas Jefferson studied Elizabeth's Anglo-Saxon grammar, but the international market for Anglo-Saxon textbooks was apparently too small: '[D]ebts that she and her brother ran up to finance their scholarship' required her eventually, after the brother's death, to flee 'to evade debtor's prison, living for years under an assumed name'.[17]

Scholars unable to fund their own research, or unwilling to follow the Elstobs into debt, have needed to convince someone—governments, trustees, students and any others who might become patrons of the (liberal) arts—that doing so will be worth the money. There is a rich and lengthy history of professors and other university leaders reaching out to potential donors for funds to support their colleges and universities. We can see the success of these efforts in names that may now be nearly as commonly associated with colleges, universities and scholarships as with their business endeavors, such as Rockefeller, Stanford, Vanderbilt, Rhodes and, more recently, Templeton, and, perhaps someday, even Gates. Beyond philanthropy, educational fees have been a regular supporter of the humanities even, or especially, when, in the case of younger professors, they might need to have been 'collected…directly and per head from [the] students'.[18]

The humanities will probably never be divorced from the need to ask for money. To attract financial support from public or private sources, particularly during economically lean times, humanities scholars may find it both true and potentially useful, at least for fundraising purposes, to show that the rigorous study of their disciplines and the insights of their research will enliven and enrich the way people think about very practical and important things, such as medicine, business, the economy and civil liberties. Much of this book, therefore, focuses on the surprising degree to which the humanities have been essential for two seemingly disparate areas of modern life: biomedical research and civil liberties. These sometimes literally life-and-death arenas involve a very large portion of our economies, and touch our daily lives. They also share a crucial common attribute. In both of these fields, a fairly small number of people routinely make decisions that directly affect the quality (and indeed the quantity) of all of our lives. That is, these two areas involve decisions with far-reaching national consequences that are often made by small, unelected and, not necessarily representative, governmental bodies. The individuals making up these powerful arms of the government have relied heavily on the work of humanities scholars to inform and justify their decisions, which are deeply rooted in the kinds of questions to which the study of the humanities has been devoted for a very long time.[19] This message, that important elements of our economy and vital aspects of our lives are based on policy choices influenced by humanities scholarship, bears repeating whenever times get tough, and people begin to say, 'What are the humanities really good for, anyway?'

What do I mean by 'the humanities'?

I am writing specifically about areas where we—all of us—need the answers to specific questions concerning public policy. The humanities that we need are those that can help governmental decision-makers reach answers that best promote the common good. I believe, for the reasons generally articulated in the many books and articles defending the humanities, that we need the humanities even more than I am setting out to defend. Those topics have been well handled by far more thoughtful and influential writers. Here, I will focus on what we need specifically in the context of the public policy questions that require answers. That is, instead of defining the humanities and then trying to describe why we need them, I am first identifying what we need, and then looking for where we can find it, which turns out to be within fields often described as 'the humanities', as well as in some others outside the STEM fields. I am, therefore, not necessarily following either the disciplinary distinctions common to many modern universities, or the various administrative choices that institutions have made to lump scholars into schools and departments or to split them into centers, programs and institutes. Those bureaucratic alignments are unrelated to the basic issue of where we might find helpful insights into the questions presented by our social and political circumstances.

The scholars whose work has been called upon by the relevant decision-makers—primarily, healthcare policy-makers and Supreme Court justices—have been professors of philosophy (both ancient and modern), law and jurisprudence, history, theology and religion, medical ethics, politics and social psychology. A closer look at the works cited by justices and other policy-makers shows that they were written as part of a broader set of academic conversations that include scholars in literature, linguistics and other fields touching on the interpretation of documents, as well as aspects of economics and sociology. This is undoubtedly only a partial list of areas commonly considered within the humanities; it leaves out the fine arts, and a number of other areas for which others have made powerful arguments; and academic observers will note the inclusion of a number of fields that often reside inside divisions or schools of the social sciences within contemporary universities. It may be worth noting that the questions to which society needs answers are much older than these specific academic distinctions.

My point, therefore, is not to propose a comprehensive or ideal definition of the humanities, or to draw a clear distinction between the humanities and other fields dedicated to studying the human condition. It is rather to locate those areas of intellectual inquiry that are likely to help us answer the key questions I have identified. If a more comprehensive definition of the humanities were necessary, I would probably lean toward offering the attractively vague approach philosopher Bernard Williams borrowed from the title of a Gauguin 'grand and, mysterious painting... *Where do we Come From?... What are we?... Where are we Going?*'[20] The last question is a difficult one for everyone, Williams noted, 'whether they are an oracle, a politician or a business analyst'. This is essentially the question raised in chapters 2 and 3, although there it is expressed in the language of rights, justice or fairness. As Williams (rightly, in my view) points out, 'What is certain... is that there is no hope for answering the last question [Where are we Going?] unless we have some ideas for answering the first two'. For Williams, the 'most basic justification of the Humanities... is that our insights into the first two questions essentially involve grasp of humane studies, in particular because the second question involves the first'.[21]

Williams' view of the humanities provides a foundation for the specific areas of research and study discussed in this book. Whether the scholars who have been so influential in leading policy-makers to the choices they made were called philosophers, historians, social psychologists or medical ethicists, they were taking part in society's continuing effort to figure out, as Williams/Gauguin put it so succinctly, 'What are We?' and 'Where are we Going?' which necessarily involves thinking about 'Where Do We Come From?' Alas, there is not enough room in one volume even to attempt to answer any of these fundamental questions. I am hopeful, however, that I can at least add some degree of clarity about where we should look for possible answers to some very specific and important elements of the question, 'Where are we Going?'

In summary, this book will range widely across a series of controversial topics, from the future of high-tech medicine to the nature of religious freedom, which may initially seem to have little in common with one another. My goal is to show how scholarship in the humanities has been at least one important common denominator. One of the biggest challenges in doing so, which is a challenge for higher education in general, is that the various disciplines have become so isolated from each other that even the most thoughtful decision-makers have lost sight of all of the various pieces of the higher education puzzle. While I certainly cannot claim to be able to provide an adequately comprehensive view, I am hopeful that my unusually diverse academic and professional background will allow me to bring some new insights into how the pieces fit together.

I have a PhD in religion and a law degree; I have taught for two decades at Princeton and Notre Dame, primarily in courses on civil liberties and constitutional interpretation; and I have written books for academic presses on the intersection of law, religion, history and politics. At the same time, I have spent over a quarter of a century founding and running biotechnology companies as an entrepreneur, executive and venture capitalist, generally seeking to commercialize academic research in the life sciences in the United States and Europe. On numerous occasions, I have met with Wall Street investors or global pharmaceutical companies during the business day, and then led a group of students through a discussion of civil liberties in the evening. While authors frequently imagine themselves to be uniquely qualified to write about the subjects of their books, I think it is at least fair to say that I bring an unusually broad perspective to this work—one that I hope will be helpful in understanding at least some of the many moving parts of modern higher education. There may be other Entrepreneurs of the Year who are fellows of the Royal Historical Society, but probably not many.

The breadth of my background only extends so far, however, and, as can be seen in this summary, virtually all of my examples are derived from the United States and the United Kingdom, where I have had the opportunity to be involved with a number of excellent companies and terrific universities. Even then, my experience has been considerably more extensive in the United States, and I apologize in advance for places where my observations or phrasing may not resonate equally well on both sides of the Atlantic. As for readers in countries outside the United States and the United Kingdom, I hope they will find some of the insights and arguments here to be useful, even if they have not been specifically directed toward the humanities as they are found around the world.

Why We Need the Humanities has been written for the legislators, education policy-makers, trustees and presidents who decide where to spend higher education's limited resources, and who have been increasingly focused on the promotion of the STEM fields. This science and technology orientation has put pressure on the humanities at a time when students have also been highly concerned about how their undergraduate education will prepare them for successful careers. It also seeks to speak to scientists and entrepreneurs in the STEM fields who may paradoxically have the most to lose from a weakening of the humanities. It is not clear that the study of the humanities necessarily takes resources away from more urgently needed scientific research, and, it may, in fact, be an essential component of STEM's long-term success. Finally, it is addressed to the humanities students and scholars whose work I am encouraging. Interestingly, as I have given talks about these topics to various types of audiences, I have encountered the most resistance from humanities scholars. Scientists, management scholars and practitioners, and the general public seem more willing to take seriously the idea that the humanities can be useful than some of the humanities scholars themselves. I am hopeful, nevertheless, that these scholars will recognize the importance of the issues discussed here, and will take this work to heart.

Donald Drakeman

Acknowledgments

Many people have contributed to the development of my thinking about the role of the humanities in the broader world. I would like to express my thanks with the caveat that they may not all necessarily agree with the ultimate direction of that thinking. And so, I recognize their contributions here with gratitude, and with more than a little emphasis on the standard disclaimer: Joel Alicea, Stephen Blackwood, Nigel Bowles, Kalipso Chalkidou, Janice Chik, Marc DeGirolami, Patrick Deneen, Vince DiMauro, Raymond Dwek, Richard Ekins, Sarah Foot, Rick Garnett, Ben Hardy, Bruce Huber, Peter Kilpatrick, Jeff Kristoff, Richard Mason, John McGreevey, William Modahl, Mark Movsesian, David Murphy, Jim Murphy, Chuma Nwokike, Nektarios Oraiopoulos, Raj Parekh, Michael Poliakoff, Helen Small, Steve Smith, John Valentino, Steve Whelan, Brad Wilson, John Wilson, Paul Yowell, Michael Zuckert and two very helpful anonymous reviewers for Palgrave Macmillan. I would especially like to thank those whose contributions to the direction, shape and existence of this book went well beyond the call of duty: Robert George, Phillip Muñoz, Stefan Scholtes, Stephen Tuck and Robert Weisbuch. Essential to the entire effort was the genuinely outstanding research and editing work of Michael Breidenbach. Additionally, I benefited from the opportunity to receive very thoughtful questions and comments during panels and presentations sponsored by the Centre for Health Leadership & Enterprise at the Judge Business School of the University of Cambridge; the ESTEEM Program and the Graduate Political Theory Colloquium, both at the University of Notre Dame; The James Madison Program in American Ideals and Institutions at Princeton University; and The Oxford Research Centre in the Humanities, whose seminar on "Where's the Virtue in the Humanities?" featured panelists—Jonathan Bate, Steven Biel and Nigel Biggar—who brought unusually deep insights into these topics. I am also grateful to Peter Cary, Jen McCall and their colleagues at Palgrave Macmillan, who made this book possible, and to Marci Friscia, Kathy Gryzeski and Colleen Riegel, without whom there would never have been a manuscript in the first place. Finally, in any household sharing nearly a dozen degrees in the humanities, there are likely to be quite a few conversations about the relationship of the humanities and the real world. I am grateful not only for the love and support of Amy, Cindy and Lisa, but also for their willingness to engage thoughtfully with the themes that appear here when they were just glimmers of ideas.

1
The Ups and Downs of the Humanities

The cartoon cover of a 1935 issue of *The Princeton Tiger* humor magazine showed Depression-era students lined up at their graduation ceremony to be handed a loaf of bread with every liberal-arts diploma.[1] A few months later, the university's alumni magazine reported on students' shifting academic interests in a table titled 'Trend Away from the Humanities'.[2] Students concentrating their studies in those disciplines were down by nearly a third from the go-go years of the 'roaring twenties'.

The humanities eventually regained their popularity, and national reports show that enrollments peaked around 1971, following a period of economic growth in the 1960s. Then came 'stagflation' and the prolonged bear market on Wall Street that accompanied it. Down went humanities degrees as well, until a bull market started its run in the early 1980s.[3] After a bit of a lag, the humanities became popular yet again until recent times, when, just as we seem to be getting over the crash of 2008, we have discovered (as if for the first time) a 'trend away from the humanities', with even Harvard fretting about declining humanities enrollments.[4]

Maybe there is a correlation here. As Americans' stock portfolios go up, so does their interest in the humanities. Then, when the bears dominate Wall Street, there is an accompanying bear market for the humanities. Perhaps, one might hypothesize, there is even a cause-and-effect relationship. We ought not to leap to conclusions, of course. But it is worth considering: is it possible that the humanities cause economic decline? Perhaps all those humanities students spent too much time with Aquinas instead of accounting, and, before you know it, we are in the midst of the Great Depression.

Or, perhaps, it is more likely that causation runs the other way. In difficult financial times, students (and their parents) might tend to seek out courses of study that increase their chances of gainful employment. In the economically depressed 1930s, Princeton's engineers tripled from the 1920s, while enrollments in English, art and classics dropped sharply. That we have seen similar shifts in more recent economic downturns may not so much signal what has been described as a 'crisis of the humanities' as simply reflect a reasonably predictable reaction to tough times, especially in the United States, where the pursuit of higher education can involve spending—and sometimes borrowing—hundreds of thousands of dollars.[5]

The good news, for those of us who believe in the importance of the humanities, is that once the bread lines disappear, people realize that they cannot live by bread alone. The important questions addressed in religion, literature, the arts and elsewhere in the humanities will always captivate us, and we will continue to return to them when we can. There is, however, an ever present need to think about how to earn one's keep, and the economic factors can appear to weigh heavily in favor of some disciplines over others, especially when unemployment rates are rising.

The decisions by students and their parents about subjects it makes sense to study at the undergraduate level take place in an environment in which abundant information about employment prospects and starting salaries is readily available, if not always completely accurate. In economically difficult eras, the potential joys of spending several years studying literature, history or philosophy will encounter stiff competition from fields promising better job prospects and well-paying careers. 'Just look at salary.com', an engineer friend advised a mathematically talented son, who was beginning to hear the siren call of a less pragmatic but more intriguing course of study. Sure enough, on one popular website, engineering holds 9 of the 12 top-earning positions, joined by actuarial mathematics, computer science and physics. The first humanities discipline, philosophy, appears in 45th position, with religious studies (my undergraduate focus) holding down 101st place, just edging out classics.[6] The situation is similar in the UK, where one report shows the salaries of humanities graduates to be substantially below the average of 'all graduates', although still ahead of non-graduates.[7]

President Barack Obama is not even sure that humanities degree holders will fare better in the job market than non-graduates in the skilled trades, saying in 2014, '[A] lot of young people no longer see the trades and skilled manufacturing as a viable career. But I promise you, folks can make a lot more, potentially, with skilled manufacturing or trades than they might with an art history degree.'[8] President Obama anticipated the predictable outcry from art historians, saying, 'Nothing wrong with art history degree. I love art history. I don't want to get a bunch of emails from everybody.' Protest emails arrived anyway, and the president responded to one University of Texas professor, who had 'emphasize[d] that as art historians we challenge our students to think, read and write critically'.[9] His (partial) apology—'I was making a point about the jobs market, not the value of art history.... [A]rt history was one of my favorite subjects *in high school*'[10] —was too much for political opponent Senator Marco Rubio, who called the apology 'pathetic', and tweeted, 'We do need more degrees that lead to... jobs.'[11] Both President Obama and Senator Rubio have undergraduate degrees in political science, #48 on the Payscale.com rankings, just below philosophy but well ahead of #94 art history.[12]

The reports of a technology-based promised land are not necessarily predictive, as undergraduates seeking to 'follow the money' may rush to the areas that are currently the most economically attractive, only to find that so many have done so that they have overwhelmed the job opportunities, even in science and engineering.[13] There can also be more to a job than simply collecting a paycheck, and the benefits of higher education may well extend beyond simply earning a high income living. According to a 2014 Gallup poll, 'liberal arts majors [in the United States] were slightly more satisfied with their jobs than were business and science majors'.[14] The University of Oxford, meanwhile, studied 11,000 of its humanities graduates, and issued a widely publicized report of their 'Hidden Impact', noting 'the breadth and variety of roles in society that they adopt, and the striking consistency with which they have had successful careers in sectors driving economic growth'.[15]

Oxford's reference to 'sectors driving economic growth' is an important reminder that governments, too, make decisions about where to invest their resources in higher education (if at all). National economies are considerably more complex than our family finances—among other things, you and I are not in a position to print money—but governments must also think about how to pay for their many expenses, from health, education and welfare to defense, foreign aid, and on and on. In light of glowing reports of the job growth and economic benefits that flow from the technology-based entrepreneurial sectors, it is easy to see why legislators would find it attractive to pour billions into, for example, medical research, which promises to deliver better health and greater wealth at the same time, making it the government's way of 'doing well by doing good'. And where better to support that research than at the universities where so many of the fundamental discoveries have occurred?

Although science departments may worry that they also are under-funded (especially outside the life sciences), advocates for science and technology research funding have recently received a more attentive audience in congresses and parliaments than proposals to promote the study of the humanities. These politicians are taking a cue from public opinion. For example, when a 2010 poll asked Britons 'which university subjects...offer the best value for taxpayers' money', the responses ranked 'medicine, education, mathematics, dentistry, chemistry and biology' at the top, 'with humanities subjects clustered at the bottom of the list'.[16] Advocates for the humanities have not been willing to concede defeat to the force of public opinion, however. The University of Cambridge and the UK Arts and Humanities Research Council commissioned an independent analysis 'of the reported impacts of arts and humanities activities conducted at...Cambridge "that will be suitable for dissemination to stakeholders locally and nationally, including at senior levels of government, *in particular to the Treasury*"'.[17] The report's primary conclusion was that 'Arts and humanities research by University of Cambridge academics has many impacts', although 'attribution of research impact is often difficult', and 'impact is difficult to predict or assess in advance'.[18] To a considerable extent, the goal of this book is to specify especially important areas where there has been, and can be reasonably predicted to be, significant impact of the kind described in the report.

The debates about whether university programs in the humanities are worth the cost to individuals or to nations—however we may choose to measure 'worth' and 'cost'—are unlikely to be resolved to everyone's satisfaction anytime soon. What may be fairly predictable, however, is that when the stock market shows signs of sustained economic growth, there is likely to be a resurgence of interest in the humanities from individuals, and perhaps from governments as well.

This link between economic health and support for the humanities is not just a recent phenomenon. In tracing the 'forgotten origins of the modern humanities' through the work of philology scholars over many centuries, James Turner notes, for example, that Scottish economic growth after 1707 furthered the work of Scottish philologists like Thomas Blackwell. Turner argues, 'Prosperity energized Scotland's ancient universities.'[19] In general, we should probably not make too much of this ebb and flow of interest in the humanities other than to note that it has roughly correlated with economic conditions at least since the 1920s, is likely to have done so in previous centuries and may well continue indefinitely into the future. The point is simply that the humanities may find themselves squeezed somewhat harder during financially exigent times than academic disciplines that claim closer links to prosperity.

Speaking up for the Humanities

One regular aspect of this periodic appearance of a crisis, or at least of a decline in student interest that may be accompanied by an actual or threatened reduction in governmental funding, is the need for the humanities to stand up for themselves during the difficult times—to articulate a rationale for students to study, for scholars to explore and for societies to support those academic fields for which a close relationship with high-paying jobs and economic growth is considerably less clear than for whatever is considered to be a more practical field of study. This 'humanities defense' literature often speaks of the need for careful reading and critical thinking, the power of a well-crafted written argument, the societal value of public displays of art and historical artifacts, the importance of civic education, the need to inculcate moral values (or, in some quarters, the need to question the inculcation of moral values) and so on—even the importance of doing something just for its own sake or for the personal joy in doing so.[20] These arguments describe, and actually even display, an impressive array of eloquent and excellent reasons for humanities scholars to do what they have devoted their professional lives to doing, and for others to follow in their intellectual footsteps.

These traditional arguments are valuable and important, and I am fully in sympathy with most of them. For those disinclined to believe in the importance of the humanities, however, they are unlikely to carry the day. Even an academic figure as distinguished as Alan Ryan, Princeton professor and former Warden of Oxford's New College, concludes that none of the most common defenses is 'completely plausible'.[21] Harvard's Louis Menand has reached much the same conclusion: 'About twenty years ago, the humanities acquired a rationale problem.... The problem was not that humanists were unable to provide rationales for their work.... The problem was that even humanists felt that those rationales were not completely persuasive to outsiders.'[22] Among other things, it is too easy to point to engineers, scientists and mathematicians, and many others with no university education at all, who exhibit the qualities of critical thinking, good citizenship, effective communication and other positive attributes that advocates claim as the special province of the humanities. These standard claims about the usefulness of the humanities simply have not been compelling enough to convince parents or treasuries to favor the humanities in economically bleak times.

My goal is to demonstrate our need for the humanities from a considerably different perspective. Rather than setting out to defend the humanities, I will point to two especially important areas of modern life where society genuinely needs the help of the humanities. That is, I am writing primarily for the people who remain unconvinced by the arguments that have been advanced by humanities scholars in defense of their academic disciplines. Those who have not been persuaded need to see that we really do need the humanities. Thus, the 'we' in the title—*Why We Need the Humanities*—refers to all of us, in particular the many of us who are not academics working in a humanities discipline. We require the insights of the humanities to help our society sort out some particularly knotty problems of public policy that affect each one of us. It turns out that the humanities and the 'real world'[23] actually intersect in more important places than either side might expect.

These policy issues arise in the realms of healthcare and civil liberties, where they influence a significant portion of our economies and affect our lives. In these areas, national policies are being made by unelected political elites who often rely on scholarship in the humanities. So that the policy-makers will receive guidance that will best contribute to the common good, we need to continue to support the scholarly research that contributes to the deep well of learning of which the humanities is justly proud.

This book will, then, be an argument for the central importance of the humanities in our economic and political lives. We need the humanities. At the same time, we would be better served by them if they were more focused on what we need them to do than they often are at the moment, a topic I will address in Chapter 4. My suggestions are more focused on shifting perspectives than overhauling a system, however. They are simply rooted in the kinds of questions that the much more expansively funded biomedical researchers have often had to address to obtain research grants over the last few decades: how does my research relate—if only indirectly, tangentially and hypothetically—to human health? Or in the case of the humanities, we might say, to the good of humanity? In the end, my hope is to convince both scholars and the rest of us to think differently about the humanities.

In summary, this book will try to show why society should pay for something as apparently irrelevant to a modern high technology economy as the humanities. The simple answer is that some of our most exciting and economically important technological advances, as well as the recognition of many of our fundamental rights and liberties, require the ongoing contributions of philosophy, politics, history and other disciplines where the key questions have traditionally been addressed. Abandoning the humanities for the sake of the anticipated ability of the STEM fields—that is, science, technology, engineering and math—to give us better lives may, paradoxically, lead to the opposite result.

What this book is about

The second chapter describes the increasingly common view of universities as engines of innovation that are stimulating the economies of the United States and many Western European countries. Over the last ten years, technology licensing from universities has had a half trillion dollar impact on gross industrial output in the United States alone, spawning thousands of spin-off companies and hundreds of thousands of new jobs.[24] For the universities, technology also contributes to the bottom line through royalties and fees that have reached $2.6 billion annually.[25] The most valuable of these products—more than 100 new medicines to treat cancer, AIDS and other devastating illnesses—have linked health and wealth in a way that makes it easy to see why there are strong temptations for higher education policy-makers to divert resources from philosophy to physiology.

The educational and economic promise of some of the STEM fields has been so strong—and the arguments for the humanities have not always been strong enough—that some universities have closed programs in philosophy, classics and modern languages,[26] and a widely published report in the United Kingdom recommended phasing out block grants for teaching the humanities.[27] The next two chapters suggest that society ignores the humanities at its peril. They focus on two seemingly disparate areas of modern life—biomedical research and civil liberties. Those important arenas share a crucial common attribute. In both of these fields, a fairly small number of people routinely make decisions that directly affect the quality (and indeed the quantity) of all of our lives. Many of us can think of areas where we, as individuals, may have selected a course of action because of our exposure to history, philosophy, theology, literature or other components of the humanities, whether we have formally studied these fields or simply paused to think about what it means to live a good life. Normally, the extent to which we seek to lead this kind of 'examined life' is up to us. But when it comes to obtaining access to new treatments for deadly diseases or determining just what kinds of civil rights and liberties we have, those decisions may be taken by central authorities who will be making philosophical judgments, whether they call them by that name or not. They need the best help the humanities have to offer.

The second chapter focuses specifically on the essential role of the humanities in the economic growth resulting from biomedical research, which is the source of most of the government grants, spin-off companies, and licensing fees in the United States and Europe. Monoclonal antibodies, recombinant DNA technology and a variety of other highly promising technologies have emerged from their births in academic laboratories,[28] and they are making progress toward creating a new generation of novel medicines for treating devastating diseases, such as cancer, Alzheimer's and arthritis. Yet whether these modern medical technologies will ever reach pharmacists' shelves—and then on to patients' bedsides—requires the complex interaction of many fields, from molecular biology and physiology to pharmacology and statistics. By analyzing how the UK's National Health Service makes decisions about paying for new drugs, which is a process that affects nearly 30 percent of the global pharmaceutical market,[29] the chapter shows how these ostensibly scientific and medical decisions are, in fact, based on very difficult, and largely unresolved, issues of distributive justice, fairness and the nature of the common good—questions that historically have been the province of the humanities. The continued efforts to grapple with those questions by scholars and the public alike are essential if the link between university research and economic growth will be maintained.

In the future, humanities scholarship may contribute to what could be very expensive governmental decisions to continue to pay premium prices for new medicines, and thus maintain the much-anticipated economic growth from biomedical research. Alternatively, political decision-makers could conclude that society can no longer afford to pay as much as it has been paying for medical innovation, in which case the biomedical economic growth that we have come to expect will stall, and then dissipate.[30] Massive private investments in the life sciences, which have been essential to that growth, will no longer yield attractive economic returns because new high tech drugs will not be worth creating. And if society decides not to fund the biomedical research that might lengthen people's lives, then universities and governments can consider redirecting some of those billions to the less expensive disciplines of the humanities—art, literature, religion and music, for example—where people have historically turned when seeking fuller and richer, even if shorter, lives.

Chapter 3 will turn to a completely different arena, but again one where the humanities have profoundly affected the quality of modern life—defining fundamental rights. The chapter looks carefully at the work of judges, the people who, in interpreting constitutions and other foundational documents of civil society, decide upon the rights of citizens. The simple question is: where do they get their ideas about the meaning of phrases such as 'free exercise of religion' or 'equal protection of the laws'. These judicial policy-makers (and sometimes other public officials) make legally enforceable decisions about everything from the nature of our healthcare and educational systems to the extent of our religious freedom. A close look at where they turn for intellectual guidance when confronted with new and complex questions will shed light on how humanities scholarship has played a remarkably important but largely unsung role in defining our rights and responsibilities. In looking specifically at how US Supreme Court justices have debated among themselves in their private conferences, and then subsequently explained their interpretations of the Constitution to the public, this chapter shows how scholars in a surprisingly diverse array of humanistic studies have supplied the core concepts that justices have transformed into the supreme law of the land.

Beyond various examples of specific legal cases and controversies, we can also see how broader questions about the proper way to interpret a document, in particular a legal document such as a statute or a national constitution, have determined which fields of academic scholarship may predominate in defining American civil liberties. Over the last few decades in the United States, for example, judges, scholars and the public have disagreed vigorously over whether the Constitution should be interpreted in accordance with the framers' intentions or, alternatively, in light of evolving conceptions of human dignity. The former 'originalist' analysis has looked to historians to provide critical insights into the constitution-making process, the meaning of the constitutional language during the era in which it was drafted and even the mind of the founding generation (assuming that it was of one mind). Meanwhile, justices who seek instead the evolving meaning of a 'living constitution' have turned to numerous philosophers and other scholars in determining the requirements of dignity in the modern world. Whichever methodology is chosen by the justices from one case to the next, and that methodological question is itself rooted in the humanities, humanities scholarship has played a significant and sometimes definitive role: well over 50 Supreme Court cases have cited philosophers, from the ancients to contemporary scholars, and dozens more have relied on history and historians. In some of those cases, we can even see the American Supreme Court looking for guidance in the decisions of the courts and legislative bodies of other countries, which, in turn, have often based their decisions on the insights of historians, philosophers and other scholars.

The fourth chapter turns to these much-needed humanities scholars. Spirited and articulate humanities scholars have already provided vigorous defenses of their fields. For these brilliant scholars, the liberal arts are not only of intrinsic value, but they are essential for training citizens to carry out their duties in democratic societies.[31] The humanities, they posit, 'rightly pursued and rightly ordered, can do things, and teach things, and preserve things, and illuminate things, which can be accomplished in no other way. It is the humanities that instruct us in the range and depth of human possibility.'[32] These eloquent arguments about character and the human condition are likely to be compelling to other humanities scholars, and I join the many people who believe that the study of these fields is both important for society and intrinsically valuable, simply worth doing for its own sake. In fact, I retired from full-time employment in business to do just that. I have, as the politicians put it, 'voted with my feet' in favor of devoting time and effort to pursuing scholarship in the humanities for its intrinsic value (or, perhaps, if that claims too much, because it is just so interesting).

In difficult economic times, however, it is important to supplement those statements of faith with instrumental arguments that will convince the people who have control of the higher education purse-strings to see more clearly the utility of the humanities in helping society make crucial decisions about the kinds of lives we live. If we want the help of genuinely thoughtful humanities scholarship, we should be prepared to pay for it. To make those instrumental arguments requires us to demonstrate that there is a solid link between what the humanities do and what a society in straitened circumstances is willing to pay for.

One of the challenges that arises in making these instrumental claims for the role of the humanities in modern society is that academic scholarship has not always resonated well with the way society deals with controversial questions. Sometimes this disconnect is simply a result of intellectual inquiry that explores arcane issues or employs cutting-edge methodologies for which there may not be a clear connection with non-academic work. As Michael Dirda has written in *The Times Literary Supplement*, in 'cultural studies and literary scholarship, the work of our freshly minted Ph.D.'s all too often seems either annoyingly hip or possessed of a deconstructionist-like power to cloud men's minds'.[33] That is simply a fact of academic life.

Of greater concern are two other facts of modern academic life. One is the degree to which there may be disincentives within the academy regarding multi-disciplinary, collaborative work in the humanities. As a result, for example, policy-makers seeking advice relevant to questions about how much society should pay for new medical treatments may hear very different analyses depending on whether healthcare policy analysts calculating the return on investment from funding life sciences research choose to collaborate with the philosophers focused on how distributive justice principles apply to the government's purchase of the new medicines resulting from that research.

The second academic fact is that, in some disciplines, currently dominant ideological assumptions may diverge from the views found in society to such an extent that there may be insufficient overlap for the scholarship to be as useful as it could be. That scholars will not necessarily follow conventional ways of thinking is a very good thing, as is a diversity of viewpoints. My concern is that, especially in those disciplines that do connect fairly clearly with real world concerns, there is not enough diversity. While there are always exceptions, it turns out that ethicists and political philosophers frequently begin with assumptions about the nature of justice that may be inconsistent with the views of a large percentage of the public. The philosophies of John Rawls and John Stuart Mill, for example, may provide a foundation for much more thinking about healthcare policy issues in the academy than outside it. Similarly, in the realm of civil liberties and constitutional interpretation, a prominent Harvard historian has likened constitutional originalism to astrology, despite its embrace by about half of the American public as well as some Supreme Court justices (as discussed in Chapter 3).[34]

The academy, particularly in the humanities, is less ideologically diverse than the general population, and there is the possibility that views at odds with the academic mainstream may receive less thoughtful attention than would be most helpful for policy decisions that will affect a more diverse and complex public. John Stuart Mill's statement, 'He who knows only his own side of the case, knows little of that', is the opening to a recent article by a group of social psychologists arguing, '(1) Academic psychology... has lost nearly all of [its political diversity...]; (2) This lack of political diversity can undermine [research] validity via mechanisms such as the embedding of liberal values into research questions and methods, [and] steering researchers away from important but politically unpalatable research topics'.[35]

A similar degree of leaning to the left side of the political spectrum has been found among humanities scholars, especially in the United States, but also in the UK and other European countries. In describing a 2005 study, an article in *The Washington Post* noted that the

> most liberal faculties are those devoted to the humanities (81 percent) and social sciences (75 percent)....The most left leaning departments are English literature, philosophy, political science and religious studies, where at least 80 percent of the faculty say they are liberal and no more than 5 percent call themselves conservative.[36]

These data are, not surprisingly, very controversial, but, generally speaking, it is hard to dispute that, in terms of their personal voting preferences, humanities faculties are considerably more liberal than the public. Those preferences are relevant here to the extent that they spill over into their scholarly work, and it seems likely that they do. Harvard Professor Louis Menand, in a chapter titled, 'Why Do Professors All Think Alike?,' noted that not only are academics 'significantly more liberal than the rest of the population', but also that '70.9 percent said that it was all right for a professor's research to be guided by his or her political or religious beliefs; only 5.1 percent of liberal professors described themselves as "ardent advocates of neutrality"'.[37] My point is not that humanities scholars should necessarily lean to the right instead of the left, although it would certainly be helpful to have more of a balance.[38]

Rather than propose that scholarship be liberal or conservative, or anything else on the political or intellectual spectrum, my goal is to encourage scholars to reflect on, and consider equally critically, the range of views found in the peoples and texts they study. Doing so will not only make scholarship potentially more helpful for policy-makers, but, following Mill, it may enliven and enrich the scholarly discussions themselves. In one of the examples cited above, where Harvard Professor Jill Lepore analogized constitutional originalism to astrology, my concern is not that she believes that originalism represents sloppy thinking and shoddy history; those issues are worth analyzing and debating. Rather, I worry that, by likening it to astrology, a field not generally considered a worthy subject of contemporary academic study, she is seeking to eliminate it as something scholars study and critique. Yet, it appears with some regularity in opinions of the Supreme Court of the United States, and polls have shown that about half of the American public supports the approach.[39] Perhaps the public and those justices are wrong, but they are unlikely to be convinced without more thoughtful engagement and persuasive explanations than a quick dismissal as so obviously flawed as to be unworthy of serious discussion.

We do need the humanities, and, during those times when there is pressure on the humanities, it may be useful for scholars to devote additional attention to issues that bear on public policy in ways that connect with the range of political preferences found in the public and their elected representatives. It will be good for society, and may well be intellectually invigorating for scholars as well.

Finally, the conclusion argues that society should be prepared to support humanities research—inside or outside academia—to be in a position to obtain the guidance it needs to address important public policy issues. In doing so, it needs to recognize that, as with the STEM fields, research can sometimes become important only many years after it has been completed, even when it may have originally appeared to be irrelevant or impractical. At the same time, it would be helpful for humanities scholars to look for opportunities to engage more regularly and effectively with the public to highlight the continuing importance of their work.

* * *

From the 1830s to the 1860s, a South Carolina slave named Dave was a potter and a poet. We only know that Dave was literate and that he was a poet because his poems have been preserved on the clay pots he made—huge jugs for farm and kitchen use. Dave's creations can be seen today not only in the Smithsonian but also in a striking series of paintings by the award-winning artist Jonathan Green.[40]

We know of 27 of his poems, and two of his main themes were religion and the usefulness of his jars. This one combines the two:

> Good for lard or holding fresh meats
> Blest we were, when Peter saw the folded sheets
>
> 3 May 1859

And, then, four score and three years after the founding:

> The fourth of July is surely come
> To blow the fife and beat the drum
>
> 4 July 1859

In those days, his poetry endured because of the commercial value of the pots; today, museums preserve the vessels because of the value of the poetry. Inscribed with rhymes about everything from the resurrection and independence to advertising slogans, these pots are just one of the visible signs of the sometimes unexpected interconnectedness of the humanities and the commercial world. My hope is that this book will bring a few more of them to light.

2
The Humanities and the Future of the Life Sciences

Philosophy and theology may once have been known as the queens of the sciences, but, today, we often look to science and technology for answers to the 'big questions'. Physicists have been on the trail of the God particle; biologists regularly dazzle the media with the discovery of one molecular Holy Grail or another; and the neuroscientists are competing with the economists to decide whether moral choices are genetically hard-wired or rationally calculated.

The sciences now dominate higher education budgets in a manner scarcely imaginable when Harvard, Princeton, Yale and a few others first decided to establish schools of science and engineering. In 1788, a Princeton professor welcomed the study of science, then called natural philosophy, as yet another way to obtain 'knowledge of the one almighty all-wise and all-good Being, who created, preserves and governs the universe'.[1] A little over 200 years later, the subject that he had blessed as 'the very handmaid of religion' is now embraced by academia with near religious devotion. The STEM fields today often play leading roles in setting academic policies and priorities, both within the universities themselves, and, perhaps more importantly, among politicians, policy-makers and other funders of higher education.

Especially when there are economic pressures on higher education, universities seek ways to cut spending and, where possible, to increase revenues. Beyond the billions in direct grants from national and international sources that some of the STEM fields have attracted, numerous universities have found that they can build an attractive business of patenting and licensing new discoveries in the life sciences, engineering, physics and some of the other STEM fields. In 2012, for example, a group of 161 American research universities received about $1.9 billion in royalty payments. This lively technology transfer activity has also spawned thousands of spin-off companies (818 companies in 2013 alone) that have also contributed to job growth and to greater economic prosperity for both town and gown.[2]

It would be hard to imagine the phenomenon of Silicon Valley, for example, without Stanford University. As a result of the success of this California cluster of entrepreneurial enterprises, wherever there are similar league-table-leading research institutions in the Western world—from Cambridge, United States, to 'Silicon Fen' around Cambridge, United Kingdom, and on to Scandinavia's Medicon Valley, Paris, Amsterdam, Flanders, Munich and numerous others—governments and universities have teamed with venture capitalists to try to create Silicon Valley-style, STEM-driven economic success. That there is no specific chemical formula for creating a fertile, entrepreneurial environment has led to creative efforts by universities, governments, trade associations and other interested parties to catalyze the process by tweaking the mix of such volatile elements as research strength, technological innovation, entrepreneurs, venture capitalists and investment bankers, not to mention laboratory space, skilled workers (and jobs for many of their spouses), lawyers, accountants and the like.

It is not surprising, with this background, that budget-cutting trustees and other decision-makers may choose to allocate their resources in ways that favor the revenue-producing STEM fields over other parts of the university, including the humanities.[3] One major point in favor of the STEM disciplines is that their contributions are so easy to see, especially for governing boards and policy-makers who are searching for metrics—something measurable by which they can try to determine success or failure. Patents can be counted; licensing revenues contribute cash to the university's financial statements; spin-off companies create measurable job growth; and new cancer treatments can lengthen life itself. Productivity in the humanities, by contrast, can be hard to measure beyond arcane academic publications that are often read by just a few other scholars, and, if one of them actually writes a best-selling book, the royalties typically end up in the author's pocket, not the university's.

In considering the relevance of scholarship to the modern world, it may be instructive to look at a snapshot of the University of Cambridge's press releases during one month in 2010. Both the arts and the sciences were well represented with announcements of important findings and events, but overall, science and medicine contributed nearly twice as many announcements as the humanities. While there are ongoing arguments over whether the humanities have (or need to have) any practical impact at all, it is hard to gainsay the potential effect of the launching of a 'Digital Library for the World', or the historical value of a newly opened polar museum. The debut of a new Cambridge play about climate change could certainly influence public attitudes about global sustainability, although that impact could well be trumped by the University's scientists and engineers, who are turning algae into a renewable energy source. Meanwhile, their STEM colleagues have established links between diabetes and heart attacks, discovered a possible new pathway for helping cocaine addicts and created a new blood test for the early diagnosis of schizophrenia—all announced within a four-week period. It is not that the humanities have nothing important to say, but that the STEM fields can regularly provide such overpowering evidence of their contributions to society's health and well-being.

Governing boards and policy-makers that elect to support the STEM fields do not necessarily do so because they believe that molecular biology is inherently more worthy of intellectual pursuit than political philosophy. Policy-makers embrace the STEM fields in the very pragmatic expectation that the resulting technological progress will contribute to the wealth of nations, starting with their own communities. Take, for example, a report from the United Kingdom's Royal Society, titled *The Scientific Century*. The report's highly instrumental, goal-oriented subtitle is especially telling: *Serving Our Future Prosperity*.[4] The Royal Society's language of investment and return is revealing: '[T]here is little doubt that advances in science and technology will continue to transform the way we live, create new industries and jobs, and enable us to tackle seemingly intractable social and environmental problems.' At present, the Society points out, 'thanks to sustained investment, we have the most productive research bases among the world's leading economies'. With the 'outputs of our research increasingly threaded throughout our economy', it would be little short of 'disastrous if... there was a withdrawal of support for our world-class universities, or the incentives which have been put in place to encourage translation, commercialization and knowledge exchange'.[5]

The kinds of numbers that stimulate policy-makers to be enthusiastic about the direct link between scientific research and economic prosperity can be seen in the effects of university patent licensing on the US economy between 1996 and 2007:

- a $187 billion impact on the US gross domestic product;
- a $457 billion impact on the US gross industrial output; and
- 279,000 new jobs created in the US from university inventions.[6]

In the words of a report to Congress by the National Institutes of Health in 2001, technology transfer from universities to companies in the life sciences has 'yielded a dramatic return to the taxpayer through the discovery of new technologies that extend life and improve the quality of life through the development of products that might not [otherwise] be available', and it has 'buttress[ed] the biomedical research enterprise that has made the US the world leader in this field'.[7] It is little wonder, writes the legislative forefather of university technology transfer in the United States, Senator Birch Bayh, that a desire to continue the trend of 'more than 6,000 new US companies formed from university invention... is a key ingredient in virtually every state economic development plan'.[8]

The life sciences appear to be responsible for a 'large majority', in the vicinity of 70–85 percent, of this university technology transfer and economic growth in the past three decades.[9] In addition to this impressive economic growth, research in the life sciences has resulted in at least '153 new drugs, vaccines, or [medical] devices' as of a 2009 report, with additional new medicines appearing every year.[10] And so, while all of the STEM fields can point to examples where basic research in academic institutions has boosted economies and has fostered commercial success (as well as the overall betterment of humankind), the life sciences, which pair the expectation of prosperity with the promise of well-being, is where most of the research dollars have been allocated, where most technology transfer has occurred, and what this chapter is about. As the United Kingdom's Medical Research Council (MRC) wrote about its goals, 'MRC will develop and sustain leading edge research programmes that will accelerate the transition of fundamental research into measurable positive impact on health, innovation and wealth creation'.[11]

Biomedical research is also the field in which the optimistic, STEM-driven economic predictions can be expected to come true only under the right conditions. Those conditions revolve around critical questions that have been addressed traditionally within the humanities, resulting in hidden variables in the prosperity equation that are often overlooked by scientists in their predictions of continuing economic growth.

Investment and return in the life sciences

In 2010, there was a controversial proposal to reduce cancer research funding in the United Kingdom by over £100 million a year. The chief executive of Cancer Research UK wrote an article for *The Times* in support of maintaining the funding. He did not begin his essay with the hopes and fears of desperate cancer patients and their families, or even with the promise of Nobel prize-winning discoveries. Instead, he wrote, 'Scientific research makes a vital contribution to the economy.' To sharpen the financial point, the article was titled, 'Years of Crucial Investment Could Fall by the Wayside'.[12]

The financial returns on scientific investment can appear so dramatic that the health benefits from biomedical research may pale in comparison. Leading economists, for example, projected over $70 *billion* of direct and indirect financial returns from a comparatively modest $380 *million* state government investment in one particular new medical technology. No wonder STEM sells so well in legislatures these days. These kinds of numbers, which were produced by distinguished scholars at a major research university, certainly make a persuasive case for investing in academic research in the STEM fields. The prospect of medical breakthroughs for patients with devastating illnesses, combined with these kinds of massive near-term and longer-term economic benefits, make for a compelling argument.

The $70 billion return on investment came from an analysis of the 2005 proposal for the State of New Jersey to launch a government-funded stem cell research initiative. Joseph Seneca and Will Irving of the Edward J. Bloustein School of Planning and Public Policy at Rutgers, the State University of New Jersey, prepared a report on the expected 'Economic Benefits of the Research Initiative' for the

Governor.[13] These economists reviewed the planned tax-supported funding program for promoting research into the use of stem cell technology for the treatment of a number of life-threatening conditions.

Through the application of what the authors termed 'conservative assumptions throughout the report', Seneca and Irving forecast financially compelling returns generated by the government's investment in this new technology. The key element required to achieve the predicted economic growth was attracting non-governmental, for-profit investment in the stem cell initiative. Of the $1.4 billion of new economic activity, over $1 billion was attributable to this 'private leveraging'. The report assumed that for every $1.00 in public spending, venture capitalists (or other for-profit investors) would invest $1.50. State money would thus prime the pump, but 60 percent of the funding needed to flow from private sources.

The report also sounded a cautionary note about the risks of not funding this particular area of research. The authors warned that the health of the state's existing biotechnology industry could be threatened if this stem cell initiative were not to take place, because many states and countries are competing for the 'biotechnology industry, with its high value added and knowledge-based workforce'. If the 'locus and focus of US stem cell work, highly competitive to start, ... centers on other locations', private capital will shift to where the most exciting research is taking place, and, the report argued, up to 20 percent of New Jersey's existing biotechnology jobs could move to the places where 'the intellectual and commercial synergies associated with proximity to others in the industry attract the new start-ups'. Without the program, then, thousands of existing jobs would be lost, along with the private capital that seeks the best new discoveries wherever they take place.[14] This initiative thus represented both an investment in the potential for new medicines emerging from a particular STEM field and a technological 'land grab' by which New Jersey, already home to several global pharmaceutical companies as well as numerous biotechnology companies, could increase its national share of well-paying biomedical jobs.

If New Jersey were to adopt the initiative, and thus avoid biotech job loss and the resulting economic decline, the financial returns to the state would go well beyond the R&D jobs created, equipment purchased, taxes paid and other direct benefits of the research initiative.

The report identified many billions more in 'broader benefits' from savings in future healthcare costs resulting from better treatments for Parkinson's disease, Alzheimer's disease, spinal cord injury and the like ($11.3 billion in overall savings, including a $1.7 billion savings to the state itself); 'work time and economic productivity savings' ($813 million) and the 'value of premature deaths avoided' ($60.7 billion).

New Jersey was not alone in seeking financial and technological benefits from investing in stem cell research. These types of stem cell economic analyses were being performed in a number of other countries, as well as in other states in the United States at roughly the same time. They typically shared the same types of broad assumptions found in the New Jersey study.[15] A report issued by the California Stem Cell Research and Cures Initiative was prepared by a pair of researchers, one of whom was the chief of health services research at Stanford School of Medicine. The detailed analysis in support of California's multi-billion dollar bond issuance for stem cell research identified 'total state revenues and healthcare savings of between $6.4 billion and $12.6 billion . . . , generating a 120 percent to 236 percent return on the [state's] investment made in the research'.[16] As in the New Jersey report, the lion's share of these financial returns to the state was expected to be derived from two sources: (1) private investment exceeding the amount of the state's funding, and (2) many billions of reduced healthcare costs as a result of the new stem cell treatments. These cost savings were based on the assumption that new therapeutic products emerging from the initiative would immediately lower, not raise, the cost of treating the patients. To make the cost-savings analysis work, the new products would need to reduce the overall cost of treating a patient by at least 10 percent, and to reduce mortality by about 7 percent.[17]

As noted in both the New Jersey and California reports, attracting sufficient levels of private capital is an essential component of obtaining enough funding to make successful drug development possible, and for generating the economic multiplier effect that is so important in increasing the overall return from the state's investment in the near term. The reports do not say why they believe that private capital will follow the public dollars, although economists have observed that, in the past, increases in public spending on medical research have generated a corresponding growth in private R&D

funding. Even if we assume that these studies are correct (which may not be the case),[18] we need to consider whether these historical data are likely to predict the responses of the investors who would consider investing in state-funded stem cell initiatives. If not, these programs will have a much smaller chance of generating the projected billions in economic growth and other benefits to New Jersey, California, and the other locations that have considered implementing similar funding initiatives. So the question is: Will private sources of capital continue to invest in new technologies for developing life-saving drugs? That question turns out to involve more questions in the humanities than might be expected.

Private capital and biomedical research

If there is one thing that is as important to the successful launching of a new drug as a breakthrough scientific discovery, it is money. Great quantities of money must be continually infused into any drug development program over the dozen or so years of testing that are required. Even with the benefit of all of the biomedical discoveries of the last few decades, the drug development process almost invariably costs hundreds of millions of dollars or more, not including the cost of the about 90 percent of drug candidates entering human clinical testing that end up failing to become new medicines.[19] Without adequate sources of capital for each stage of this lengthy process, the likelihood of ultimate success—already quite low, probably as low as a fraction of 1 percent of early research-stage products—diminishes further.

Money for the research and development efforts that lead to new biotech medicines comes from a variety of sources.[20] The earliest, most basic research typically takes place at a university or other academic research center, and one estimate, which is probably a conservative one, finds that 31 percent of scientifically novel new drugs were based on patented university discoveries.[21] The university research is most likely to have been funded by the government or by charities that raise funds for medical research. While some of the research is designed specifically to identify potential new treatments for various diseases, it generally involves much more basic research in a wealth of fields, such as biochemistry, microbiology, physiology, molecular biology and immunology. This type of grant-funded academic research only occasionally yields a notion about the possible diagnosis or treatment of disease that is commercially interesting enough to lead the university to file for patent protection, which is generally the first step toward attracting interest from the private sector.[22] As discussed in the previous chapter, many thousands of grant-funded projects are likely to yield only a few hundred patents. Whether to pursue a patent filing for a research discovery is often decided by the university's technology transfer and licensing department. This office initially serves as a bridge to patent attorneys; it later introduces the discovery to biotech and pharmaceutical companies, and to the venture capitalists who focus on creating new life science companies.

Great numbers of discoveries from STEM research in the life sciences, even patented ones, fail to attract any commercial interest, but, from time to time, a venture capitalist who hears about an especially interesting technology or potential product may consider starting a new biotech company to take advantage of that discovery. The venture capitalists are typically the first sources of the money that fund new job growth at entrepreneurial companies; they represent a significant share of the $1.50 in private capital expected by the economic forecasts to match each dollar of public funding.

To understand the likelihood of venture capital investments, we need to focus briefly on how venture capital firms operate. Much as university scientists compete for a limited amount of funding available from government grants, venture capitalists in the life sciences compete with many other investment firms to raise the funds that they invest in entrepreneurial companies. Venture capitalists need to convince these funding sources that they will obtain a better financial return from investing in life science companies than they would by putting the same money into stocks, bonds or any other form of investment. Venture capitalists are almost invariably partnerships in which a handful of individuals serve as general partners responsible for the day-to-day business of investing in (and often starting) entrepreneurial companies. They invest funds that they have obtained from a group of limited partners, which are typically large institutional investors. Most of these investors are pension funds and university endowments, which, following modern theories of financial portfolio management, place their money in a diverse array of investment opportunities. The bulk of their money is often invested in the traditional types of stocks and bonds that are listed on various exchanges around the world, but they may elect to put a small portion of their funds in venture capital on the promise of a better financial return than would be expected from investments in less risky and more liquid (that is, more easily bought and sold) financial instruments.[23]

Some of the endowments that invest in venture capital in the life sciences are the same research universities—Harvard, Princeton and Stanford, for example—that are generating many of the new biomedical ideas in the first place, although only rarely do they link their endowment investments to any research performed on their campuses.[24] Instead, they seek out the best performing venture capital firms (in which performance is measured solely in terms of financial returns), and they leave the investment decisions to the general partners. It is important to note that pension and endowment funds are very sophisticated investors with billions to invest. They can pick and choose their investments for what they believe will be the best possible financial return; they will therefore expect to be very well compensated for investing in something as risky, illiquid and time consuming as life sciences venture capital. As a result, venture capitalists must pick investment opportunities with the prospects for high enough returns to compensate for the risks involved since so many new drug prospects turn out to be failures.

When a venture capitalist is enthusiastic enough about an academic research discovery to make an investment, the next step will often be to start a new company dedicated to that technology or product, with the venture capitalist receiving shares of stock in the company in return for the cash that is invested. Initial investments in these kinds of start-up companies can range from a few hundred thousand dollars of 'seed capital' to tens of millions of dollars. With the newly found cash, the company can begin hiring experienced scientists and managers, thus creating the high-paying jobs sought by the policy-makers who are supporting STEM-related research. The spin-off company works to advance the research so that it moves in the direction of becoming a new medicine, all the while buying equipment and supplies, hiring additional scientists and otherwise stimulating the economy.

Somewhere in this process—ideally within the typical ten-year life of a venture fund—the venture capitalists will attempt to sell the company to a large pharmaceutical company, or, if market conditions are favorable, to have the company complete an initial public offering (IPO). In either case, the goal is for the venture capitalist to exchange its ownership of the company's stock for cash. The IPO involves a stock market listing, which, if things go well, will create the liquidity that the venture capitalist needs to be able to sell its shares to stock market investors. These IPO opportunities, or 'windows', appear infrequently and unpredictably for early stage, research-oriented companies in the life sciences, and, therefore, a 'trade sale' to 'big pharma' has usually been the principal goal.[25]

The sale of the biotech company to a pharmaceutical company provides what is known as an 'exit opportunity', that is, it allows the venture capitalists to cash in their stakes in the spin-off company and to send money back to their limited partners, that is, the pension and endowment funds. When everything goes well, a promising technology has the chance to be transformed into a new medicine; the economy has grown by the addition of new jobs; the pension and endowment funds have more money with which to fulfill their institutional missions of paying for people's retirements or funding academic programs; the venture capitalists have potentially achieved a good enough investment track record to be able to raise another investment fund that will allow them to continue investing in the life sciences; the pharmaceutical company's business prospects have improved, potentially creating additional economic growth; and patients have obtained access to a medicine that might not otherwise have existed. This is obviously a very attractive scenario. It is especially attractive to the governments that originally invested in the basic research: the economy is healthier, and all of that economic growth sends taxes back to the government, which can then, if it chooses, continue to fund life sciences research.

The problem is that these happy endings occur so rarely. Only a tiny fraction of grant-funded research programs yields patentable results, and an even smaller number look promising enough to get as much as a quick glance from venture capitalists, who may invest in just a few percent (at most) of the biotechnology opportunities they consider. Then only a minority of venture-backed biotech companies will be sold at a profit, and only a fraction of the companies or products sold by venture capitalists to pharmaceutical companies will generate profitable sales of new medicines.[26] What makes this entire cycle possible is belief: in particular, the reasonable belief by the people who control the flow of cash—largely the pharmaceutical companies and the venture capitalists (including especially their investors, the pension and endowment funds)—that a product that beats these daunting odds and effectively treats disease will be approved for commercial sale by the regulatory agencies in the most important pharmaceutical markets. Moreover, they must believe that such an approval will create sales of the product at high enough levels that the resulting profits will provide an attractive return on the very substantial investment required to pay not only for this successful drug development effort but also for all of the numerous unsuccessful ones as well. If any of these beliefs and expectations no longer seems reasonably possible, then the flow of money pouring into commercializing biomedical research will come to a halt, and the associated economic growth will stop along with it.[27] In 2012, this amount of commercial investment in biomedical research was about $170 billion worldwide, over 70 percent of which is in the United States and Europe.[28]

Surprising as it may seem, the humanities need to help us with precisely those dilemmas. But first, a brief note. Some scholars might prefer to see their academic departments permanently disbanded than to provide aid to an enterprise that is based so much on finance capitalism or involves the creation of medicines whose cost, at least initially, may be beyond the means of many people around the world. That is a perfectly fine choice—just not one that leads to STEM-related prosperity. The next chapter on constitutional rights may offer a more attractive position from which to defend the humanities. My point is simply that many policy-makers justify their current support of the STEM fields on the grounds that the large costs required to maintain a modern university's scientific research programs will essentially be repaid to society not only through improved healthcare but also from increasing economic prosperity. Recall the aims of the United Kingdom's MRC: 'measurable impact on health, innovation *and wealth creation*'.[29] If such a goal-oriented approach strengthens the STEM fields only by weakening the humanities, and thus diminishing our ability to understand the relationship between healthcare innovation and wealth creation, such an imbalance may—paradoxically—reduce the chances of achieving those medical and economic goals.

There are many interesting and sometimes highly controversial ethical issues associated with drug development, including questions involving access to healthcare, the profitability of the pharmaceutical industry, the ethics of animal testing, the use of stem cell and cloning technologies and so on, all of which are worthy of close attention from scientists and humanities scholars alike. These questions are important but fairly easy to see. The crucial issue for this discussion resides in an area where mathematical equations may be masking fundamental questions solidly within the domain of the humanities.

The STEM promised land: New drugs and improved healthcare

Seeing how the humanities figure in these biomedical and mathematical discussions requires a little further exploration of some of the opportunities and challenges associated with the drug development process. Even the most exciting technological advancements have created (or perhaps enhanced) a major problem whose solution cannot be found in the laboratory, at least not any time soon: cost. These products are breathtakingly expensive, for four major reasons. First, and most important, many potential products do not actually work when they are tested in human clinical trials. Second, of the few products that are found by the appropriate regulatory agencies to be safe and effective enough to be approved for commercial sale, they generally only help some of the patients; we usually cannot tell in advance which patients will be the fortunate ones, since the progress toward personalized medicine has been disappointingly slow. Third, many of the important new products emerging from biotechnology research are very costly to manufacture. And fourth, they often are added to existing treatment regimens, especially for patients with life-threatening diseases, resulting in an increase in overall healthcare costs.

Numerous studies have shown how remarkably expensive it is to develop a new pharmaceutical product. In 2003, the consulting firm Bain & Company put the number at $1.7 billion.[30] A report from the Tufts University Center for the Study of Drug Development in 2000 estimated the cost at nearly a billion dollars. A recent study updated the Tufts estimate by adding increased regulatory burdens, inflation and other costs, and by adjusting the projected success rates downward to reflect the decreasing numbers of product approvals, yielding a new drug cost of over $3.9 billion in 2008 dollars.[31] These amounts need to be invested over a 12–15-year period. The costs can be divided into three major components: the opportunity cost, the expenses of the numerous failed projects for every successful one and the costs of developing the drug that ultimately turns out to be a Food and Drug Administration (FDA) approved treatment. The largest aspect of these costs is the so-called time value of money. That is, roughly half the cost of developing a drug, as calculated by economists, is attributable to the earnings (such as interest payments) that the company did not receive because it invested its money in drug development instead of in interest-bearing government bonds. This is the financial 'opportunity cost' of the new drug.

The second largest element of cost is all of the money spent on the highly promising research discoveries and product candidates that turn out to be unsuccessful. About 10 percent of products reaching human clinical testing demonstrate the required safety and efficacy to qualify for regulatory approval. These clinical stage products have typically been derived from many hundreds or thousands of research-stage programs that, for any of a wide range of possible reasons, do not advance even as far as clinical trials.

The final component is the discovery and development cost of the new drug itself. It is remarkable that the expenses associated with the creation of a successful new drug are lower than the costs of failed drugs, but that is a natural consequence of the remarkable attrition rate for even the most promising ideas for new products. A report in *Science* points out that a 'staggering 99.9 percent of compounds wash out of the development pipeline'.[32]

Research may have become increasingly high tech, but all we have learned through the war on cancer, the mapping of the human genome and similar efforts has not made drug development any faster or cheaper. Rather, it is increasingly costly: lengthy and expensive drug development pathways—including many years of human clinical testing—remain the norm, and, if anything, overall costs and timelines have increased. As a 2014 study concluded, 'Since the human genome was sequenced ten years ago, the number of compounds in development has increased 62 percent and total R&D expenditures have doubled. And yet, the average number of new drugs approved by the [FDA] per year has declined since the 1990s.'[33]

I have estimated (based on a series of important and probably controversial assumptions) the 'allocated R&D expense per FDA-approved' new drug deemed a 'priority' product by the FDA. Those are the products that represent a significant improvement in the treatment of 'a serious of life-threatening condition'. According to my analysis, the cost for one new medicine is $1.63 billion for biotech companies and $6.30 billion for pharmaceutical companies.[34] These amounts include the cost of failed programs, but they do not account for the opportunity costs discussed above.

The fact that not all patients are helped by the new treatments is likely the result of numerous factors, from the toll such diseases and their standard treatments have already taken on the patient's body to the challenges of fashioning just the right biological tool for a disease-related target. No small part of the problem is due to the fact that the highly publicized mapping of the genome did not really create 'the instruction book of human life', despite the enthusiastic announcement of 2000 to that effect from the heads of the governments of the United States, United Kingdom, Japan, France, Germany and China.[35] However valuable it may be, it is not yet the book of life. The on-going work of scientists to identify and catalog potential disease targets is an immense task, and, even when one of those genes (or the protein for which it is the code) is determined to be related to a particular disease, that knowledge merely begins the 15–20-year process to try to turn that insight into a new therapeutic product.

Even after a highly promising disease target[36] has been at least presumptively identified, it turns out that, in cancer, for example, different patients with the same type of tumor (that is, lung cancer, breast cancer and so on) will have different amounts of the target molecule on their tumor cells, from virtually none to many tens of thousands. The same target may also play different roles in different patients' diseases, as it interacts with other molecules in the body. In short, there is only occasionally a way, using today's technology, to tell in advance whether a particular patient will respond favorably to a new treatment, especially in life-threatening diseases. The mapping of the genome has therefore not (yet) either reduced the cost of development or substantially increased our ability to predict which patients will benefit from most new products.

Further adding to the cost of new medicines is the fact that many of the most innovative treatments emerging from biotechnology research cost thousands of dollars just to manufacture enough of the material for use in one patient. Whereas conventional pharmaceutical products are typically made in fairly well known and reasonably inexpensive chemical synthesis processes, biological products are manufactured through the use of a complex fermentation process involving genetically engineered living cells. Because scientists and engineers have not yet worked out how to reduce this manufacturing process to the levels associated with traditional, chemically synthesized drugs, new biotechnology-derived cancer treatments can cost thousands of dollars more per patient than currently prescribed regimens of chemotherapy.

Finally, new biotech products for cancer and other life-threatening conditions are often additions to current treatment regimens rather than replacements, resulting in overall higher treatment costs per patient than before the new products came onto the market. Such drugs are often first approved by regulatory agencies for the patients who have reached the latest stages of disease when all existing treatments have failed. Such an approach may be rooted in the desire to provide medicines where they are most urgently needed. Or it may be due to the fact that the FDA and other regulatory agencies have often required smaller, shorter clinical trials in late stage patients than in early stage, relatively healthier patients, thus creating a faster and potentially less expensive way for companies to begin generating sales revenues. Either way, the new product emerges as an addition to, rather than as a replacement for, existing therapeutic regimens. Then, once the product is approved for sale, the company selling the product may have a greater financial ability, and may also have an increased desire, to conduct the larger, far more expensive clinical trials in earlier stage patients where there may be a better chance of achieving not only greater improvements in patients' health but also lower overall costs of treatment.[37]

In considering all of these factors that bear on the cost calculations, we should pause to compare the outcomes of research in the life sciences with similar efforts in electronics, computer science, advanced materials and the other components of the revolution in information technology. In fields outside the life sciences, technological advances often lead to ways to do things faster, better *and cheaper*. In computer engineering, this phenomenon is often referred to as Moore's Law, based on Intel co-founder Gordon Moore's original statement that the 'number of transistors incorporated in a chip will approximately double every 24 months'.[38] This technological prediction has been expanded to encompass not just doubling transistor density, but simultaneously 'increasing functionality and performance and decreasing costs'.[39] Advances in healthcare seem mostly to tack in the other direction. First, new medical products are also likely to be much more expensive to create than new products in the information technology field. According to a 2008 report, 'the average out-of-pocket cost of a new [pharmaceutical] product approval is $400 million... whilst in other highly innovative sectors, such as IT and communications technologies, an investment of £4 million allows companies to bring new products to the market'.[40] Second, unlike new information technology products that deliver cheaper and better 'solutions' to the user, medical technology has certainly led to improved treatments, but at often significantly higher costs than prior, less effective, treatments. In many cases—and particularly in connection with high-tech biomedical products that extend life or create substantial improvements in people's quality of life—novel products are often far more expensive than existing treatments.

With this background, we can return to the New Jersey and California stem cell initiatives. The economic return requires sizeable amounts of private investment. Venture capitalists gauging their level of comfort in making these kinds of investments will be asking just how confident they can be that someone—patients, insurance companies, or governments—will pay enough for a successful new stem cell treatment to make the investment sufficiently attractive in light of the risks involved. This analysis will not only consider historical patterns but will also consider the trajectory that attitudes of healthcare payers may follow in the future, as these payers have increasingly been balking at high-priced, high-tech products. The New Jersey report supporting state investment in stem cell technology moves obliquely in that direction by noting that successful 'biotechnology therapies are estimated to have generated $3 billion in sales per drug over the patent life'. Yet, the report appears optimistically to assume that the $3 billion will be available from future healthcare budgets, presumably because it is a fraction of the $11.3 billion that would otherwise have been spent on less effective treatments.

For many of the reasons discussed above, however, any new treatment generated by New Jersey's or California's initiative is probably more likely to increase overall treatment costs for the patients than to decrease them, at least in the early years. Finding a novel therapy for a usually intractable condition such as Alzheimer's or spinal cord injury can therefore be a two-edged sword: once it is proven effective, it may not necessarily replace existing inadequate treatments, but is more likely to complement them. As a result, brand new money is needed to pay for the brand new treatments. Whether healthcare payers will allocate $3 billion dollars to just one new product over a 7-year period beginning 11 years after the investment is made, is a difficult question in any economic environment. In light of these concerns, as well as the global financial crisis in the end of the first decade of the twenty-first century, the overall pool of capital available for biomedical investments began to shrink. Investors became increasingly worried about whether blockbuster sales (several billion dollars over the life of the patent, in the New Jersey example) can continue to be available for new products. Not surprisingly, how much insurance companies and governments are willing to pay for new treatments for serious diseases is a critical question that arises when biotech venture capitalists seek to raise new funds from their investors.

In the end, then, potential investors' excitement over the promise of stem cell technology—or any other new technology in the life sciences—must be combined with their belief that a new product will generate enough sales to repay the lengthy and technologically risky investment. That belief can only come from a firm sense that the governments and insurance companies that pay for these kinds of treatments will provide an adequate return for the risk taken. If not, life science venture capital firms will not yield good returns to their investors; as a result, the pension funds will be less able to fulfill their commitments to people's retirements, and the endowments will have less money to pay for academic programs. Moreover, these pensions and endowments have plenty of other places where they can invest their money, so poor returns driven either by product failures or by the lack of a viable commercial market for successful products will be followed by an inability of venture capitalists to raise funds to invest in the life sciences. And so, in considering the availability of the private capital that is necessary to make the STEM-to-prosperity equations work properly, we must bear in mind that venture capitalists invest not only in the dream of medical progress arising from new technologies but also in the belief that healthcare payers—largely insurance companies and governmental policy-makers—will find the money to pay premium prices for the fruits of pioneering research.

Those policy-makers, as noted above, are not just making decisions about near-term economic growth when they consider something along the lines of the New Jersey or California stem cell initiatives. Their judgments about the value of life and how they should balance healthcare costs with other spending priorities will need to be guided and informed by close attention to questions deeply within the realm of the humanities. Not only must they confront the highly controversial religious and ethical debates over the use of embryonic stem cells, for example (more on that shortly), but they also need to consider the value to society (philosophical, theological, economic or otherwise) of paying billions of dollars for what is perhaps most likely to be a modest-but-real benefit to the patients. That benefit could, at least in the early years, actually increase overall healthcare costs rather than decrease them, despite the assumptions in the reports discussed above.[41] In sum, the enthusiastic New Jersey and California reports in support of government funding for stem cell research rely on the largely self-evident prediction that society will pay lower prices for better health. That is an easy assumption. The more likely and significantly harder question is how much *more* will we pay for the possibility of better and longer lives.[42]

Policy-makers need not resolve those issues in favor of higher spending on new high technology drugs, but, if they do not, then the much-anticipated 'leverage' from private investment—the added $1.50 for every dollar of government funding—will likely disappear, and its multiplier effect on economic growth in the biomedical STEM fields will quickly dissipate. As we saw with the New Jersey and California stem cell initiatives, the assumption that government investment in the STEM fields will lead to economic growth depends on how much confidence private investors have in society's (often government's) future commitments to paying a sufficiently high price for each additional year of life for someone with cancer, Alzheimer's or Parkinson's disease.

This state of affairs brings us to a place where the humanities take center stage.

Healthcare and the humanities

We have arrived at the intersection of the humanities and the life sciences because judgments about the value of life are resulting in governments not paying for drugs whose discovery and development were initially paid for by, in some cases, those same governments. In many countries, new medicines, including high-priced, high-tech ones, must meet strict cost-effectiveness standards to qualify for payment, as is the case with the United Kingdom's National Health Service (NHS).

To take a real life and death example, we can look at some of the most promising new molecular medicines. Scientists at the government-funded MRC laboratories in Cambridge, England, won a Nobel Prize for discovering the technology for making monoclonal antibodies. Antibodies are, in many respects, the eyes and ears of our immune systems, and we have billions of them. They bind to disease-causing agents such as viruses and bacteria, and thereby mark them for destruction by potent killer cells such as macrophages (literally 'big eaters'). *Monoclonal* antibodies are laboratory-made versions of naturally occurring antibodies, and this technology allows scientists to create new antibodies that will attach themselves specifically to tumors or infectious agents in cases where the patients' bodies have not made enough of the right kinds of antibodies to combat the disease.

It is likely that more entrepreneurial companies have focused their research on monoclonal antibodies than on any other single technology emanating from biomedical research in the last 50 years. These companies range from Cambridge Antibody Technology, which AstraZeneca acquired in 2006 for over a billion dollars, to Genentech, the company that launched the biotech industry by completing the first IPO of a research-stage biomedical company, and which is now a part of pharmaceutical giant Roche, following an acquisition in 2009 for nearly $50 billion. While it is difficult to obtain an exact number, it is fair to estimate that, at the very least, hundreds of biotech companies and many thousands of well-paying jobs have been created with the goal of developing monoclonal antibody-based drugs. Even decades after the original Nobel Prize-winning discovery, the field of antibodies remains exciting enough to continue to attract start-up investments from venture capitalists around the world.

Monoclonal antibodies are such an unusually potent method for fashioning novel drugs that the technology has led to more than 20 new treatments for cancer and other life-threatening and seriously debilitating diseases, and hundreds more are in development by a wide range of companies.[43] In 2013, monoclonal antibody drugs had worldwide revenues of $63.4 billion, and six of the top ten global pharmaceutical products that year contained monoclonal antibodies.[44] The point of this extended discussion of monoclonal antibodies is that, on the one hand, this one technology has led to a great deal of the economic growth that has emanated from academic research in the life sciences. Moreover, most of the technology transfer from academic research to industry has been in the life sciences, thus making antibodies one of the most vital drivers of all STEM-related economic growth. Yet, monoclonal antibodies are often so expensive that the NHS and similar organizations in other countries have refused to pay for them. Whether these kinds of high-tech drugs are available to patients in the United Kingdom depends on a multi-step cost-benefit analysis.

Taxes set by Parliament fund the NHS, which turns to the National Institute for Health and Care Excellence (NICE) for advice on how to parcel out the inevitably limited resources available to pay for healthcare. In considering how this system works, it is important to bear in mind that a similar mechanism for approving the cost of new treatments is in place in a number of other countries and could someday also include the United States, currently the world's single largest market for pharmaceutical products.

As of 2010, a new product was likely to be recommended for reimbursement by NICE if its cost is less than about £30,000 for a 'Quality Adjusted Life Year' (typically known as a 'QALY').[45] The concept of the QALY is to combine 'both quantity (length) of life and health-related quality of life into a single measure of health gain', thus providing a 'common currency' for comparing different treatments for the full range of illnesses. That is, NICE will calculate how much it will cost for a new drug to extend a patient's life by one 'quality year' (a fully active life being more valuable than the same year in a coma, for example), thus allowing the NHS to compare the value of a new cancer drug to a new treatment for heart disease. As a result of the QALY calculations, some of the potentially life extending monoclonal medicines that were based on the discoveries of the Cambridge Nobelists do not qualify for NHS use because they cost too much.

One side of the QALY equation is a fairly straightforward collection of costs: the new drug itself, any hospitalization required, medical personnel, whatever medications may be needed for dealing with likely side effects, and anything else that allows NICE to estimate the comprehensive cost of the treatment and its expected consequences. These numbers are then weighted according to the probabilities associated with the various events, as with a side effect that only requires medication a third of the time. There may be lively debates among participants in the relatively new field of pharmacoeconomics about how to do these allocations and calculations, but it is the other aspect of the QALY question that falls more distinctly in the traditional domain of the humanities. How should a government agency decide what a year of life is worth in an era of straitened resources for healthcare?

The sensible and straightforward nature of these largely fact-based cost calculations should not obscure the really difficult moral and political judgments that are essential to the NHS's final decision about whether to pay for a new medication. NICE's recommendation, once implemented by the NHS, inevitably involves choosing whose 'life years' will be extended and whose will not be. Will every citizen be allocated an equal amount of the national medical budget, or will the chronically ill get a bigger share? Will rich and poor receive equal opportunity for new medicines? Should both taxpayers and the unemployed be treated the same? Are some diseases less worthy of expensive treatments than others? Should saving lives trump treating debilitating but non-fatal conditions? These questions—and many more of a similar nature—are not the focus of degree programs in medicine, statistics or pharmacology. They are, however, just the kinds of issues with which the humanities have traditionally wrestled, from literature and history to religion, philosophy and politics. Those are the fields that ask us to reflect on the value of life, and how we deal with genuinely difficult choices when some lives may end up being lost in the interest of saving others. (Whether humanities scholars are adequately addressing these issues is a different question—more on that in Chapter 4.)

NICE has recognized the degree to which these are challenging questions. A thoughtful document published by NICE, titled *Social Value Judgements: Principles for the Development of NICE Guidelines*, seeks to address them. The *Social Value Judgements* document begins by recognizing that NICE must make not only scientific value judgments but also social value judgments, which it defines as ones that 'relate to society rather than science'. The document lists four 'widely accepted moral principles' that have been adopted by NICE 'because they provide a single, accessible, and culturally neutral approach that encompasses most of the moral issues in healthcare'. The four principles are:

- respect for autonomy
- non-maleficence
- beneficence
- distributive justice.

After listing these principles, the *Social Value Judgements* document points out that none of them is especially hard and fast. Autonomy, for example, cannot 'be applied universally or regardless of other social values', and neither the principle of non-maleficence nor that of beneficence will avoid the need to 'balance the benefits and harms'. The widely accepted moral principles of respect for autonomy, non-maleficence and beneficence, therefore, are not expected to yield compatible outcomes in all cases, and will therefore need to be held in balance, although the *Social Value Judgements* document does not explain how that weighing process will take place.[46]

The document's discussion of the fourth principle, distributive justice, is more extensive, and this is where the humanities need to do the most work. Noting that the 'mismatch between demands and resources in healthcare leads to the problem of "distributive justice," or how to allocate limited healthcare resources fairly within society', the *Social Value Judgements* document observes that there exist 'broadly, two approaches that can be taken to resolve such problems in publicly funded healthcare systems': utilitarianism and egalitarianism. A utilitarian allocation would distribute 'resources to maximize the health of the community as a whole'. Yet the efficiency of utilitarianism can be 'at the expense of fairness' the document argues. It 'can allow the interests of minorities to be overridden by the majority, and it may not help in eradicating health inequities'. The egalitarian option, by contrast, distributes 'resources to allow each individual to have a fair share.... It allows an adequate, but not necessarily maximum, level of healthcare, but raises questions as to what is "fair".' In other words, the *Social Value Judgements* document sets out two common approaches to addressing the societal issue of how to achieve distributive justice, but expresses the concern that each of them can lead to potentially undesirable or unpopular outcomes.[47]

How does the document resolve this political and philosophical conundrum? The basic problem is that there 'is no consensus as to which approach provides the more ethical basis for allocating resources'. Since there is no general agreement on how exactly to achieve distributive justice, the document opts for transparency: the goal is 'procedural justice'.[48] That is, if the reasoning is explicit and the processes for making the decision are transparent, there need be no attempt to delve into the deeper issues of conflicting rights, duties and obligations.

The goal in seeking procedural justice is not to resolve conflicts between differing conceptions of distributive justice, but rather to ensure that 'the processes by which healthcare decisions are reached are transparent, and that the reasons for the decisions are explicit'.[49] It is not clear, however, that procedural justice always provides a sufficient basis for decision-making. One United Kingdom local health authority has actually asked for help from the humanities. Wrestling with the fact that 'the question of how scarce health-care resources should be allocated cannot be solved by specifying the criteria for a just process', the health authority concluded that the process needed to include 'guidance from philosophical analysis in coming to decisions'.[50]

However those decisions are made, with or without the help of the requested philosophical analysis, procedural justice is designed to provide for 'decision-makers to be "accountable for their reasonableness"'. The *Social Value Judgements* document specifies that this accountability for reasonableness requires NICE's decisions to exhibit 'four characteristics': publicity; relevance (that is, the grounds for decision 'must be ones that fair-minded people would agree are relevant'); challenge and revision of 'decisions that are unreasonable'; and some form of regulation to make sure that all of these characteristics are present.[51]

All of the difficult questions that the *Social Value Judgements* document attempts to resolve have been the stock-in-trade of the humanities for a very long time. Fundamental issues of justice have ancient roots, from the knotty questions we find in Plato's *Republic* to the sacred texts of various religions, including Micah's famous injunction 'to do justice'.[52] It would certainly be difficult to imagine NICE's modern principle of non-maleficence arising without reference to Hippocrates' injunction to 'do no harm', for example. Humanities scholars and their students have been discussing and debating these basic principles for millennia. Each new era raises additional issues concerning how to apply even the most basic and simple concepts, such as 'do *no* harm', a requirement that is a simply impossible goal for physicians to follow absolutely, given the side effects associated with even the highest technology medicines.

The NICE principle of distributive justice also has a distinguished heritage in various fields of the humanities, and it is such a challenging area of philosophical inquiry that scholars are unable even to agree on when the concept first arose. A recent study dates the modern conception of distributive justice to the last 200 years, but some scholars have suggested that key elements of the doctrine actually go back to the debates of theologians and canon lawyers in the twelfth century over 'the doctrine of necessity'. Others argue that more than two millennia ago 'Aristotle and Plato wrote on the question, and the Talmud recommends solutions' to issues of distributive justice.[53]

The basic idea of distributive justice (also sometimes called economic justice or social justice) is that there are 'normative principles designed to guide the allocation of the benefits and burdens of economic activity'. In modern times, governments are typically the decision-makers about which principles should apply since 'they continuously make and change laws affecting the distribution of economic benefits and burdens in their societies'. Because almost every law, 'from the standard tax and industry laws through to divorce laws hav[e] some distributive effect', governments are essentially 'always faced with a choice about whether to stay with current laws and policies or to modify them'.[54] There are many schools of thought about how economic benefits should be distributed by governments: from libertarians, who generally want the state to leave the economy alone as far as possible, to a range of often conflicting policies, the goals of which may be to advance egalitarianism, to be as fair as possible, to better the lives of the least fortunate, to eliminate gender or racial inequities, to ensure that people get what they deserve and so on. Even if there were broad agreement on the basic principles of distributive justice, there are inevitably tricky questions involved in applying them and measuring the outcomes.[55]

Whether we end up tracing the concept of distributive justice as far back as Aristotle and the Talmud, or Huguccio and Guillaume of Auxerre in the twelfth and thirteenth centuries, or perhaps more recently to Adam Smith or Rousseau, Kant, Hobbes, Locke and other writers of the last few hundred years, the point remains that the humanities have been working on—and not yet resolving, but providing thoughtful analysis and rational reflection about—this difficult issue for quite some time. While distributive justice sounds as if it should be solidly within the domain of political philosophy, the often conflicting principles of social justice not only are subjects with which religious ethicists, philosophers, and political theorists continue to wrestle, but they also attract the attention of scholars of history, literature, economics and sociology. Literature scholars, for example, have observed that Virginia Woolf's 'implied views on distributive justice permeate her novels and diaries', and these issues percolate through a number of postcolonial novels as well.[56] Scientists and physicians can figure out whether a new drug actually extends lives, and mathematicians can calculate the costs, but the STEM fields, by themselves, cannot provide a considered judgment about who should have those benefits and at what price.

That these traditional questions within the humanities must now be applied to ever more sophisticated scientific discoveries does not fundamentally alter the nature of the issues, nor does it necessarily shift the deep thinking process to people with degrees in science, medicine or mathematics. That is, people do not need to know how to create a monoclonal antibody—or even have any idea about what one looks like—to think about the value of extending lives with antibodies versus spending the same amount on other social goods and services. It turns out that applying these issues to the question of how governments should allocate limited resources for healthcare is so hard that NICE's *Social Value Judgements* document admits that it has not figured out how best to do it, and the two Harvard scholars (a philosopher and a physician) who developed the concept of procedural justice in healthcare that was adopted in that document observe that 'no democratic society we are aware of has achieved consensus on . . . distributive principles for healthcare'.[57] And so, not only does NICE and its (current and future) counterparts in other countries need to bring greater expertise about these moral and social judgments to their recommendations, but, in the end, the real decisions-makers will be the country's elected leaders, when fair-minded and not so fair-minded people declare NICE's recommendations to be unreasonable, unjust, too politically unpopular or simply not to their liking. Both the members of the public making the complaints and the policy-makers will be thinking about the value of life without needing to contemplate the specific nature of life-changing technology.[58]

When patients are denied what they believe are potentially life-saving treatments by the NHS, Members of Parliament come under considerable pressure to address the desires of dying patients and their families. A number of the very expensive new molecular medicines have been developed to treat cancer, for example, and NICE's QALY-based evaluations have meant that the NHS has not approved some of those treatments. Patients and their families have put pressure on their elected representatives to make those medicines available, nevertheless. The result was the establishment in 2010 of a 'Cancer Drugs Fund', a multi-year, multi-hundred-million pound 'work-around' of NICE's distributive justice-based budget allocations.[59] The political need for Parliament to vote for this additional funding, which provides a special benefit only for cancer patients, demonstrates how complex these issues of distributive justice in healthcare can be. A national poll reported in 2013 that the 'NHS beat both the monarchy and the Olympics to take gold in the patriotism stakes', with '[s]eventy-two per cent of people declar[ing] the NHS to be "a symbol of what is great about Britain and we must do everything we can to maintain it" '.[60] On the one hand, there is a public endorsement, in principle, for the NHS and its commitment 'to providing best value for taxpayers' money and the most effective, fair and sustainable use of finite resources'.[61] On the other hand, cancer treatments deemed not to be cost-effective are now funded outside the normal NHS decision-making process. The intense pressure leading to the Cancer Drugs Fund—essentially a politically created exception to some of the principles at the heart of the United Kingdom's most popular institution—demonstrates just how hard these questions are, and provides additional evidence that society has not figured out how best to address the difficult issues of distributive justice in healthcare.

That the public seems, at least in the case of cancer treatments, to be of two minds on the subject of how best to allocate limited healthcare resources increases the pressure on Parliament to struggle with the very same issues of distributive justice—as yet unresolved—that the *Social Value Judgements* document highlighted. And while NICE's governing board is heavily weighted toward physicians and public health experts, the country's elected government is nearly STEM-free. It turns out, instead, that a great many Members of Parliament have been steeped in humanities subjects during their university studies. For the nearly 500 members of the House of Commons in 2010 for whom information about university degrees is available (of a total of 650), only about 10 percent hold a degree in a STEM field. Of the remaining 90 percent with non-STEM degrees, the most popular fields of study are law, politics, history, economics and English, with over a dozen members of the House of Commons holding PhDs in traditional humanities subjects.[62] (Interestingly, *Times Higher Education* has estimated that three of the fields most popular with MPs—law, English and history—are among the five 'areas where universities [have] proposed cutting . . . to create extra STEM provision'.[63]) In dealing with the problem of distributive justice, these public servants will, virtually of necessity, draw on their own educations in the humanities. Moreover, they regularly seek advice from prominent humanities scholars whose work they or their political advisers may have first encountered at university. In a study by the RAND Corporation, for example, about two-thirds of humanities faculty surveyed at the University of Cambridge responded that they had influenced policy-making, and the librarian for the House of Commons 'stated that he and his colleagues would often access written outputs from peer-reviewed academic research when providing a member of parliament with information on a particular subject'.[64]

The future of STEM-driven jobs and economic growth in medicine and the life sciences will thus be very substantially influenced, and potentially severely limited, by politicians and policy-makers who may never have been in a modern laboratory, and they will be debating the moral and political effects of healthcare allocations in discussions that require no sophisticated scientific vocabulary. While their STEM-focused classmates were conducting experiments, they were reading literature, history, politics and any number of other humanistic fields, and those studies will likely inform their views about the value of life, the importance of economic growth relative to other social goods and how to weigh conflicting moral and political imperatives. And even in the unlikely event that a future Parliament or Congress were to be composed exclusively of scientists and engineers, the members would have no choice but to wade into these humanistic waters. Ultimately, with no mathematical formula on which to rely, these elected and appointed leaders will decide what justice (or politics) requires: how much our lives are worth, how long stem cells will keep us going and how many of the STEM-related jobs will continue to grow or even to exist.

How policy-makers ultimately parcel out the healthcare budget inevitably raises questions of distributive justice even more than it relates to issues of medical science. A failure by policy-makers to decide appropriately when confronted by this central question of political philosophy and ethics could be as bad for society as NICE's inability to understand the medical or economic benefits of the treatment, or, perhaps, even as unhappy a result as medical science's failure to create a new drug in the first place. For the vast majority of United Kingdom citizens, the NHS's decision not to approve payment for a new drug is, practically speaking, the equivalent of the drug never having existed in the first place. Only a fairly small percentage of people will have sufficient personal wealth or private insurance to cover the high costs of new medicines if the NHS does not elect to pay for them. In fact, knowing that the drug exists but is inaccessible to patients covered by the NHS—while it is available to wealthier neighbors or to patients in more prosperous countries—may seem less fair and reasonable to the public than if the drug never existed at all. It will probably feel like cold comfort for patients covered by the NHS to know that the United Kingdom's economy was stimulated by research funding that contributed to the development of a new drug used to treat patients in other countries if that stimulus was not financially potent enough to allow the nation to afford the drug itself.

How these questions are answered by elected officials will not only have profound medical, moral and political consequences, but there can be substantial and fairly immediate implications for economic growth as well. NICE's recommendations currently influence government reimbursement decisions in about 30 percent of the global pharmaceutical market.[65] If enough NHS-like organizations, or the politicians who decide how much funding to allocate to them, refuse to pay for these expensive new medicines, then the pharmaceutical companies will cease trying to create them, and they will stop acquiring them from biotech companies. If the large pharmaceutical companies thus lose interest in accessing new products and technology from entrepreneurial biotechnology companies, venture capitalists in the life sciences will have poor financial returns, which will cause the pension and endowment funds to dramatically decrease their investments in those venture capital firms. Shutting down the flow of private investment capital into the venture firms focused on medical research, in turn, will reduce or eliminate the number of university spin-off companies and the amount of licensing income. New jobs will stop appearing, and previously created jobs in the biotech and pharmaceutical industries, and in related fields from venture capital to contract research, will disappear. The link between science and prosperity will be broken, at least in the life sciences. And it is important to remember that life sciences research represents about 70–80 percent of the spin-off companies and licensing income associated with STEM-related academic research.[66]

Unless dramatic breakthroughs in life sciences research occur in ways that reduce the cost of new biomedical treatments by an order of magnitude or more, our economies will need to grow in other areas just to keep healthcare expenditures at their current level of GDP spending. (To see how these costs fit into the overall economic picture, it may be useful to note that, in 2011, for example, the amount of GDP spent on medicines was 2.1 percent in the United States and 1 percent in the United Kingdom.[67]) Alternatively, the need to ration healthcare will grow, in which case the state of our future health will not be decided by physicians or scientists; it will be determined by policy-makers employing arguments and making judgments about the relative values of various people's lives, and about the responsibilities of governments and citizens to one another.

How policy-makers signal to investors and companies that they will answer these questions in the future will have a dramatic effect on the willingness of private capital to invest in developing new drugs. The near-term economic growth promised by government funding for biomedical research therefore depends on credible evidence of a longer-term commitment—or at least a reason for private capital to believe in that potential commitment—to paying for the often expensive fruits of those labors. Failure by policy-makers in enough of the world's major pharmaceutical markets to show a reasonable degree of willingness to make those longer-term financial commitments will rapidly diminish the economic growth that has been projected to be derived from discoveries in the life sciences.

Lest this sound too much like a commercial message in favor of profits for the biotechnology industry, a place where I have spent most of my business career, let me pause to clarify my goals here. This is an argument for the importance of the humanities and their relevance to modern life, including their critical role in helping us decide whether to support life sciences research and to pay for the products derived from that research. Even if higher education leaders and government policy-makers agree with me that the humanities are critically important in addressing essential questions in the STEM-to-prosperity continuum, that does not mean that the best thing the humanities has to offer should inevitably serve the cause of economic growth and wealth creation. That is a subject for another day. The goal of this book is to make as clear as possible that the pathway from science to prosperity will require policy-makers to make some difficult decisions for which the knowledge and insights traditionally provided by the humanities will be essential, and for which expertise in STEM fields alone is inadequate. By the same token, if policy-makers decide, from their study of the humanities or otherwise, that those decisions required to realize the STEM-driven economic growth are the wrong ones, then they may need to re-evaluate their enthusiasm for the investments now being made in scientific research because the societal returns may be far lower than expected.

Policy-makers' failure to recognize the importance of the humanities in the STEM-based health-wealth connection will not let them avoid making those difficult decisions; rather, it will mean that the judgments, when made, will be at risk of being over-simplified and ill-informed. Financial support for the humanities may seem like a luxury in an era where those same resources could be channeled into the cure for cancer and a high-flying economy, but the price of ignoring the importance of the humanities will be paid not only in the loss of the cultural contributions that we often associate with these fields but will also potentially endanger the same economic prosperity that appears to be grafted exclusively onto the STEM fields.

Even more issues of bioethics

Despite this chapter's primary focus on government funding and incentives for life sciences research and how those decisions need to be linked to critical thinking about the payment for new medicines, we should not overlook other important areas where moral and political judgments can affect the development of new treatments for deadly diseases. The New Jersey and California stem cell research funding initiatives, for example, were proposed specifically because the United States' government had strictly limited the extent to which federal funds could be used for stem cell research. These restrictions resulted from well-publicized protests stimulated by ethical and religious objections to the use of human fetal or embryonic stem cells.

A 2004 report of the President's Council on Bioethics provided a 'Brief History of the Embryo Research Funding Debate'. It notes that in 'the immediate aftermath of the Supreme Court's 1973 Roe v. Wade decision legalizing abortion nationwide, some Americans... became concerned about the potential use of... embryos... in scientific research'. These concerns led to a moratorium on federal funding of research involving human fetuses or living embryos that was instituted by the precursor to the Department of Health and Human Services (HHS). A year later, Congress enacted a law providing for such a 'temporary moratorium' and establishing a National Commission for the Protection of Human Subjects of Biomedical and Behavioral Research. Chaired by Kenneth John Ryan, MD, Chief of Staff at Boston Hospital for Women, it included a diverse group of biologists, bioethicists, lawyers, physicians and others. Following the commission's report, the moratorium ended, and an Ethics Advisory Board was established to consider to what extent federal funding would be used for human embryo research, especially in light of recent developments in in-vitro fertilization. This board called embryo research 'ethically defensible but still legitimately controverted'. The Board's approval was required prior to any federal funding for embryo research, and when the Board's charter expired in 1980, so did the prospects for funding until another body, the Human Embryo Research Panel, was convened over a decade later, in 1994.[68]

The new Panel supported funding for embryo research under certain circumstances, including the controversial concept of creating human embryos 'with the explicit intention of using them only for research purposes'. The next year, before any federal funding was authorized, the United States Congress passed the Dickey Amendment to the HHS appropriations act 'prohibiting the use of any federal funds for research that destroys or seriously endangers human embryos, or creates them for research purposes'. Congress has adopted this Amendment each year since 1996.[69]

Not long thereafter, scientists at the University of Wisconsin reported that, in experiments funded solely by private sources, they had isolated human embryonic stem cells, and these cells could be grown and propagated according to standard laboratory techniques. Then, in 1999, HHS took the position that human embryonic stem cell research could receive federal funding, despite the Dickey Amendment, if the activities involving embryo destruction were supported only with private funds.

The guidelines implementing this policy were put into practice during the administration of President George W. Bush, who took the position that federal funding could only be used for research involving laboratory stem cell 'cell lines', or continually propagating groups of cells creating stem cells in laboratory vessels that already existed. That is, there would be no federal funding for the creation of new embryonic stem cells or cell lines. Many researchers believed that these guidelines were so restrictive that medical progress would be impeded, hence the various proposals in New Jersey, California and elsewhere to provide state funding for stem cell research.

The controversy over stem cell research continues. President Barack Obama issued an executive order in 2009 expanding the areas of research eligible for federal funding.[70] In response, the National Institutes of Health released draft guidelines that would make eligible for funding any 'research using human embryonic stem cells that were derived from human embryos created by in-vitro fertilization ... for reproductive purposes and were no longer needed for that purpose'. Opponents then sued in federal court on the grounds that the breadth of the guidelines violated Congress's express mandate in the Dickey Amendment. In August 2010, a federal district judge issued an injunction blocking the implementation of the guidelines, holding that they contravened the provisions of the Dickey Amendment.[71]

This brief history of how research funding policies have repeatedly shifted as a result of a vigorous ongoing debate about stem cell research shows how complex issues of science, medicine, theology, philosophy and public policy may be initially resolved, then reopened again and again, by elected officials, administrative agencies and judges. Each branch of the federal government has participated in the debates over the complex ethical, scientific and legal issues. Moreover, these policies often appear to shift based not only on results in the laboratory, but also, in considerable part, on the most recent election returns. In fact, each of the last few presidents has created a different advisory council of biomedical and bioethical experts to help sort out these difficult questions.

President Clinton, for example, established by executive order the National Bioethics Advisory Commission in 1995 to provide advice on 'bioethical issues arising from research on human biology and behavior', which was chaired by Harold T. Shapiro, an economist then serving as president of Princeton University. Its members included professors from a wide range of academic subjects, including religious studies, genetics, law, medicine, nursing and ethics. This commission issued a report, the gist of which was to permit a fairly broad swath of the then on-going research involving human embryonic stem cells, the area generating the most public controversy.

Several years later, in 2001, President George W. Bush constituted a new advisory body with fairly different viewpoints called the 'President's Council on Bioethics', charged with advising the President on bioethical issues that may emerge as a consequence of advances in biomedical science and technology. Philosopher and physician Leon R. Kass of the University of Chicago chaired this council, and it contained an equally diverse but quite different group of scholars, including professors of biochemistry, internal medicine and neuroscience, as well as those in ethics, jurisprudence and philosophy. It is not difficult to imagine that each President will use the power of appointment to create an advisory council that will provide the advice that may be more palatable to that President than advice that might have come from a predecessor's advisory panel.

It is beyond the scope of this book to explore all of the potential moral and political controversies that may be associated with biotechnology research, and the many political, administrative and judicial responses to them. But it is valuable to bear in mind that politically charged controversies affecting biotechnology research have periodically arisen in a variety of areas, from these issues surrounding embryonic stem cells to concerns over cloning technology, employing animals for medical testing or the use of genetically modified organisms in food crops. In each case, policy-makers in various countries have directly or indirectly restricted the use of new technologies because of political pressure unrelated to the scientific potential of the approach or its purely financial costs. Whatever may be the merits of the ethical objections that have been raised, venture capitalists and pharmaceutical companies will discount the expected returns from investing in new technologies by the added risk arising from the possibility that political decisions made in response to ethical controversies will affect the future value of a product. Serious concerns over the possibility of burdensome regulations, or even a possible ban on a new product in the commercial marketplace, will significantly diminish investors' enthusiasm for supporting such a project, especially since it will undoubtedly involve a considerable dose of technical risk as well.

Some scientists have argued that ethical and religious issues should have no role in scientific decision-making, and that protesters and legislators do not understand the scientific issues well enough to interfere with technological progress, but those arguments have not always been persuasive in the halls of government. Either as a result of political pressure, or perhaps motivated by their own ethical values, or both, public officials have taken positions on these controversial issues, and investors are forced to figure out how the resulting policy decisions will affect the viability of potential investments in controversial fields. As noted earlier, investors contemplating an investment in a new biotechnology opportunity will need to be confident that they will be handsomely rewarded for taking the massive risks associated with the simple but daunting 'Will it heal the sick?' question. Worries that a new drug will surmount the inevitably long odds and become approved for sale but not eventually become profitable—either because there is no money in the healthcare payers' budgets or because lawmakers or judges declare it to be based on forbidden technology—will simply reduce investors' enthusiasm for biomedical research and development altogether.

The point is not to ignore ethical issues or to allocate unlimited funds to healthcare costs: governmental policy need not be one of freely paying for all new drugs and freely granting permission for any and all research. Rather, the message from this analysis is that governments need to take into account these 'downstream' effects of public policy decisions when predicting dramatic economic growth as a result of priming the research pump in the near term. And taking such matters into account will require the insights of the humanities, even when the issues appear on their face to be primarily a set of scientific questions.

All government all the time?

Since so much of this chapter has focused on the importance of private investment in healthcare research, it may be valuable to reflect in closing on an entirely different scenario. Governments could decide to 'cut out the middleman' and essentially nationalize (or even multinationalize) pharmaceutical research. Instead of primarily supporting basic research and then looking to private companies and investment capital to provide the funding and expertise to develop, market and sell the resulting drugs, governments could become fully integrated drug developers. Eliminating pharmaceutical profits would certainly make medical costs lower, especially for high margin, patent protected products.

It is unlikely that it would be politically possible throughout the world to make it unlawful for for-profit companies to develop and commercialize pharmaceutical products, although enough governmental limitations on approvals or payments for new drugs could have virtually the same effect. And, of course, nothing currently prevents governments from developing drugs, either alone or in collaboration with academia or industry. In a number of cases, governmental research that has been licensed to for-profit companies has ultimately led to a successful product, and, in the future, governments could decide to take a more active role in those further development efforts.

Whether governmental research in the absence of a significant effort by commercial entities would be a better, more efficient way to develop new drugs would be an intriguing topic to consider, but is well beyond the scope of this work. What is more pertinent is how a substantial move by governments to get into the drug development business might affect STEM funding in higher education. Since such funding is typically promoted as providing a foundation for significant near-term economic growth—as in the state stem cell proposals discussed above—it is important to note that the multiplier effect of private investment will be largely or completely eliminated. At present, for example, the pharmaceutical and biotechnology industries provide nearly 60 percent of the total amount of biomedical research funding in the United States.[72] This amount, over $58 billion per annum, would likely disappear in this scenario, along with hundreds of thousands of jobs. The government could certainly replace these positions in national laboratories, but doing so would involve an annual expense of many tens of billions of dollars, even if the new government scientists were to earn less than they did when they worked in private industry, since salaries are only a fraction of the cost of drug development.

In such a nationalized approach, universities would not only lose some of the industrial grants and contracts that they currently receive for life sciences research, but the much-heralded economic growth from spin-off companies and new job creation would disappear as well. STEM research would, of course, retain its value as an opportunity to expand the breadth of human knowledge, and it would likely still contribute to the creation of new medicines (assuming policy-makers decide that advancing medical care is a politically desirable legislative goal). But the projections of an effervescent, entrepreneurial, job-creating economic stimulus driven by scientific discovery would no longer be a valid part of the financial models. A $380 million state program, as proposed in New Jersey, would no longer be expected directly to yield $1.4 billion of total economic growth. The 'leverage' or 'multiplier effect' driven by a concurrent investment by venture capitalists equal to 150 percent of the government funding would simply not exist. Life sciences research would then more closely resemble other government funding programs, such as new roads and bridges—and perhaps research and teaching in the humanities. They are public goods, all of which are important, indeed often compelling, but not directly linked to the short-term economic growth that has been attributed to the STEM fields, since that rapid growth toward prosperity has required large influxes of private capital, something that would evaporate in such a nationalized approach.

The STEM-to-prosperity continuum

In summary, then, the STEM-to-prosperity continuum over the last few decades has been fueled primarily by a potent combination of biomedical breakthroughs and a heavy infusion of private investment capital. This degree of job-creating investment requires a strong belief by the investors that society will pay handsomely for new medicines that treat life-threatening and seriously debilitating diseases. Accordingly, especially in countries where the government funds both the universities and the purchase of new drugs, as we have seen with respect to the United Kingdom (and as is happening increasingly in other countries), STEM-driven economic growth in the biomedical fields needs to be paid for twice, once at the beginning of the research enterprise, and then again at its successful conclusion in the creation of a new treatment for disease. In between, the private sector will provide the funds to create the jobs and the companies that will transform the basic biological research into therapeutic products. Deciding whether to make that double investment in STEM-driven success will require policy-makers to make judgments for which a thoughtful understanding of critical issues within various humanities fields is essential. And a failure to contribute enough financial support to allow the humanities to provide those insights into what society should do with its scientific developments—all in the name of diverting limited funding into the high-impact STEM fields—may end up inadvertently breaking the bond that has so far joined the promise of exciting STEM research to the politically attractive prospect of economic prosperity.

3
The Humanities and the Law

During US Supreme Court Justice Elena Kagan's 2009 confirmation hearings, Senator Jon Kyle asked:

> [T]he president ... said that in hard cases, adherence to precedent and rules of construction and interpretation will only get you through the first 25 miles [of a marathon] .... He says the critical ingredient in those cases is what is in the judge's heart .... [D]o you agree ... ?

In response, now-Justice Kagan said, '[I]t's law all the way down .... [P]eople can disagree about how the constitutional text or precedent ... apply to a case. But it's law all the way down, regardless.'[1]

This dialogue, which was televised, and then widely reported, raises the interesting question of what the law actually looks like 'all the way down'. Perhaps Supreme Court justices are equipped with special scientific or other observational tools that allow them to see with unusual clarity the objective constitutional facts that command a particular decision in difficult cases. Or, Justice Kagan may simply have been trying to sidestep some of the controversy generated when President Obama announced that he would appoint justices who would bring, in his view, a desirable degree of empathy to the judicial process, a position attacked by conservative politicians as allowing justices to substitute their own values for the ones enshrined in the Constitution.

The concept of the law 'all the way down', and nothing but the law, leads us to think about where 'down' is compared to the grand

(and often impressively vague) principles found in the Constitution's text. It sounds as if justices are specially trained to ignore political controversies and policy debates so as to unearth the one true meaning at the core of the Constitution. That is, great expertise resulting from years of intensive training and study will enable the discovery of clear and correct answers that are hidden from the view of the rest of us. In fact, modern judicial confirmation hearings are invariably full of testimony about the nominees' scholarly credentials, from their class rank and other academic prizes and honors to learned articles published in scholarly journals. Somehow it seems natural that high honors graduates of Princeton or Harvard, who then excel at Harvard or Yale law schools—a description that applies to all four of the most recently appointed Supreme Court justices—will likely have the capacious understanding of the law as well as the scholarly skills to discern legal fact from fiction. The Constitution is thus analogous to the Internal Revenue Code and its voluminous regulations: the right answer is in there somewhere, but only highly skilled and experienced tax lawyers know exactly where to look and how to understand the labyrinth of sections, clauses and subclauses. Yet, that straight-A-student portrait of a justice's job is not an especially good one. The most significant interpretive challenge involving the Constitution is not the text's complexity or obscurity, but, rather, its simple, broad statements.[2]

The entire constitutional text involved in many of the most important (and often the most politically controversial) cases decided by the Supreme Court about the freedom of religion, speech and press is the following: 'Congress shall make no law respecting an establishment of religion, or prohibiting the free exercise thereof, or abridging the freedom of speech, or of the press; or the right of the people peaceably to assemble, and to petition the government for a redress of grievances.' Forty-five words. That is all there is to what we call the First Amendment. (The first federal Congress that initially adopted this language in 1789 actually called it the Third Amendment, but the states refused to ratify the two amendments that Congress had placed ahead of this one.) And the key provisions of the Fourteenth Amendment that have been the subject of high profile cases over racial and gender discrimination or the controversial 'privacy' cases involving sexual activity and assisted suicide are usually just summed up in a pair of constitutional concepts: 'equal protection' and 'due process'.

The complete text of these provisions contains barely 30 words, and no further illumination about, for example, how to measure equality, or even why a provision about process might lead to extensive discussions of the nature of a substantive right to privacy.[3]

When the Supreme Court needs to apply these words to a particular case, how does it discern the Constitution's proper meaning? The answer is that the justices have turned with impressive frequency to scholarship in the humanities not only for inspiration, but also for direct guidance as to the meaning of the supreme law of the land. The precise language of the text may provide a general sense of the interpretive metes and bounds, but the shape and substance of the constitutional landscape has come from historians, philosophers, sociologists and other scholars.[4]

History and politics

The first case involving the first section of the First Amendment—the religion clauses—did not arise until the 1870s, nearly a century after the amendment was adopted. The case revolved around 32-year-old newlywed George Reynolds, and it concerned his recent wedding to Amelia Jane Schofield, as well as his earlier marriage to Mary Ann Tuddenham. With his second marriage vows, Mr. Reynolds, private secretary to a series of Mormon leaders, violated a recent federal law designed to stamp out polygamy, which was the remaining American 'relic of barbarism' after slavery had been abolished.[5] These congressional concerns about polygamy resulted in part from a wildly popular lecture tour throughout the East by 'The Rebel of the Harem', Ann Eliza Young, who wrote the bestseller, *Wife No. 19: Or the Story of a Life in Bondage, Being a Complete Exposé of Mormonism, and Revealing the Sorrows, Sacrifices and Suffering of Women in Polygamy, by Brigham Young's Apostate Wife*.[6]

The unfortunate Mr. Reynolds was nominated by the frequently married elder statesmen of the Mormon Church to serve as the defendant in a test case of the new anti-polygamy law. Reynolds was convicted, and his appeal to the Supreme Court provided Chief Justice Morrison Waite with the Court's initial opportunity to interpret the first portion of the Bill of Rights, which reads, 'Congress shall make no law respecting an establishment of religion or prohibiting the free exercise thereof.' Could Mr. Reynolds' constitutional right to religious freedom as a member of the Church of Jesus Christ of Latter-day Saints, which made it his duty to have plural marriages, exempt him from a federal law criminalizing polygamy?[7]

Judging by the frequency of modern headlines over high profile church–state issues—from the constitutionality of 'under God' in the Pledge of Allegiance to whether peyote use in Native American rituals is insulated from federal drug laws—how could it take nearly a century for a religious freedom case to reach the Supreme Court? Church–state battles certainly raged during the intervening years, but they occurred within individual states and towns. The justices had declared in an 1845 case involving the display of Roman Catholic caskets that the First Amendment did not apply to local disputes, which were the sole province of state constitutions and courts.[8] In this case, however, Mr. Reynolds lived in the federal territory of Utah, which had failed in its bid to become the new state of Deseret. The Constitution would, therefore, apply directly to his case, and the Chief Justice assigned himself the task of writing the Court's opinion in this case of first impression. Lacking guidance from either precedents or the kind of clearly applicable rule of construction that President Obama, himself a former law professor, suggested would carry a justice for the first 25 miles of a constitutional marathon, the Chief Justice turned instead to his next-door neighbor.

The Chief Justice, Morrison 'Mott' Waite, had arrived at the Court with the profile of a classic Washington outsider. He had prospered primarily as a railroad lawyer in Toledo, Ohio. During a tight presidential election, President Grant picked him as a stealth nominee from this perennial swing state after the chief justiceship had been embarrassingly vacant for eight months. Waite's biographer, C. Peter Magrath, observes that his 'primary qualification [was] his obscurity'.[9]

When he moved to Washington, Waite initially rented a house on H Street where he became quite friendly with one of his neighbors, the patrician statesman and historian George Bancroft. One of the first group of nineteenth-century Americans to receive a PhD from a German university, Bancroft ultimately became Minister to Great Britain and Prussia, Secretary of the Navy, Secretary of War and author of a ten-volume *History of the United States*. When he was living next to the Chief Justice, Bancroft was hard at work on a multi-volume history of the Constitution. He undoubtedly appeared to Waite to be an ideal 'back door' source of historical context for the Court's pioneering interpretation of the First Amendment.[10]

Bancroft painted a clear picture of the First Amendment's intellectual origins for the Chief Justice. Referring to the Commonwealth of Virginia's Statute on Religious Freedom, which had been drafted by one of Bancroft's heroes, Thomas Jefferson, the historian wrote in a personal note to the Chief Justice that '[t]he Virginia law, which guided the Virginia members of the [constitutional ratifying] convention, shows the opinion of the leading American statesmen in 1785'.[11] The message to Waite, then, was that Congress's adoption of the religion clauses in the Bill of Rights in 1789 (ratified by the states two years later) was rooted in local church–state battles in the Old Dominion and inspired by a Jeffersonian conception of how religion and government should relate to each other.[12]

With this guidance, Justice Waite embarked on his own independent research into Jefferson's views. (This was a time before the justices had law clerks to help with legal research, and so it is likely that the Chief Justice himself searched for the historical sources.) One of the items he found was a nine-volume compilation of Jefferson's papers, a scholarly resource that had been prepared by H. A. Washington, a professor of history and political economy at the College of William and Mary. In the index compiled by Professor Washington, Waite made a historic find: The first entry under the heading 'Religion Should Be Free' is a reference to an 1802 letter then-President Jefferson wrote to a group of Baptists in Danbury, Connecticut. This letter, which was not widely known during the nineteenth century, is now the most famous of all American documents on church–state relations.[13] In it, Jefferson proclaimed that the Constitution built a 'wall of separation between church and state'.[14]

The Chief Justice made this letter the centerpiece of his opinion, arguing, 'Coming as this does from an acknowledged leader of the advocates of [the First Amendment's religion clauses], it may be accepted almost as an authoritative declaration of the scope and effect of the amendment.'[15] Thanks to Bancroft's advice to Justice Waite about the Jeffersonian inspiration of the religion clauses, and thanks also to Professor Washington's inclusion of the previously obscure 1802 presidential letter in his collection of the third president's papers, nearly every Supreme Court case about religion since the *Reynolds* case has invoked the image of Jefferson's 'wall of separation'.[16]

Since Jefferson was not even in the country when the Bill of Rights was adopted, Waite needed to create a rationale for granting Jefferson such an authoritative role in the inspiration of the Constitution's religion clauses, and he followed Bancroft's clue about the 1785 religious freedom statute to learn more about church and state in the Commonwealth of Virginia.[17] That useful background came from a relatively recent *History of Virginia* written by Robert Reid Howison, a Virginia lawyer, minister and college professor, whose local pride made it easy for him to believe in the Old Dominion's inspiration of the entire Bill of Rights.[18] Howison told the story of how Jefferson teamed up with James Madison to defeat a broad-based tax to support Virginia's churches, leading to the adoption of Jefferson's religious freedom statute. And, then, a few years later, when several states were lobbying for amendments to the federal Constitution, primary credit goes to Virginia, declared Howison, since 'nearly every material change suggested by Virginia was adopted', including 'one article of amendment [which] provided for freedom in religion'.[19] Howison's history thus reinforced Bancroft's advice that the ideological origins of the First Amendment could be found in the founding fathers from Virginia.

A majority of the Supreme Court justices had spurned Reynolds' constitutional claims that his religious duty of polygamy provided sanctuary from federal prosecution, so Waite ultimately had to work around the ringing odes to religious liberty that he found in Jefferson's statements in the Virginia Statute for Religious Freedom, which proclaimed that 'Almighty God hath proclaimed the mind free.'[20] He accomplished this goal by, once again, turning to academic sources. He looked to the highly regarded legal *Commentaries* written by Columbia University's first law school professor, James Kent, where he found an opinion about how polygamy 'fetters the people in stationary despotism'. According to Justice Waite, this view was based upon the work of Professor Francis Lieber, whom the Chief Justice cited by name.[21] At the time, Professor Lieber, a pioneering political scientist and Columbia University professor, was playing a critical role in the development of political science as an academic discipline. One modern scholar calls Lieber's *Political Ethics* 'arguably the very first... treatise on the state in America'.[22] Waite actually quoted Kent who, in turn, quoted Lieber, but Waite did not employ quotation marks, so the language derived directly from the academic publication appears to be the Court's own opinion about the constitutional question, which is explicitly based on the authority of Professors Lieber and Kent. One of Waite's biographers notes that the Chief Justice's familiarity with Professor Kent's *Commentaries* dated back to when he was an undergraduate at Yale.[23]

In the end, Mr. Reynolds lost his case, and he was sentenced to prison. Beyond this profound effect on George Reynolds, there are two principal legacies of the Chief Justice's opinion, and both show how the work of scholars has directly—but nearly invisibly—shaped the nature of First Amendments rights. Professor Lieber's distinctly negative view of the social and political consequences of the practice of polygamy turned out to be the foundation for the Court's decision about the extent of religious freedom in America. Faced with a First Amendment text mandating that '*no* law' shall prohibit the 'free exercise of religion', Justice Waite carved out an exception for polygamy, despite the amount of space he devoted to Jefferson's encomia on behalf of religious liberty. The Chief Justice used the material in Kent's *Commentaries* and Lieber's *Political Ethics* to establish a constitutional rule that the religion clauses would not be a get-out-of-jail-free card, at least for polygamists who violated federal laws. A century later, this principle first enunciated by Chief Justice Waite would form the precedent for the Supreme Court to declare more broadly that the religion clauses would provide no shelter from criminal laws of 'general applicability', such as laws against illegal drug use.[24] Both the content and the intellectual history of this important area of American civil liberties law is thus traceable directly to the published work of two nineteenth-century Columbia University professors.

Constitutional cases in the area of religious freedom have almost always been controversial, both in Waite's era and in our own, and whether we agree with the extent to which religious freedom has been limited by the *Reynolds* approach is not relevant for our present purposes.[25] It is also possible that Chief Justice Waite and other judges were not motivated solely by the academic work that they cited, but by any of a host of other factors, from personal policy preferences to the plain text of the Constitution or sympathy for one of the parties. Whatever may be the actual motivation for reaching a decision, we can clearly see that the Court, in announcing the decision in the *Reynolds* case, believed that it would be beneficial to invoke the authority of Professors Kent and Lieber. The critical point for this book is the extent to which the history of the *Reynolds* case shows how scholars and academic scholarship have either directly influenced the nature of the Court's decision, or have at least been pressed into service by the Court in its published opinion to help justify a potentially controversial decision to the public. We cannot be sure, but this latter approach may have been the one taken by the Chief Justice in his use of the polygamy material from the Columbia professors since there is some evidence that Justice Waite had initially voted in Mr. Reynold's favor, and then subsequently changed his vote so that he could write the Supreme Court's opinion in the first major case involving the religion clauses.[26]

At the same time that the *Reynolds* case put the burgeoning field of political science to constitutional use, it also imprinted virtually all future constitutional church–state disputes with the image of Jefferson's 'wall of separation', thanks to historians Bancroft, Washington and Howison. One remarkable fact is the extent to which Bancroft ends up being a completely silent, but nevertheless extremely influential, partner in the Chief Justice's constitutional interpretation efforts. We have no reason to believe that Chief Justice Waite had any particular church–state agenda in mind before reaching out to his friend and neighbor for historical guidance. He seemed genuinely to be seeking knowledge about the original understanding of the religion clauses from George Bancroft, who appeared to be uniquely well positioned to provide it, thanks to his distinguished reputation for historical scholarship. In the end, Bancroft received a thank-you note from Chief Justice Waite stating, 'As you gave me the information on which the judgment in the Utah polygamy case rests, I send you a copy of the opinion that you may see what use has been made of your facts.'[27] However, there is no mention of it in the opinion itself. It took another 50 years before another historian, Bruce Trimble, discovered the Bancroft–Waite correspondence while conducting research for a biography of the Chief Justice.[28]

Many attacks over the years have labeled the Virginia-inspired interpretation of the religion clauses that Chief Justice Waite adopted from Bancroft's insights as little more than an example of 'law office history'.[29] That is, it is merely a narrow, one-sided view of history employed by lawyers solely to benefit their clients' cases. Yet, we can see that Justice Waite's church–state history was neither more nor less than what the historians he consulted had to offer at the time. These historians may have been a bit myopic themselves: They overlooked the New Englanders who played key roles in the drafting of the religion clauses, and, in discussing the intellectual background to the First Amendment, they ignored the very non-Jeffersonian church–state views prevailing among many American leaders at the time.[30] Instead, Bancroft went out of his way to position his hero, Jefferson, at the center of the constitutional action, while Howison similarly claimed full credit for his beloved home state. Right or wrong, they nevertheless provided Waite with their best professional judgments. The history may have been oversimplified, or even wrong, but it was the real thing—history as it was being written in the mid- to late nineteenth century by some of the best historians of the time, and it, quite literally, became constitutional law because of the close personal relationship between George Bancroft and Chief Justice Waite. Thus, we can see that when the Supreme Court needed to find the meaning of a never-before-interpreted provision, it turned to eminent scholars, either in person or via their published work. This pattern would be repeated in the next major church–state case, where, once again, what the Court finds, when it looks 'all the way down' for the law, is what humanities scholars say is there.[31]

Everson v. Board of Education (1947) arose at a time when the Court had changed its mind about the reach of the Bill of Rights; by this point, the justices had decided that the First Amendment did, in fact, regulate the affairs of state and local governments. The issue confronting the Court was whether the State of New Jersey could pay to bus children to Roman Catholic and other religious schools, and the case is most important for its extensive treatment of First Amendment history.[32]

Justice Wiley Rutledge is primarily responsible for the historical focus of the case, since his history-laden, dissenting opinion draft was the catalyst that prompted a historical response from Justice Hugo Black, who wrote the majority opinion, and whose initial draft was nearly free of constitutional history. Justice Rutledge did not go much further than next door for his historical sources. A good friend from Rutledge's days as dean of Washington University's law school was historian and newspaper editor Irving Brant, the author of a highly regarded multi-volume biography of James Madison. Brant was a vocal supporter of President Roosevelt, and he had personally lobbied the president to appoint Rutledge to the Supreme Court. Like Rutledge, Brant was an outspoken civil libertarian, and he was not shy about making Madison sound quite a bit like a twentieth-century Midwestern progressive. He also liked to place Madison at the center of pivotal historical events. His description of Madison's role in introducing a Bill of Rights in the First Congress allowed him to accomplish both of these goals: 'Madison had the satisfaction of developing his own previous declarations [in support of religious freedom in Virginia] into the sweeping prohibition of state support of religion and protection of individual rights found in the first amendment.'[33]

Much as Bancroft had found Jefferson's church–state views at the heart of the First Amendment, Brant's focus on Madison led to yet another Virginian's starring role in the adoption of the religion clauses. In *Everson*, Brant's biography of Madison so inspired Justice Rutledge that the fourth president's name appears more than 50 times in the opinion, and Brant's biography of Madison is cited numerous times as well. Rutledge pays particular attention to Madison's 'Memorial and Remonstrance Against Religious Assessments', written in opposition to a state tax to support churches that was debated in the Virginia legislature five years before the Bill of Rights was adopted. For Rutledge, the 'Memorial and Remonstrance' represents 'Madison's complete . . . interpretation of religious liberty [and] a broadside attack upon all forms of "establishment of religion," both general and particular, nondiscriminatory or selective'.[34] Rutledge then imports Madison's entire 'Memorial and Remonstrance' into his constitutional analysis because '[a]ll the great instruments of the Virginia struggle for religious liberty . . . became the warp and woof of our constitutional tradition . . . by the common unifying force of Madison's life, thought and sponsorship'. And there is little doubt that Madison, as he appears in the Brant/Rutledge portrait, would have been against the practice of busing children to parochial schools, especially since 'Madison opposed every form and degree of official relation between religion and civil authority', even if as little as a contribution of 'three pence'.[35]

Meanwhile, his judicial colleague, Hugo Black, was initially inclined to write a short opinion for the five justices voting to uphold the law, and he had no plans even to touch on history. When faced with Rutledge's deluge of footnotes, however, he too embraced a historical analysis that relied on Madison, Jefferson and Virginia's history. Justice Black's rapid review of the development of religious freedom in America cited a number of historians, from Macaulay's *History of England* to William Warren Sweet's *Religion in Colonial America* and Sanford Cobb's *Rise of Religious Liberty in America.*[36] Not only does he cite Madison's 'Memorial and Remonstrance', but he also draws on a fairly recently discovered cache of Madison's later writings to the effect that the 'Memorial and Remonstrance' had 'met with the approbation of the Baptists, the Presbyterians, the Quakers, and the few Roman Catholics, universally; of the Methodists in part, and even of not a few of the [Anglican] Sect formerly established by law'.[37] Ultimately, however, Justice Black veered away from Madison's strict 'three pence' approach to a marginally more flexible Jeffersonian 'wall of separation between church and state'. He averred that the wall was 'high and impregnable' but, in the end, said that while '[W]e could not approve the slightest breach', the busing program constituted 'public welfare legislation', and, therefore 'New Jersey has not breached [the wall] here'.[38]

Although Justice Black penned the majority opinion that upheld the parochial school busing program, he was anxious to provide clear constitutional guidance that the religion clauses would not permit broader governmental aid to religion. (Or, as the justice who frequently referred to himself as a 'hillbilly' from Alabama put it colloquially when speaking with his judicial brethren, 'I won't go in a whole hogically way to contribute to a church—only this far.'[39]) He accomplished this goal by providing a lengthy summary of the meaning of the establishment clause: it clearly stated that neither the state nor the federal government 'can pass laws which aid one religion, aid all religions, or prefer one religion over another'.[40] This bold (and ultimately quite controversial) interpretive statement, which goes on in a similar vein for 150 words, very closely tracked language that Black found in historian Charles Beard's 1943 book, *The Republic.*[41] While Black did not use quotation marks or mention Beard by name, the language was appropriated by the justice nearly verbatim. Justice Black was a great fan of Beard's volume, and Black's biographer, Roger Newman, who discovered the link between Black's opinion and Beard's volume, notes that the justice had once said that *The*

Republic should have been titled 'The Origin and Aim of the American Constitution'.[42] Law professor A. E. Dick Howard calls Black's (really, Beard's) statement 'the most famous *dictum* in any Supreme Court opinion on the meaning of the Establishment Clause'.[43]

Once again, as in the *Reynolds* case, a Supreme Court justice transformed scholarship about the founding era into constitutional law. And, again, the fact that a historian's insights were the basis for the decision remained completely invisible for decades until another scholar discovered the link. As we saw with George Bancroft's critical role in pointing Chief Justice Waite toward Thomas Jefferson's views of church–state relations, the remarkable influence of Professor Beard's scholarship on the Supreme Court's majority opinion was only unveiled half a century later when the research for a scholarly biography provided an occasion for a thorough review of the justice's private papers and correspondence.

In both of these religion clause cases—in Waite's opinion in *Reynolds*, which is essentially the Supreme Court debut of the religion clauses, and then again in *Everson*, which launched the modern era of church–state jurisprudence—the justices actually looked past the arguments of litigants and lawyers for insights into the meaning of the First Amendment. On their own initiative, they sought out learned scholars—historians, political scientists, law professors and other men of letters with no interest in the parties or lawsuits—whose insights would then inspire the justices' views of constitutional law. Despite its remarkable effect on the development of the law, that academic influence was, in these cases, mostly hidden from view until generations of scholarship later when more recent historians were able to identify the intellectual origins of these constitutional principles.

Throughout these church–state cases, history has been particularly influential, and, as a general rule, its use in constitutional decision-making in modern times has been both important and highly controversial. Whether the Constitution should—indeed, must—be interpreted in light of how historians have portrayed the founding fathers' intentions is a vigorously debated topic, with those of a politically liberal bent typically rejecting what conservatives have embraced as the jurisprudence of original intention (or, more recently, original meaning).[44] Yet, in these two cases involving the religion clauses, historians Bancroft, Brant and Beard bestowed on modern church–state jurisprudence a distinctly liberal, wall-of-separation cast, leaving conservatives who favor school prayer and other faith-based initiatives on the historical defensive.

One of the conservative counteroffensives can be seen in Chief Justice Rehnquist's opinion in a 1985 case: 'Thirty-eight years ago this Court, in Everson . . . summarized its exegesis of Establishment Clause doctrine' in Thomas Jefferson's 'wall of separation between church and state'.[45] The Chief Justice, dissenting in a case striking down an official prayer in the public schools, continued, 'It is impossible to build sound constitutional doctrine upon a mistaken understanding of constitutional history, but unfortunately the Establishment Clause has been expressly freighted with Jefferson's misleading metaphor for nearly 40 years.'[46] For Justice Rehnquist, the 'true meaning of the Establishment Clause can only be seen in its history',[47] but, in his view, that history is better reflected in a constitutional commentary by Harvard professor (and, at times, simultaneously, a Supreme Court justice) Joseph Story, who wrote 'An attempt to level all religions, and to make it a matter of state policy to hold all in utter indifference, would have created universal disapprobation, if not universal indignation.'[48] Ultimately, Chief Justice Rehnquist concluded that '[n]othing in the Establishment Clause . . . , properly understood, prohibits any generalized endorsement of prayers'.[49] A proper reading of the history, he wrote, is that the 'Framers intended the . . . clause to prohibit the designation of any church as a "national" one. [It] was also designed to stop the Federal Government from asserting a preference for one religious denomination or sect over others.'[50]

Nearly 30 years later, these historical issues continued to arise in church–state cases. In a case replete with citations not only to the framers and the records of the First Federal Congress but also to a host of scholars discussing that history, the Court upheld, over several dissenting opinions, prayers at a town board meeting.[51] With these church–state issues continuing to animate the Court, it is likely that volumes of church–state history will continue to appear in the continuing dispute over the original meaning of the establishment clause. How this particular constitutional battle will end is anyone's guess, but what is clear is that humanities scholars—both inside and outside the academy—have had, and are likely to continue to have, a profound influence on what religious freedom in America means.

The burden of history and the benefits of social science

History has not always been as constitutionally convenient for progressive-minded Supreme Court justices as it was in the New Deal era religion cases. In what may be the most famous case in American jurisprudence—the 1954 case of *Brown v. Board of Education,* where the Court held racial segregation in the public schools to be unconstitutional—history presented a significant problem for the justices, all of whom eventually voted to strike down laws providing for segregation of schools.[52] The relevant constitutional provision was the Fourteenth Amendment, which had been enacted in the 1860s, shortly after the Civil War. This Amendment guaranteed that every state would provide all citizens with the 'equal protection of the laws'. The question presented in the collection of school segregation cases from around the country that became consolidated as *Brown* was whether the Court would abandon its late nineteenth-century 'separate but equal' approach to the equal protection clause,[53] a doctrine that would permit segregated schools as long as the evidence showed that characteristics such as funding and facilities were equivalent.

The 'separate-but-equal' interpretation of the Fourteenth Amendment originated in *Plessy v. Ferguson,* an 1896 case in which the Supreme Court upheld the constitutionality of a Louisiana law 'providing for separate railway carriages for the white and colored races'.[54] The opinion in *Plessy* pointed out that laws 'permitting, and even requiring [the separation of races] in places where they are liable to be brought into contact do not imply the inferiority of either race to the other, and have been generally, if not universally, recognized as within the competency of the state legislatures'.[55] In support of this conclusion, the *Plessy* Court had cited the 'most common instance of this [legal understanding, which] is connected with the establishment of separate schools for white and colored children', a practice that, the opinion noted, 'has been held to be a valid exercise of the legislative power even by courts of States [such as Massachusetts] where the political rights of the colored race have been longest and most earnestly enforced'.[56]

The difficulty facing the justices who favored striking down segregation in *Brown* was that, as *Plessy* had pointed out, a considerable body of historical evidence suggested that the framers of the

Fourteenth Amendment did not think that it required desegregation. In fact, the Congress that had voted for the equal protection clause had itself endorsed a system of racially segregated public schools in the District of Columbia, where the federal Congress was directly responsible for the school system.[57] As Justice Clark said during the justices' private conference in the *Brown* case, 'I was surprised at the legislative history. I had always thought it obvious that one of the purposes of [the] Fourteenth Amendment was to abolish segregation. But the history shows differently, and we can't use that.'[58] At best, then, the history could be seen as 'shed[ding] a mixed light', as Justice Douglas remarked during the justices' discussions.[59]

The *Brown* Court eventually issued a unanimous decision proclaiming that 'in the field of public education, the doctrine of "separate-but-equal" has no place. Separate educational facilities are inherently unequal', and therefore violate the equal protection clause.[60] As segregated schools were common throughout the South at that time, the decision was enormously controversial, and the Chief Justice, a former governor of California, crafted an opinion that he knew would be the center of public attention. Legal historian Lucas Powe, Jr., has pointed out that the opinion in *Brown* was uncharacteristically short for a major Supreme Court case in the twentieth century—'a mere eleven pages... because [Chief Justice Warren] wanted it that way. A short opinion could be reprinted in full by any newspaper in the country. Warren, the politician knew the importance of getting his message to as many people as possible.'[61] One of the Chief Justice's key messages was that recent scholarship strongly supported the Court's rejection of segregated schools.

After the initial arguments in the case, the historical issues had loomed to such an extent that the Court had asked the lawyers to engage those questions in a second set of briefs and arguments. Specifically, the Court asked, 'What evidence is there that the Congress which submitted and the state legislatures and conventions which ratified the Fourteenth Amendment contemplated, or did not contemplate, understood or did not understand, that it would abolish segregation in public schools?'[62] Despite requesting all of this additional information, the Court's opinion ultimately devoted impressively little attention to the nineteenth century, and, while the Chief Justice began with a nod toward the historical background, he quickly moved to neutralize the problematic aspects of it. The history of the framing of the Fourteenth Amendment's equal protection clause may 'cast some light' (echoing Justice Douglas' comments during the judicial conference), but the history 'is not enough to resolve the problem with which we are faced. At best, [the sources] are inconclusive.'[63] After thus diminishing the potentially negative force of the nineteenth-century legislative context, Chief Justice Warren then opted for a more helpful historical perspective. He called on several scholars of the history of higher education to show how different public education had been in the late 1860s, when the Fourteenth Amendment was adopted, from what it was when the *Brown* case arose in the 1950s. In particular, 'the movement toward free common schools, supported by general taxation, had not yet taken hold' when the amendment became part of the Constitution, and, since 'public school education at the time of the Amendment had advanced further in the North, ... the effect of the [post Civil War Fourteenth] Amendment on the Northern States was generally ignored in the congressional debates'.[64] It was, therefore, 'not surprising that there should be so little in the history of the Fourteenth Amendment relating to its intended effect on public education'.[65]

The Chief Justice based these observations on several books on the history of education, all written by distinguished professors, who were cited in a footnote to the opinion: R. Freeman Butts and Lawrence Cremin of Columbia University; Howard K. Beale, a professor of history at the University of Wisconsin; Edgar W. Knight, a professor of education at the University of North Carolina; and Ellwood Patterson Cubberley, Dean of Stanford's school of education.[66] (Interestingly, despite the fact that the Court cited these studies in support of its desegregation decision, the volume by Professor Knight, which was written in 1922, had originally been brought to the justices' attention in the brief submitted by the states defending segregation because it 'offered a derogatory view of South Carolina's brief experience with racially mixed public schools in the Reconstruction era'.[67])

Chief Justice Warren next had to confront the precedential value of the 'separate-but-equal' doctrine, which had been on the jurisprudential books for nearly 60 years. In a number of mid-twentieth-century cases involving public education, the Court had found that the putatively 'separate-but-equal' schools were not really equal at all; it was, therefore, able to decide those cases without directly confronting the

Plessy precedent. But in this case, 'there are findings . . . that the Negro and white schools . . . have been equalized, or are being equalized'.[68] By declaring that the schools were being considered by the Court to be equal in *Brown*, Justice Warren set them squarely within Plessy's 'separate-but-equal' doctrine.

The Chief Justice then rephrased the issue in a way that would allow him to find the answer to the Court's constitutional question in the scholarly literature. He stated the issue thus: 'Does segregation of children in public schools solely on the basis of race, even though the physical facilities and other "tangible" factors may be equal, deprive the children of the minority group of equal educational opportunities?'[69] Based on recent scholarship in the fields of social psychology and sociology, Chief Justice Warren concluded that 'the policy of separating the races is usually interpreted as denoting the inferiority of the Negro group. A sense of inferiority affects the motivation of a child to learn.'[70] As a result of this sense of inferiority, '[s]egregation with the sanction of law . . . has a tendency to [retard] the educational and mental development of negro children and to deprive them of some of the benefits they would receive in a racial[ly] integrated school system'.[71]

Clearly declaring that advances in scholarship have the power to change constitutional outcomes, the Chief Justice proclaimed, 'Whatever may have been the extent of psychological knowledge at the time of [the "separate-but-equal" case] *Plessy v. Ferguson*, this finding is amply supported by modern authority.'[72] It is at this point that the Chief Justice inserted one of the Supreme Court's most famous footnotes. He cited a series of books, articles and reports written by scholars to support his conclusions about the effects of segregated schools. The footnote reads in its entirety as follows:

> K. B. Clark, Effect of Prejudice and Discrimination on Personality Development (Mid-century White House Conference on Children and Youth, 1950); Witmer and Kotinsky, Personality in the Making (1952), c. VI; Deutscher and Chein, The Psychological Effects of Enforced Segregation: A Survey of Social Science Opinion, 26 J. Psychol. 259 (1948); Chien, What Are the Psychological Effects of Segregation under Conditions of Equal Facilities?, 3 Int. J. Opinion and Attitude Res. 229 (1949); Brameld, Educational Costs, in Discrimination and National Welfare (MacIver, ed., 1949), 44–48;

Frazier, the Negro in the United States (1949), 674–681. And see generally Myrdal, An American Dilemma (1944).[73]

The opinion then concluded that any 'language in *Plessy v. Ferguson* contrary to this finding is rejected'.[74] The relevant authority was found in the published scholarship cited in the footnote, which included reports of psychological studies in peer-reviewed journals, and a survey of leading social scientists, as well as more wide ranging analyses by distinguished scholars, such as E. Franklin Frazier's *The Negro in the United States* and Myrdal's *An American Dilemma: The Negro Problem and Modern Democracy.* As columnist James Reston wrote the next day in the *New York Times*, 'Relying more on the social scientists than on legal precedents... the Court insisted on equality of the mind and heart rather than on equal school facilities. The Court's opinion read more like an expert paper on sociology than a Supreme Court opinion.'[75]

The footnote is famous not only for its specific content but also for the controversy it engendered over the nature of how the Supreme Court should engage in the process of constitutional interpretation. James Jackson Kilpatrick declaimed in *The Southern Case for School Segregation*, that in

> one stroke, the Warren court violated [the] precepts of judicial restraint and constitutional interpretation which it most frequently has insisted on in the past.... Abandoning law, the court wedded sociology, discarding eighty years of unbroken precedent, members of the court substituted their own notions of psychological and moral fitness for the plain and palpable meaning of the Fourteenth Amendment.[76]

While most of the commentary—both pro and con—about the influence of the social sciences in *Brown* has been directed at the studies cited in footnote 11, historian Richard Kluger has identified an equally important, yet otherwise invisible, scholarly contribution to the Chief Justice's opinion. Sandwiched between the footnotes featuring first the historians and then the social scientists was the critical conclusion that segregation 'with the sanction of law' had a profound effect on children's education. This ultimately critical concept of the importance of the force of law in sanctioning segregation had entered the record in *Brown* during the trial of the case when, as Kluger notes, 'a thirty-four year-old sociologist with strong credits in psychology by the name of Louisa Pinkham Holt, then serving as an assistant professor in the psychology department at the University of Kansas' gave her testimony.[77] She said that the

> fact that [segregation] is enforced, that it is legal, I think, has more importance than the mere fact of segregation by itself because this gives legal and official sanction to a policy which is inevitably interpreted both by white people and by Negroes as denoting the inferiority of the Negro group.... A sense of inferiority must always affect one's motivation for learning.[78]

In reaching their decision, the trial judges felt compelled by the *Plessy* precedent to uphold the constitutionality of the 'separate-but-equal' schools, but the opinion, nevertheless, contained 'findings of fact' that would be quite helpful to those challenging segregation. One of these findings was later embraced by the Supreme Court in the opinion in *Brown,* and it bore a striking resemblance to Professor Holt's testimony:

> Segregation... in public schools has a detrimental effect upon the colored children. The impact is greater when it has the sanction of the law; for the policy... is usually interpreted as denoting the inferiority of the Negro group. A sense of inferiority affects the motivation of a child to learn. Segregation with the sanction of law, therefore, has a tendency to retard the education and mental development of Negro children and to deprive them of some of the benefits they would receive in a racially integrated school system.[79]

The crucial portion of the Supreme Court's constitutional argument about the negative effects of 'segregation with the sanction of law' was thus a quotation from the trial court's finding of fact, which itself was a close paraphrase of Professor Holt's testimony. As Richard Kluger has written, Professor Holt

> did not speak for very long, but none of the hundreds or more witnesses who testified in the cluster of cases that would eventually go

> down as a landmark in legal history under the collective name of *Brown v. Board of Education* spoke words that had a more detectable impact on the phrasing of the final decision in the case.[80]

And, once again, as we saw with the influence of historians George Bancroft, in the polygamy case, and Charles Beard, in the school busing case, the most profound effects on the course of constitutional law have come from scholars who do not even make it into the footnotes of the cases, and whose critical contributions only become visible many decades later when a subsequent generation of scholars digs deeply into the archival record.

Irrespective of whether all the academic insights that played a role in *Brown* were formally acknowledged or silently appropriated, the studies referenced in the Chief Justice's opinion have been the subject of continuing controversy, especially since the research cited in footnote 11 may not have been as definitive as the Court suggested. These observations have come not only from die-hard segregationists but also from scholars who fully support the outcome in the case, but who wish the Court had given better reasons for its decision, as in the recent collection of essays by several distinguished law professors in a volume titled, *What Brown v. Board of Education Should Have Said*.[81]

The study most directly relevant to the *Brown* opinion was Kenneth Clark's research involving school children asked to choose between a black or white doll based on which was 'nicer'.[82] Clark, a professor at City College in New York and the Hampton Institute, tested students in the segregated schools involved in the various cases leading to the *Brown* decision, and, when he observed that the African-American students picked the white doll as nicer, he concluded that legally enforced segregation caused these students to have lower self-esteem. Yet, critics have pointed out that other results from Clark's published research 'included findings that African-American children attending schools in northern states (that is, states without... state-sponsored school segregation) were even more likely to prefer white dolls than the African-American children attending state-sponsored segregated schools in the South'.[83] If that is the case, the Court's key point about the feeling of inferiority caused by *legally mandated* segregation was not necessarily supported by all of the available data. The justices, however, were convinced of the proper constitutional outcome, and while they could not 'use' the history of the Fourteenth

Amendment to get there, as Justice Clark had pointed out in their conference discussions, the Chief Justice clearly felt that he could use the authoritative appearance of a series of scholarly publications instead.

The extent to which these academic studies actually motivated the justices to reach their decision in *Brown* is not entirely clear. During one of the judicial conferences, Justice Black had said that 'I can't escape the view that the reason for segregation is the belief that Negroes are inferior. I do not need books to say that.'[84] Yet, some authority was needed to provide the justices with a credible reason for putting aside a large amount of unhelpful constitutional history and for abandoning the quite clear but contrary precedent of the *Plessy* case. As Justice Frankfurter said at one of the justices' conferences, 'History speaks clearly, and the question arises—does history determine this question?... Principles must be capable of another application than this version.... Psychological changes... that is what this is about.'[85]

Whatever may have moved each of the individual justices to come together to issue a unanimous opinion in *Brown*, it is clear that the Chief Justice's opinion in this extremely controversial case relied upon research in several scholarly disciplines to provide the case's logical linchpin. And, even beyond the cited works, we can see the critical and largely invisible role played by Professor Holt, whose expert testimony in the trial court was transformed by the Chief Justice into a statement of constitutional principle. Thereafter, thanks to *Brown*'s highly visible application of academic research to constitutional law, social science research would become as much of a mainstay in lawsuits involving education as history has been in church–state cases. As law professor Michael Heise has recently pointed out, over 50 years after the *Brown* decision, 'modern sophisticated litigation seeking to enhance educational equity and opportunity... increasingly draws on empirical social science'.[86] Equality under the Constitution has thus often become a measurable mandate, and academia's social science has provided the tools and expertise to make those quantitative determinations. (As discussed at some length in the preface, these fields focusing on our understanding of the human condition, irrespective of where they fall in the administrative structure of modern universities, fall generally within my broad definition of the humanities.)

Classical and modern philosophy

One of the major political and jurisprudential debates over the past quarter century of American constitutional law has been between those who believe in what Justice William Brennan has called a 'living Constitution', and others who are devoted to the approach Attorney General Edwin Meese dubbed the 'jurisprudence of original intention'.[87] For General Meese, the process of constitutional interpretation should be straightforwardly historical: 'Those who framed the Constitution chose their words carefully, they debated at great length the most minute points. The language they chose meant something. It is incumbent upon the Court to determine what that meaning was.'[88] Otherwise, judges will be tempted to substitute their policy choices for the ones adopted by the legislature. Justice Brennan disagreed, calling Meese's approach 'a view that feigns self-effacing deference to the specific judgments of those who forged our original social compact'.[89] To the contrary, he charged, 'in truth it is little more than arrogance cloaked as humility' because the historical record is often 'far from clear'.[90] More importantly, restricting 'claims of right to the values of 1789 specifically articulated in the Constitution turns a blind eye to social progress and eschews adaptation of overarching principles to changes of social circumstance'.[91] For Justice Brennan, the Court's 'eternal quest' is to 'achieve ... a comprehensive definition of the constitutional ideal of human dignity', in light of the fact that 'the demands of human dignity will never cease to evolve'.[92]

For those who seek to follow the original meaning of constitutional provisions, the study of history is essential. Someone must unearth the archival materials and then situate them within their eighteenth- or nineteenth-century context. The historian's work is often informed or supplemented by the efforts of scholars of literature, language and political theory, which can offer a richer framework for the understanding of the linguistic and intellectual milieu of the constitutional framers. Sometimes, these historical judgments literally become part of the Constitution as a result of their influence on the justices' opinions.

Meanwhile, justices more favorably disposed toward adopting Justice Brennan's concept of a 'living Constitution' need to seek evidence of social progress and the evolving meaning of the concept of human dignity. It is, therefore, not surprising that, in education cases, the kind of sociological and psychological research made prominent in *Brown v. Board of Education* has been a recurring theme. At the same time, the concept of human dignity has formed a fertile area for the research and writing of legal and political philosophers. Whether seeking to chart a constantly changing course of human dignity, or, instead, explicating what they believe to be the fixed and timeless laws of human nature, philosophers, ethicists, theologians and others who provide the intellectual raw material for justices need to consider how constitutional language about 'due process' or 'equal protection' should be interpreted in controversial areas, such as 'right to life' or 'right to die' cases.

The Supreme Court has regularly sought the wisdom of a variety of ancient and modern philosophers. We will never know how much philosophy may have indirectly influenced the Court's decisions in difficult constitutional cases, but two scholars, Neomi Rao and Thom Brooks, have found nearly 70 Supreme Court opinions in which a leading philosopher is mentioned by name, from the ancients to quite active modern philosophers.[93] Inasmuch as Supreme Court opinions have become longer and more detailed over time, it may not be surprising to find that more than half of the cases in which philosophers have been invoked by the justices have occurred since 1950.

Montesquieu was an early favorite of the justices, with his works garnering seven references in the nineteenth century, but his views on the nature of limited government may have fallen out of fashion during the New Deal's nationalizing impulses, because he has not appeared since 1926. Overall the Court's most popular philosophers, each of whom has been cited by name five or more times, are: Plato, Aristotle, Montesquieu, Kant and Bentham. While these great philosophers certainly did not write with the framing of constitutional law in mind, modern philosophers have not been reluctant to enter the fray directly through *amicus curiae* briefs submitted to the Court, especially in cases involving high profile social issues. One such friend-of-the-court brief was filed by a 'Who's Who' of modern academic philosophy—Ronald Dworkin, Thomas Nagel, Robert Nozick, John Rawls, Thomas Scanlon and Judith Jarvis Thomson. They urged the justices to declare a constitutional 'right to die' in a pair of 1997 cases involving assisted suicide.[94] While the justices declined to follow the philosophers' advice—or even to refer to their brief—in those cases, the Court did cite the 'Brief of Amicus Curiae Bioethicists', a group of over two dozen scholars, about half of whom were identified as professors of philosophy.[95]

The author of the Court's majority opinion in this 'right-to-die' case, Chief Justice Rehnquist, generally foreswore philosophy in favor of a considerable focus on history. He noted that the justices 'have regularly observed that the Due Process Clause specifically protects those fundamental rights and liberties which are, objectively, "deeply rooted in this Nation's history and tradition"... and "implicit in the concept of ordered liberty," such that "neither liberty nor justice would exist if they were sacrificed"'.[96] Assisted suicide, according to Chief Justice Rehnquist's review of the relevant 'history and tradition', was not one of those deeply rooted fundamental rights. But, the philosophers were not completely ignored. Justice Stevens, in a concurring opinion, picked up on themes from one of the principal authors of the philosophers' brief when he argued for giving 'proper recognition to the individual's interest in choosing a final chapter that accords with her life story, rather than one that demeans her values and poisons memories of her'.[97] In support of that particular reading of the Fourteenth Amendment's 'due process' clause, Justice Stevens quoted from Professor Dworkin's *Life's Dominion*:

> Whether it is in someone's best interests that his life end one way rather than another depends on so much else that is special about him—about the shape and character of his life and his own sense of his integrity and critical interests—that no uniform collective decision can possibly hope to serve everyone even decently.[98]

The enduring attraction of history

From ancient philosophy to the modern empirical social sciences, and from linguistics and literature to psychology and political science, an impressive range of scholarly disciplines have become embedded within modern American jurisprudence.[99] Of all these fields, history is likely to play the most significant continuing role in constitutional decision-making, despite the lively and ongoing 'living constitution' debates, not least because opinion polls show that about half of the American public believes that 'the US Supreme

Court should base its rulings on its understanding of what the US Constitution meant as it was originally written'.[100] It turns out that history's appeal extends even beyond the half who believe that it should determine the Supreme Court's understanding of the Constitution. I commissioned a survey in 2012 to discover whether people in the remaining 50 percent discount historical approaches entirely, or whether they believe that an originalism analysis should play at least some role in the justices' thinking. The answer was that 'over ninety percent of all respondents believe that the original meaning should play at least some role in the Supreme Court's decision-making'.[101] From the public's point of view, history (and historians) should be a prominent part of constitutional law. If nothing else, this popular viewpoint is likely to encourage politicians to look for historically-minded 'originalist' judges to appoint to the federal courts.

The justices and the public nevertheless need to be thoughtful about Justice Brennan's concern that the historical record is often 'far from clear'. There have, however, been occasions when the justices, upon following the law 'all the way down', at least to its historical bottom, find the history to be both clear and compelling. In 1983, the Court decided that the practice of having official chaplains in state legislatures did not violate the Constitution, largely because the First Congress had appointed chaplains at essentially the same time as it adopted the First Amendment. In the justices' internal conference discussions, Chief Justice Burger began by recounting the key elements of this historical record in support of upholding the chaplaincy practice, and the conference notes show how three additional justices found this historical evidence to be definitive:

> *White*: I agree with the Chief Justice. History weighs heavily with me.
>
> *Rehnquist*: The 'page of history' theory requires [me to uphold the practice].
>
> *O'Connor*: History is my basis.[102]

Even when particular justices are ambivalent about whether history should determine the outcome of a modern constitutional case, they may believe that they will speak more persuasively in their opinions if they cite historical sources. Their target audience might be their originalist colleagues on the Court, or perhaps the 90 percent of the general public who believes that the framers' understandings of fundamental rights should be a relevant factor in the Court's interpretation. As Chief Justice Warren was well aware in the *Brown* case, the American public follows the Supreme Court's rulings in high profile cases, and the opinions—or at least excerpts from them—are often printed in newspapers, and, nowadays, are available virtually immediately on the internet.[103]

Nowhere can this embrace of historical analysis by not-usually-originalist justices be seen more clearly than in the 2008 case, *District of Columbia v. Heller,* where dueling majority and dissenting opinions invoked a host of academic articles and monographs in support of diametrically opposite readings of the original meaning of the 'right to bear arms' described in the Second Amendment.[104] While such an approach might normally be expected of the Court's historically minded justices, the framers' words flowed just as freely from Justice Stevens, probably, at that time, the Court's least likely devotee of the conclusive authority of the framers' intentions; and eventually, all nine justices joined one or another of the odes to original meaning.

At issue was a District of Columbia prohibition on the possession of handguns. The constitutionality of this law arose under the rarely litigated Second Amendment, which reads, 'A well regulated Militia, being necessary to the security of a free State, the right of the people to keep and bear Arms, shall not be infringed.' The key question was whether the introductory language about the 'well regulated Militia' meant that the 'right of the people to keep and bear arms' was limited to firearms used in connection with militia or other military service. The Court, in a five to four decision, held that the District's 'prohibition on the possession of usable handguns in the home violates the Second Amendment to the Constitution'.[105]

Justice Scalia is one of the Supreme Court's most prominent modern originalists, as can be seen in both his judicial opinions and his academic writings, where he once proclaimed himself merely a 'faint-hearted' originalist for being reluctant to countenance flogging under the Eighth Amendment's ban on 'cruel and unusual punishments' clause, despite the practice's popularity at the time of the Constitution. He wrote an enthusiastically historical majority opinion in the *Heller* case. His 64-page majority opinion, which qualified Justice Scalia as a 'real historical writer' in the opinion of legal historian Joyce Lee Malcolm, contained literally scores of references to historical materials.[106] Justice Scalia's extensive collection of sources reached back several centuries to Samuel Johnson's eighteenth-century dictionary of the English language and forward to a 'forthcoming' law review article, and included articles, monographs and edited collections from scholars in numerous fields—history, law, politics, lexicography, linguistics, English literature and others. In the end, after a detailed analysis of the constitutional language and its historical context, Justice Scalia concluded that the Second Amendment contains 'an inherent right of self-defense', and that the District's ban of handguns, 'the most preferred firearm in the nation to keep and use for protection of one's home and family', violates the Constitution.[107] Justice Scalia's review of English and American history had convinced him that, at the time of the Constitution, the right to own firearms was held by all citizens, and that the 'prefatory clause' about the importance of the militia did not restrict that right to people in military service.

Justice Stevens' dissenting opinion, joined by three other justices, plunged just as deeply into a careful, step-by-step originalist analysis, with, again, history and historians appearing on virtually every page of his 46-page opinion. As sure as Justice Scalia was that the history pointed directly to the existence of an individual right to possess firearms, Justice Stevens was at least as confident that the Second Amendment was only about the 'right of the people of each of the several States to maintain a well-regulated militia'.[108] From looking especially carefully at the various drafts of the language that became the Second Amendment, as well as the arguments employed by the framers who were speaking in favor of the provision, he concluded that the amendment's origin was simply 'a response to concerns raised during the ratification of the Constitution that the power of Congress to disarm the state militias and create a national standing army posed an intolerable threat to the sovereignty of the several states'.[109] Accordingly, for Justice Stevens, since the District's ban on handguns would not interfere with a state militia, it should be upheld as a valid legislative act.

Justice Breyer added a dissenting opinion that was joined by the three other dissenters. He combined yet another historical argument with a large amount of contemporary social science research about gun crimes. In the end, he concluded that, even if Justice Scalia's 'individual right' reading of the Second Amendment were correct, the District of Columbia handgun law would nevertheless pass constitutional muster. When he carefully reviewed the gun-related laws in effect in the various states during the founding era, Justice Breyer pointed out that 'colonial history... offers important examples of the kinds of gun regulation that citizens would then have thought compatible with the "right to keep and bear arms" '.[110] Major population centers had restrictions on firing guns within city limits, as well as regulations on storing gunpowder that would usually have put quite a distance between gun owners and their ammunition. And, therefore, for Justice Breyer, 'historical evidence demonstrat[ing] a self-defense assumption' in the Second Amendment 'is the *beginning* rather than the *end*, of any constitutional inquiry'.[111] That further inquiry revolves around 'whether the statute imposes burdens that, when viewed in light of the statute's legitimate objectives, are disproportionate'.[112] He concluded that the District of Columbia's handgun restrictions were consistent with the Second Amendment based on a lengthy review of modern gun-related injuries and crimes. Justice Breyer's analysis cited a wide body of literature, including books and articles published by scholars of public health, medicine, criminology, public policy, law, sociology and economics. In the end, his conclusion, based on all of the data and analysis contained in these scholarly sources, was that the District of Columbia's law was 'a proportionate... response to the compelling concerns that led the District to adopt it'.[113]

* * *

To return to this chapter's original question, What does constitutional law look like 'all the way down', the answer seems to be that, in some of the most important and controversial cases, it is a complex mix of facts, methods and arguments derived from a host of fields of scholarly study. The language of the Constitution, on its face, does not tell us what it means for citizens to have the equal protection of the laws, how freely religion can be exercised, what constitutes a law 'respecting an establishment of religion' or who gets to 'keep and bear arms'. Nor does it delineate any clear set of rules by which justices can discover whether the death penalty (or flogging) is 'cruel and unusual', or if pornography, flag burning, political speeches and commercial advertisements are all equally deserving of constitutional protection. Time and again, the justices have reached out to works of scholarship when they talk about what the constitutional language *did mean* at the time of the founding, or what it *should mean* in our far more complex modern society.

New scholarship has even helped propel the Court to change its mind over fairly short periods of time (at least by judicial standards). The Supreme Court declined to strike down criminal sodomy laws in a 1986 case in which the justices relied heavily on the history of similar statutes throughout English and American law.[114] Within two decades, the Court reversed its position in *Lawrence v. Texas*, based, in part, on the fact that '[i]n academic writings, and in many of the scholarly *amicus* briefs filed to assist the Court in this case, there are fundamental criticisms of the historical premises relied upon by the...opinions' in the earlier case.[115] With new history neutralizing the old history, the Court, in an opinion by Justice Kennedy, then looked (somewhat controversially) to the outcome of similar cases in other countries, including the United Kingdom's Parliament and a decision of the European Court of Human Rights, in which one opinion cited John Stuart Mill as well as more modern philosophers of law.[116]

Justice Kennedy's international focus is an important reminder that the appropriate definition of fundamental rights is a critical question for every country, and the key questions, as well as the methods used to answer those questions, are often common to the various constitutional courts. The same issue presented in the American *Lawrence* case, for example, led the Constitutional Court of South Africa to wrestle with the meaning of 'equality' and 'dignity' in the context of South Africa's history, with the Court concluding that 'Just as apartheid legislation rendered the lives of couples of different racial groups perpetually at risk, the sodomy offence builds insecurity and vulnerability into the daily lives of gay men', and, therefore, 'it is a palpable invasion of their dignity'.[117] In Zimbabwe, by contrast, the High Court of Harare applied an essentially originalist analysis 'to reject a claim that laws criminalizing sexual acts between males were unconstitutional under the prohibition on sex discrimination'.[118] Noting that 'because the law predated the Constitution and because Zimbabwe's Constitution...did not explicitly prohibit sexual orientation discrimination', the Court concluded that the 'framers did not intend to invalidate sodomy laws'.[119] And so, we can see that, while the particular framers or the specific philosophical traditions may differ from country to country, the jurisprudential toolkit remains much the same as constitutional courts from around the world wrestle with difficult and controversial issues of civil rights and liberties. Inside that toolkit are the facts, analyses, theories and opinions of scholars, typically made available to the courts via the conventional modes of scholarly discourse, namely peer-reviewed publications.

What sharpens the edge of these challenging constitutional questions is not only the fact that many people disagree strongly about how to answer them, but also that, at least in the American judicial system, these issues only reach the Supreme Court when someone wants the justices to strike down a law.[120] Since the Court is empowered under the Constitution only to decide specific 'cases and controversies', the justices are not in a position to render hypothetical legal advice about proposed policy choices. Therefore, when they do set out to render an opinion, it means that they have been asked to invalidate a law that has been duly adopted by a legislature made up of elected representatives, and that has been signed by an elected governor or president. In other words, 'We the people', through a constitutionally ordained legislative process, have spoken; the people's representatives have adopted a particular policy, and the resulting lawsuit puts the Supreme Court in the position of being asked to deny the people the results of that democratic process because someone has asserted that the law contradicts language—or perhaps principles—found in the Constitution. That language, however, is often impressively vague (or at least terse), and what is 'all the way down' to its textual core is not always clear. It is at this point that scholars have supplied the Court either with the Constitution's meaning or, at least, with the endorsement of scholarly opinion for the Court's opinion: through the medium of the Supreme Court, scholars may at least help determine whether legislatures will, in fact, be permitted to implement what they have voted for.[121]

However the Supreme Court justices reach their conclusions about the constitutionality of a law, it is certain that, once a controversial decision is announced, many people will scrutinize and criticize it. In this hothouse environment, it is impossible to know whether, in any particular instance, the Supreme Court justices are appealing to scholarship—to the historical, sociological, philosophical or other published literature—to lead themselves to the correct constitutional conclusion, or whether instead their political inclinations (or gut feelings) determine the outcome of the case, and the scholars and their footnotes are then invoked primarily to provide intellectual cover for the foregone conclusions, what The Mikado's Pooh-bah referred to as 'corroborative detail . . . intended to [bestow] "artistic verisimilitude" '.[122] Either way, scholarship in a wide range of disciplines will undoubtedly continue to be the Court's constant companion in difficult constitutional cases. Scholars have yet to sort out exactly what the framers meant by many of the Constitution's most heavily litigated provisions, while, on the 'living Constitution' front, evolving notions of human dignity are, by definition, constantly in motion, and thus demand on-going philosophical attention. And so, for each of these two leading schools of constitutional interpretation, the humanities will need to continue to provide illumination when the justices follow the law, as Justice Kagan put it, 'all the way down,' much as she did, in one of her first opinions in a First Amendment case, where she invoked James Madison and Samuel Johnson's English dictionary, as well as recent historical scholarship about the founding era.[123]

4
Toolboxes, Preferences and the Humanities

So far, the focus of this book has been on showing that we—all of us, as in 'We the People'—need the humanities. We need the depth of learning and the critical thinking found in the best humanities scholarship. In particular, we need that scholarship to be able to help us understand and deal with practical issues that affect the economy and other important elements of our daily lives. Some of those issues are the ones I have described in the areas of healthcare and civil liberties, which are likely to remain important and controversial well into the future. At the same time, these questions stand for the broader class of policy issues where a small number of powerful people—generally, high-level policy-makers appointed by our elected political leaders—will decide how the rest of us will live.

In our modern democracies, we expect those who wield that kind of power to do so under a set of conditions—constitutions, statutes, regulations, treaties and so on. These written instruments are essentially the commissions by which we set the limits of their authority. Then, even when they do act within the proper bounds of the power we have delegated to them, we expect the policy-makers to exercise that authority based on their best understanding of the common good, and not necessarily just in accordance with their own preferences.[1]

As we have seen in chapters 2 and 3, policy-makers have often looked to humanities scholarship for help in interpreting the charters by which they act on behalf of the public, and in selecting the best substantive course of action to serve the common good, especially when the issues have involved deeply contested issues of public policy. These decision-makers have turned to the work of scholars not only for the possibility of obtaining valuable information and guidance, but also (and perhaps equally importantly) for the appearance of independent external support for decisions about controversial topics. Scholars' ability to provide the imprimatur of objective, expert advice may be especially valuable when the policy-makers' choices run counter to the instincts of many citizens. As the current President of Princeton University, then writing as a professor of law and public affairs, Christopher Eisgruber, has said about the Supreme Court of the United States, 'When the judge's decision flies in the face of national electoral majorities, the task of reconciling justice and American public opinion will be especially challenging. Here historical argument may play a special role. By appealing to history, judges may attach a popular pedigree to unpopular decisions.'[2]

There are several ways to think about this comment, especially since this recommendation comes in a book where he generally argues against the idea that the Supreme Court should use history as a guide to interpreting the Constitution. On the one hand, the 'popular pedigree' statement offers a rhetorical strategy for the politically powerful, such as justices of the Supreme Court, to use arguments derived from historical scholarship to provide a publically acceptable justification for a decision that the Court has made, irrespective of whether the Court had actually been influenced by historical evidence. On the other hand, this strategic advice raises the question of why the demands of justice, as perceived by the nine Supreme Court justices (or perhaps only a majority of five of the nine), might 'fl[y] in the face of national electoral majorities'.[3] How can we explain the fact that the justices' knowledge or reasoning can be so different from the thinking of a majority of the public?

This disjunction between the Court's and the public's conception of justice may have a variety of causes. It could be that the justices simply have the intellectual capacity to identify the demands of justice with unusual clarity. That vision, combined with both personal and political courage, may enable them to choose the just path, even in the face of the contrary preferences, or the clamoring, of a misguided public. In these cases, the people may be mistaken, may have been swayed by demagogues or may have become content to choose expediency or short-term self-interest over a just but unpopular course of action.

At the same time, it is also possible that a decision that flies in the face of 'national electoral majorities' may result from a viewpoint that is shared by the members of the nation's highest court (and perhaps other intellectual elites) but not by the public, where alternate conceptions of justice may have strong support. That is, while there are cases where the public may be wrong, it is also possible that, on some issues, there is a broader universe of sincerely held and potentially valid beliefs about the nature of justice and the common good than may be found in the views that are most popular with judges or other high-level policy-makers.

Since we have seen that scholarship can be a powerful force in shaping the decisions of the women and men who hold positions of particularly concentrated policy-making power, the question for this chapter is whether today's body of scholarly literature is sufficiently sensitive to the range of potential issues, methodologies and preferences to best serve the common good. I will assume that scholarship is important not only as intellectual cover for a foreordained policy choice, but also for genuinely providing the kinds of in-depth study and critical analysis for which government decision-makers may lack the time or the training. (This is an optimistic assumption, but one that is supported by the examples in the earlier chapters.) Will the policy-makers obtain the insights allowing them to appreciate the range of concerns that hold sway with society at large?

There are at least two reasons that scholarly input might not encompass as broad a perspective as would ideally be helpful. One is that administrative barriers and methodological differences may inhibit experts in one field of study from taking into account potentially valuable perspectives from their colleagues in other scholarly disciplines. Although interdisciplinary research appears to be increasing in popularity, the lack of regular connections between far-flung departments or faculties may make it difficult even for diligent scholars to be fully aware of all of the issues that may be relevant to a particular policy decision, and, therefore, they may not consider the kinds of interdisciplinary collaborations that could be productive. The second possibility (and there may well be more than just two) is that the social and political views that, from time to time, dominate scholarly discourse may differ substantially from the perspectives held by the public. Varying assumptions about the role of government in society, the proper nature of civil and political liberties, the attractiveness, or not, of market economies and so on are the kinds of preferences that can significantly affect how a particular policy will be analyzed by scholars and the public.

The value of diversity

Professor Scott Page, of the University of Michigan, has written one of the most powerful arguments for the value of diversity in policy-making. Simply stated, his book, *The Difference*, argues that the ideas that '"collective ability equals individual ability plus diversity" and that "diversity trumps ability" are mathematical truths, not [just] feel-good mantras'.[4] Accordingly, the wide range of perspectives, tools and attitudes that comes with a diverse group will allow it to solve problems better than less diverse groups. As he writes, 'When we say that diversity leads to better outcomes, what do we mean? Do we mean better solutions to hydraulic engineering problems? Do we mean better weather forecasts? Do we mean better government welfare policies? Yes, yes, and yes.'[5] Professor Page divides these differences into the somewhat related categories of 'toolbox' diversity and 'fundamental preference' diversity.

Toolbox diversity says that if we could get a variety of academic disciplines to become more engaged with each other, potentially better policy analyses and solutions might emerge. As Professor Page writes, '[C]onsider four current large-scale issues: environmental sustainability, world poverty, international security, and disease'.[6] For there to be '[s]ignificant breakthroughs in any of these areas', he argues, 'we need the perspectives of physicists, chemists, biologists, psychologists, sociologists, immunologists, economists, and political scientists—and more'.[7] (The 'and more' could well refer to much of the humanities.) The most important thing, he points out, 'is sharing perspectives, heuristics, interpretations, and predictive models across the disciplines'.[8]

Even beyond this kind of toolbox diversity, many of the important perspectives the humanities can offer to policy-makers fall within the more challenging realm of diversity, which Professor Page calls 'fundamental preference diversity'. He points out that groups where people disagree sharply about which goals are the most important can be significantly more diverse than those where everyone is aligned on a common goal. At the same time, however, these differing preferences are likely to create conflict. For example, are we trying to create such wealth in the community that, over time, the proverbial 'rising tide will lift all boats', and everyone will ultimately be able to afford the best healthcare? Or is our goal to maximize the equality of access to all medical treatments right now, even if doing so might diminish the community's ability to create as much wealth in the future as it would otherwise? Those focused on wealth-building are more likely to emphasize different tools and techniques than experts in the equality of distribution, and therefore, fundamental preference diversity can contribute to toolbox diversity. But, while fundamental preference diversity can be a good thing, it can be painful when it brings together people with clashing values.

Governments have no choice but to deal with these fundamental disagreements because their citizens hold such a wide range of views. As a result, legislatures typically reflect (often messily) these diverse and conflicting preferences. Professor Page sees this as a good thing:

> If we believe that most preference diversity is fundamental, then putting together a committee to make a decision that has society-wide impact [for 'committee', we can also read: 'legislature'], we want representatives with diverse preferences. In fact, we want [those] preferences . . . to *reflect* those of society so that any choice . . . will be acceptable to most of society.[9]

The policy arenas that have been discussed in this book involve society-wide decisions about issues where there is considerable fundamental preference diversity evident in public opinion, yet those decisions are not being made by large, diverse representative bodies. Instead, they are being taken by powerful policy-makers who may not fully reflect society's complex and conflicting values. For help, these decision-makers have regularly turned to leading universities where, it turns out, humanities scholars are also considerably less diverse than the public, at least in their fundamental political preferences, as discussed at greater length below. If Professor Page's analysis is right, this compounded lack of diversity may result either in less good decisions, or, at least, in decisions that may not always be easily 'acceptable to most of society'.[10]

If scholarship is unable to provide the full range of methodologies and expertise that policy-makers need to consider, or if scholars fall too far out of touch with the public's understanding of social and political values, then the usefulness of the humanities to society could be diminished. First, scholarly contributions to public policy (both individually and in the aggregate) may be more narrowly focused and less thoughtful than they could be. Second, even when the scholarly analysis is thorough and complete, as well as being genuinely learned and wise, it may proceed from basic assumptions so inconsistent with those held by the majority of the public that it will be difficult for both the scholars and the policy-makers to convince the public of the virtue of the right course of action.

As can be seen in the chapters on distributive justice in healthcare and civil-liberties issues, public acceptance does not always smoothly follow from the policy decisions. In the United Kingdom, the Cancer Drugs Fund is a legislative work-around to the basic equality and cost-effectiveness analyses of the National Health Service. Even an extremely popular approach to distributing healthcare fairly can run headlong into the public's simultaneous desire to adjust the system to compensate for the fact that some potentially life-saving cancer products were deemed not to be cost-effective.[11] Meanwhile, the church–state decisions of the Supreme Court in the 1950s led to a call by 49 of the country's 50 state governors for a constitutional amendment that would lower the wall between church and state. For humanities scholarship to be useful not only in problem-solving, but also in finding ways to convince the public that the policy solutions are the right ones, we need it to consider a wider range of toolboxes (interdisciplinary analyses) and fundamental preferences (social and political views) than may always be the case today.

Diversity in academia?

Chapter 2 discussed the advice government policy-makers have received from scholars about the financial benefits of funding research in the life sciences, on the one hand, and the advice taken by other policy-makers about the allocation of national health resources, on the other. It demonstrated that basic assumptions about the nature of a good society—how healthcare markets should function, the role of new medicines in job creation, and the appropriate distribution of health resources—differed enough to put those two sets of academic advice on a potential collision course.

In analyzing whether New Jersey and California should fund stem cell research in the hopes of creating new medicines, the reports from scholars at Rutgers and Stanford calculated the likely future financial return to the state from technology royalties, taxes collected, jobs created and lives saved.[12] One calculation based the state programs' projected future royalty revenues on medical market projections prepared by an investment banking firm.[13] These projections, created by stock market analysts to advise their clients on investments in biotech company shares, assumed that there would be a robust and expanding future marketplace for the purchase of new treatments. The New Jersey and California reports, therefore, projected that each drug emerging from the funded research would achieve revenues of $3 billion. Additionally, to estimate the economic value of life-years saved by these new therapies, the scholars relied on calculations first made in an analysis of the benefits of the Clean Air Act by the Environmental Protection Agency, leading to an economic value per life-year saved of $198,000.[14] Nowhere in the report is there a consideration of the burdens on payers, especially government payers, that might result from the additional costs of the new treatments (a toolbox issue), nor is there a discussion of whether pharmaceutical markets that distribute healthcare on the basis of people's ability to pay represent a more just, more politically desirable, or even more likely future approach than a system that seeks to distribute healthcare without regard for citizens' finances (fundamental preference issues).

At about the same time, organizations such as NICE, the UK's National Institute for Health and Care Excellence, were relying on experts in moral philosophy and public health to figure out how to allocate limited governmental health resources fairly. Those experts did not, at least in the first instance, discuss how these allocation decisions could negatively affect the government's expected returns on its investments in life sciences research, or on the possible benefits to society from wealth creation by pharmaceutical companies developing costly products (the other side of the toolbox issue).[15] Moreover, a life-year saved would be valued at around $50,000, not $198,000, and government policy, rather than private markets, would allocate the nation's limited health resources.[16] The result is that some of the breakthrough drugs that the investment banking report projected to generate billions in revenues were not recommended for payment by the National Health Service, thus diminishing the size of the market that would repay taxpayers for investing in the basic scientific research. In short, political commitments to a substantially egalitarian health system, combined with cost-effectiveness analyses employed to ration limited healthcare resources, influence the global marketplace for new drugs, and, therefore, affect the financial returns from governmental investments in scientific research. The scholars advising on the proposals for government-funded research had assumed an open and expanding market, and did not discuss alternative approaches to the pharmaceutical market or the effects of expensive new medicines on national health systems; meanwhile, the scholars focused on distributing health resources did not dwell on the effect of their approach to distributive justice on the economic benefits to society of the life sciences research. As the latter scholars write,

> Just how to balance public interests and private incentives is a difficult policy issue that requires careful thought about how to assign private property rights in technologies that build on publicly funded research and careful public examination of generally proprietary information about drug development strategies and costs employed by pharmaceutical companies. We refrain from speculation on them here.[17]

Although these debates would seem to be much more about money and finance than the humanities, the differences in the two reports are rooted in different, and potentially competing, moral and political philosophies as they relate specifically to wealth creation and the distribution of limited health resources. Restricting payments for breakthrough drugs in the interest of minimizing healthcare costs and equitably distributing health resources could make life sciences R&D not worth the financial investment, or at least not worth governmental subsidies. Alternatively, subsidizing research to create high-paying jobs and expensive new treatments may ultimately either bankrupt the payers or lead to an unacceptably poor return on the research investment in light of other governmental priorities.

Those health and wealth policy judgments are based (either explicitly or implicitly) on policy-makers' judgment about the best way for government to serve the common good. To do so most effectively, the policy-makers (and their scholarly advisers) responsible for public health, on one hand, and those charged with creating wealth, on the other, need to be in closer communication. They need to share their analytical tools, and to explore the degree to which preferences for certain forms of distributive justice and wealth creation may come into conflict. That they may not always have done so could result solely from silos within government itself, but it could also be caused by a degree of scholarly specialization that obscures the topics that far-flung academic disciplines may actually have in common.

Fundamental preference diversity

Beyond the issue of disciplinary boundaries, the lack of diversity in the political values of humanities scholars may add a further challenge to providing policy-makers with the best possible insights into dealing with controversial issues. At the moment, for example, humanities scholars employed as university faculty members (which, as discussed in the Preface, include a considerable number of those studying the human condition within academic departments labeled 'social sciences', as well as those falling within divisions or faculties of the 'humanities'), tend to hold considerably more liberal political preferences than the views found among the public. Although the most extensive data is available from the United States, this phenomenon has also been observed in the United Kingdom and in a number of other countries. There is, therefore, the possibility that, at least in some fields, more moderate and conservative perspectives held by many in the public will be discounted or ignored.

This lack of fundamental preference diversity would exist whether the humanities scholars' politics were to the left or right of the public, irrespective of how left and right may be defined from time to time. Because the relevant humanities scholarship *currently* reflects assumptions about the common good that fall considerably further to the left of the political spectrum than the views of the public, there needs to be greater consideration of those found on the right. But if the situation were reversed, and conservatives dominated the academic humanities to the extent that liberals do today, more progressive views would be needed. My goal is to encourage scholars to help policy-makers figure out how best to understand and grapple with the complex views found among the citizenry, not necessarily to advance any particular conception of the good life, either for individuals or societies. For the humanities to be as useful as we need them to be, humanities scholarship bearing on public policy—a far broader swath of scholarship than might appear on the surface to be 'policy-related'—needs to understand what *we* think, and why we might think it. The public may well be wrong, in which case being able to show how peoples' assumptions are incorrect, or how their analyses are incomplete, will be a valuable contribution of scholars. In the long run, society will be better off if the few who wield power over the many consider the values and attitudes of the people who granted them that authority, even if they do not always adopt or follow those views.

At the moment, humanities scholars do not exhibit a very large range of fundamental political preferences. University of British Columbia Sociology Professor Neil Gross has produced the most recent studies of the political orientation of American professors. Since political views are his principal topic, Professor Gross makes a point of identifying himself as 'a Democrat with very liberal social attitudes and more center-left views when it comes to issues like government regulation of the market and criminal justice policy'.[18] In his summary, the political preferences—and the effect of those preferences on scholarship—are clear: 'Most social scientists and humanists are on the left, and... [these] left and liberal [scholars] have clearly stamped their political mark on their disciplines.'[19] Moreover, as Gross explains, 'In academic life,... intellectual movements are better able to get off the ground when they are started by established scholars holding positions at major research universities', and, for quite some time, 'education researchers have known that there is an association between academic status and liberalism, with more leftists and liberals located near the top of the academic hierarchy—in elite, PhD-granting institutions—and more conservatives located near the bottom'.[20] That is, at the most prominent research universities, where a great deal of the influential scholarship is generated, faculty members in the humanities are overwhelmingly left of the political center and that leftward orientation influences their scholarly fields.

The phenomenon of faculty being more liberal than the public is not unique to the United States, although it is more difficult to obtain detailed data on the political orientation of humanities scholars in other countries. Among other things, left and right, liberal and conservative, may well have different meanings from country to country. University of Exeter professor Jeremy Black writes, for example, that 'in the British context "conservative" means something very different from that which has become common in the United States: it does not, for example embrace attachment to strong fundamental Christian teachings and it has no "right to life" attachments'.[21] An intriguing approach to assessing academic political preferences internationally has been taken by Indiana University professor Clem Brooks, who has used survey data from several countries to compare the social and political attitudes of university faculty (not just humanities and social science professors) to the views of the general public in their own countries. On the subject of civil liberties, for example, 'professors in all countries are well to the left of their respective national publics',[22] he concludes. This gap is sufficiently pronounced 'across diverse national contexts' that Professor Brooks suggests that the survey 'results signal that individuals with a long-standing preference for both political and personal autonomy may tend to select into academic employment'.[23] This preference for 'political and personal autonomy' is likely to find its way into their scholarship, as well, if they follow the trend of US academics, where a significant majority of faculty members, '71 percent [,] ... endorse[d] the view that it is acceptable for professors to be guided by their political or religious values in their choice of research topic'.[24] That is, not only do faculty members tend to lean further to the left than the public, but they are also likely to think that their personal beliefs are a reasonable basis for the direction of their research.

Among professors in all fields in the United States, only 9 percent identify themselves as conservative, with those conservatives concentrated outside the humanities, primarily in business and the health sciences. In the humanities and social sciences, self-identified conservatives are 4 percent and 5 percent, respectively.[25] We can make a rough comparison of the political self-identifications of faculty described in a recent book by Gross and Solon Simmons, *Professors and Their Politics*, with a 2014 Gallup Poll of the American public, as follows:[26]

	Liberal	**Moderate**	**Conservative**
Humanities professors	52	44	4
Social science professors	58	37	5
Public	23	34	38

These data, which show that faculty members are well to the left of the public, may actually understate the prevalence of academic liberals, according to an analysis by Stanley Rothman and S. Robert Lichter.[27] The large 'moderate' category in the Gross and Simmons study was comprised of all respondents who self-identified as 'moderate', plus those who called themselves only 'slightly' conservative or liberal. Rothman and Lichter looked at the respondents' scores on a values test, and they concluded that slight liberals and slight conservatives were both to the left of 'moderate', thus making the academic 'middle of the road', in their words, 'actually well along the left fork of the road'.[28] When the data were re-cast by Professors Rothman and Lichter based on respondents' answers to questions about their positions on social and political issues, only those self-identifying as 'strong' conservatives—about 1 in 20 humanities or social science professors—were to the right of the public's political center.[29]

The Rothman/Lichter interpretation of the data thus shows an even greater difference between academia and the American public, and they remark, 'one out of four professors in the humanities and social sciences is by self-description a radical or activist, and one out of seven social scientists (including one out of four sociologists) a Marxist'.[30] While radicals are in the minority, the professoriate clearly skews toward the left side of the political spectrum, and '[f]ormer Harvard president and Clinton treasury secretary Larry Summers has said that in Washington he was "the right half of the left," while at Harvard he found himself "on the right half of the right"'.[31]

The finding that professors are more likely to be politically liberal than the public has not gone unnoticed by those on the right. Whereas many conservative critiques of the liberal orientation of the professorate have focused on the potential effects on classroom education,[32] my concerns relate to the degree to which research in the humanities may ignore, overlook or misunderstand center-right views because those social and political perspectives are found so infrequently among humanities scholars' professional peers, especially at elite, research-intensive (and, therefore, opinion-leading) academic institutions.[33] That is, studies have shown that women and men to the right of the political center make up just one in 20 humanities faculty members throughout all of academia, and they are much less common at elite universities than at less prestigious institutions; conservatives, therefore, comprise substantially less than one in 20 humanities professors at our best universities.[34] As a result, it seems likely that serious engagement with politically conservative views, or even more moderate center-right views, may be difficult for humanities scholars at our leading universities for lack of intellectual sparring partners, if nothing else. With so few of their professional peers holding themselves out as right of center, it would not be surprising for academics at opinion-leading universities in these fields to overlook or discount the degree to which those political perspectives may be attractive to significant portions of the public.[35]

Academic preferences and public preferences

One of the risks of that lack of engagement is that mainstream academics may assume that the attitudes they share with their peers are not only true, but also equally mainstream throughout the rest of society. If the 'academic bubble', as it is sometimes called, is taken to be a representative microcosm of the rest of society, scholars may not see a need to take seriously arguments that challenge their own fundamental preferences. Here it may be useful to review some examples of that mainstream scholarship, ideally from the very best, most thoughtful, scholars, as they address topics that have a clear connection to issues of public importance. The question is not whether the academic scholarship is right or wrong, but whether it is sensitive to the existence of as broad a range of potential viewpoints as may be found among the public. A good place to start is an area where, at least in the United States, disputes about public policy are contentious, and scholarship has been influential: the proper relationship of church and state.

Humanities scholarship has been a major building block in the development of the US Supreme Court's approach to church–state issues, as we saw in Chapter 3. *Religious Freedom and the Constitution* is an influential scholarly contribution to this discussion. It was written by Christopher L. Eisgruber, when he was a professor of public affairs at Princeton, and Lawrence G. Sager, then Dean of the University of Texas at Austin School of Law.[36] Published by Harvard University Press in 2007, this book has already been cited hundreds of times by both scholars and judges. It is just the kind of opinion-leading scholarship on important issues of public policy that I have been encouraging in the earlier chapters. Moreover, the authors are terrific scholars, who occupy the 'translational' space between the realm of ideas and practical reason. Eisgruber was also a professor in Princeton's University Center for Human Values, and Sager had co-founded New York University's Program in Law, Philosophy and Social Theory. Much like the physician researchers in the life sciences whose 'translational medicine' carries discoveries from their laboratory benchtops to patients' bedsides, Professors Eisgruber and Sager apply insights from philosophy, literature, history and other humanities disciplines to pressing issues of public policy. They clearly worked hard to ensure that their philosophically rich book about justice and constitutional interpretation would exhibit the intellectual rigor expected by the academy, while being written in such a lively manner that policy-makers and the public could profit by it as well.

Professors Eisgruber and Sager begin by observing that the US Constitution contains three separate commitments to religious freedom, 'and that [n]o other element of justice receives such lavish treatment in the Constitution'.[37] Since the country's early years, when religious prejudices could lead to strife and even violence, society has 'made considerable progress', they note. 'In many settings, religious hatred has given way to distaste, distaste to acceptance, and acceptance to welcome.'[38] Conflicts over religion continue to occur, however, and the authors offer a comprehensive approach to resolving them through their concept of 'Equal Liberty'.[39]

Under the Equal Liberty approach, religious beliefs, practices and institutions can be protected by the Constitution, but they will receive no special benefits on account of their religiousness. The authors argue that

> it is a sign of America's progress in the domain of religious freedom *that most Americans prefer to defend their views on grounds that assume or are at least consistent with the equal status of all believers and non-believers,* rather than on the ground that some subset of believers should enjoy a preferred constitutional status.[40]

Framed in this way, the constitutional standard of Equal Liberty is derived from a belief shared by most Americans that the Constitution should treat believers and non-believers identically. In working to combine American 'constitutional values' with 'our instincts about what is just',[41] Professors Eisgruber and Sager mean all of us (or at least most of us).[42]

This description of Americans' widely shared understandings provides the foundation for the rest of the book, which applies the principle of Equal Liberty to various church–state issues 'that have roiled American politics for more than three decades',[43] including prayers in public schools and the display of religious figures on public property during the Christmas season. Their concern is that 'by sponsoring religious displays or ceremonies, the government affiliates itself with or endorses a particular theological perspective and implicitly disparages other ones'.[44] The determination of whether a 'ritual or display' violates the Equal Liberty mandate is based on its social meaning, which 'is the meaning that a competent participant in the society in question would see in that event or expression'.[45] Social meaning, the authors point out, is 'not about the intentions of particular speakers, nor about the perceptions of particular audiences, but rather about the social meanings of rituals, practices, and religions'.[46] Social meanings 'flow... from the cultural characteristics of religions in America—their comprehensiveness; their tendency to treat people as either "in" or "out"; their use of symbols and rituals to signal who is "in"; and, finally, the profound stakes they attach to the status of "in" or "out" '.[47] Public school prayer, municipal Christmas displays and the like are unconstitutional, therefore, because of their social meaning of disparaging non-believers. 'In our national community', the authors assert, 'the structure of religious belief and affiliation is such that endorsements carry with them the taint of disparagement'.[48]

Religious Freedom and the Constitution proved very influential in a 2010 challenge to the National Day of Prayer statute. In *Freedom From Religion Foundation, Inc., v. Obama,*[49] Federal District Judge Barbara Crabb considered the constitutionality of a 1988 statute reading:

> The President shall issue each year a proclamation designating the first Thursday in May as a National Day of Prayer on which the people of the United States may turn to God in prayer and meditation at churches, in groups, and as individuals.[50]

Judge Crabb declared the National Day of Prayer statute unconstitutional, and relied explicitly on the book's arguments to do so. The opinion concluded that 'religious expression by the government that is inspirational and comforting to a believer may seem exclusionary or even threatening to someone who does not share those beliefs'.[51] Judge Crabb emphasized that this feeling of exclusion 'is not simply a matter of being "too sensitive" .... Rather', the opinion continued, 'as explained in a recent book by the Provost of Princeton University and the Dean of the University of Texas School of Law, it is a consequence of the unique danger that religious conduct by the government poses for creating "in" groups and "out" groups.'[52] Judge Crabb then quoted from the book at considerable length, and devoted another paragraph to a discussion of how the authors employ the concept of social meaning.

To apply the broad language of the First Amendment's religion clauses to a specific statute, Judge Crabb thus turned to some of the very best scholars of law and religion for their thoughtful analysis of the Constitution in light of the role religion plays in contemporary American society. That scholarship led the judge to declare unconstitutional a 25-year-old statute, which reflected a 200-year-old practice of declaring national days of prayer. In overturning such a well-established practice, the judge is likely to have relied both on the authors' insights, and on the authority of their distinguished positions in academia, which she made a point of describing.

The decision striking down the National Day of Prayer statute was appealed to the Seventh Circuit Court of Appeals, where a three-judge panel overturned Judge Crabb's ruling.[53] The appellate judges directly addressed the question of whether the plaintiffs were 'injured because they feel excluded, or made unwelcome, when the President asks them to engage in a religious observance that is contrary to their own principles'.[54] This is where Judge Crabb had employed the concept of 'social meaning' to conclude that such feelings of exclusion are a consequence of the unique danger that religious conduct by government poses'.[55] Quite to the contrary, argued the appeals court, 'It is difficult to see how *any* reader of the 2010 proclamation would feel excluded or unwelcome.'[56]

That the National Day of Prayer conveyed a message disparaging non-believers was not merely Judge Crabb's personal opinion. She imported the concept of social meaning from *Religious Freedom and the Constitution*, where it is defined as 'the meaning that a competent participant in the society in question would see in that... expression'.[57] As the authors say of a display of the Ten Commandments on public property, 'no competent member of these communities could have failed to understand the [disparaging] social meaning of... the display'.[58] Yet, the three federal appellate judges, two appointed by a Republican president and one by a Democratic president, would seem to be competent members of the community, and they unanimously agreed that there was no message of exclusion or disparagement despite a contrary finding by Judge Crabb.

Eisgruber and Sager root the 'social meaning' of a governmental action in a factual inquiry: what would all competent participants in the relevant community understand as the meaning? Here, the three appellate judges disagree with the authors and Judge Crabb on the basic fact of how the National Day of Prayer statute will be understood by the community. How can we interpret such a sharp difference of opinion about what members of a community would understand?[59]

While Professors Eisgruber and Sager define 'social meaning' in terms of essentially all members of society, they note at the outset that 'our arguments in this book are not directed to theocrats or others who believe, as a matter of justice, that one or another faith deserves a privileged status; our argument is directed to readers who take for granted that people of diverse faiths are entitled to equal citizenship'.[60] In fact, in their community—the community of scholars at America's greatest universities—it is likely that nearly everyone shares their view that the government's endorsement of religion (through promoting prayer or religious displays, for example) is inappropriate, and disparages those who are not religious.

Gross and Simmons report, for example, that although 75 percent of all professors in America believe that 'religion does not belong in public schools, and that public schools should not be allowed to start each day with a prayer',[61] on this issue, 'the difference between elite doctoral schools and community colleges was especially dramatic, with 92.1 percent of professors at [elite doctoral universities] taking the secular view'.[62] It is not surprising, then, that it would seem in the academic community that most Americans would not favor religion over non-religious values and practices, and that all competent members of the community would share the belief that the social meaning of school prayer or public displays of religion is to endorse religion and to unjustly disparage non-believers. That is the view of virtually all the members of the authors' community of academic peers at research universities.[63]

The National Day of Prayer case suggests that *Religious Freedom and the Constitution* may have accurately reflected the attitudes of scholars at our best universities, but may have misjudged, as a purely factual matter, the beliefs of 'most Americans', or what all competent members of the broader national community understand when the government provides for a national day of prayer. Polls show that a substantial majority of the American public sides with the appellate court. A 2010 Gallup Poll, for example, concluded that only 5 percent opposed the practice of a national day of prayer, with 57 percent in favor and 38 percent saying that it 'doesn't matter'.[64] Similarly, a 2014 Gallup poll concluded that '[s]ixty-one percent of Americans support allowing daily prayer to be spoken in the classroom', and 75 percent favor '[a]llowing students to say prayers at graduation ceremonies as part of the official program'.[65] A sizeable majority of Americans thus welcomes whatever government endorsement of religion comes from this kind of public prayer.[66]

It therefore becomes challenging to apply the insights of *Religious Freedom and the Constitution* directly to real-world issues because its premises are statements of fact about what most Americans think. Yet, as the polls make clear, those statements describe primarily what most leading scholars believe, and may not reflect as well what most other Americans think. Because the public—rightly or wrongly—holds different fundamental preferences about the place of religion in society than the scholars, it is difficult to find a point of common contact between the public's attitudes and the remainder of Eisgruber and Sager's careful analysis.

The authors might argue at this point that the general public's attitudes are so incompatible with the demands of justice that they are not a reasonable basis for governmental policy, or that if the public thought about these questions more carefully, a much larger group would come to the scholars' position. In that case, it may be fruitful for them (or other like-minded scholars) to consider expanding their arguments in ways that would meet the public on common ground in hopes of moving public opinion in the right direction. That is, if we assume that Professors Eisgruber and Sager have correctly identified the demands of justice, then it appears that they—and their peers in the leading American universities—have arrived at the correct result ahead of the American public. Their conclusions are not, in fact, based on what most Americans think, but they can certainly argue that it is what most Americans *should* think. As a result, it would be a valuable contribution to scholarship and public policy for them to engage the arguments of scholars, not all of whom have appointments at elite universities, who have defended positions that more closely track the majority's preferences.

Another approach would be to employ rhetorical tools that might not have appealed to the authors, but could help convince the public of their conclusions. As Professor Eisgruber previously pointed out, history can 'attach a popular pedigree to unpopular decisions'.[67] He is clearly right: history, has, in fact played a prominent role in the Supreme Court's church–state jurisprudence, especially where the justices' opinions have mandated a stronger separation of church and state than the public wanted. Voters' enthusiasm for the founding fathers has been a potent force in shaping popular attitudes about the Constitution, and it is not surprising that books about Washington, Jefferson, Adams and their fellow founders tend to sell very well. What *is* surprising is the degree to which leading academic historians have disavowed these jurisprudential appeals to history, especially since it would give the historians themselves a chance to occupy center-stage in highly visible public policy discussions. Whereas the philosophical underpinnings of the health policy issues discussed earlier are not always obvious, even to the participants in the debates, the appeals to originalism in many constitutional cases are so common that it would seem to be one of the most prominent places where humanities scholars could trumpet their impact on the real world. That has not necessarily been the case.

Jill Lepore, Harvard's David Woods Kemper Professor of American History, is an outstanding scholar who has won many prizes for her work. Moreover, she has played a very effective translational role in which path-breaking historical research and analysis has become accessible to the public, both through her lively books and her writings for popular audiences in *The New Yorker* and elsewhere. In 2011, Princeton University Press published Professor Lepore's *The Whites of Their Eyes: The Tea Party's Revolution and the Battle Over American History*, which won an impressive collection of awards and prizes. In writing about the strongly conservative contemporary American political movement called the Tea Party, Professor

Lepore took the opportunity to talk about the divergence between the way the Tea Party has recruited the Founders to their cause, and the approach taken by professional historians: '[T]he Tea Party's version of American history [bears] almost no resemblance to the Revolution I study and teach', she writes.[68] While acknowledging that American political movements of various stripes have invoked the framers—'When in doubt, in American politics, left, right, or center, deploy the Founding Fathers'[69] —the Tea Party had gone beyond the pale: their '[h]istorical fundamentalism is marked by a belief that a particular and quite narrowly defined past—"the founding"—is ageless and sacred and to be worshipped; [and] that certain historical texts...are to be read in the same spirit with which religious fundamentalists read...the Ten Commandments'.[70] Beyond being historical fundamentalists, the Tea Party sees 'the academic study of history (whose standards of evidence and methods of analysis are based on skepticism) as a conspiracy, and furthermore, blasphemy...'.[71] Professor Lepore's book is thus 'an argument against historical fundamentalism'.[72]

One of Professor Lepore's many strengths is her ability to put the Tea Party/academic divide in a variety of interesting contexts. The Tea Party, she notes, 'was the product of a reactionary...version of American history that took hold during the crisis of the bicentennial [of the American Revolution in the 1970s], as a reaction to protests from the left'.[73] As Lepore comments, 'Historians mocked the Bicentennial as schlock and its protests as contrived but didn't offer an answer, a story, to a country that needed one.'[74] Instead, she notes, '[b]eginning with the rise of the New Left in the 1960s, women's history, labor history, and the history of slavery and emancipation—the study, in one way or another, of ordinary people, of groups, and, especially, of conflict—dominated the academic study of American history'.[75] That shift of focus by historians 'left plenty of room for a lot of other people to get into the history business'.[76]

An aspect of that amateur history that especially troubles Professor Lepore is originalism, 'the idea that the original intent of the Framers is knowable and fixed and the final word'.[77] Noting that '[c]onstitutional scholars generally date the rise of originalism to the 1970s and consider it a response to controversial [Supreme Court] decisions', Professor Lepore calls it 'lousy history': 'set loose in the culture, and tangled together with fanaticism, originalism looks like history, but it's not. It's historical fundamentalism, which is to history what astrology is to astronomy, what alchemy is to chemistry, what creationism is to evolution.'[78]

Despite her unhappiness with the Tea Party's version of the framers, and the aspersions she casts in the direction of originalism in general, Professor Lepore opens the door once or twice to the idea that, as she puts it, 'Jurists and legislators need to investigate what the Framers meant.'[79] This statement, which comes over half-way through the book, appears as quite a surprise since so much of the volume decries the alchemy and astrology of originalism. If it really is like alchemy and astrology, then scholars—and jurists and legislators, as well—should cast it aside, and look for better ways to understand the Constitution. But, if it is not alchemy at all, but just chemistry-done-poorly, then Professor Lepore has a chance to provide a better formula. Here is where one of our best contemporary historians could have shown us how history—'picky, demanding, and vital'[80]—can best be employed by those judges and members of Congress who, even she admits, need to learn what the framers meant.

Professor Lepore provides a glimpse into that method when she touches on Republican Presidential candidate Mitt Romney's accusation that 'modern-day secularists [are] "at odds with the nation's founders," and [have] taken the doctrine of separation of church and state "well beyond its original meaning" by seeking to remove from the public domain any acknowledgment of God'.[81] For support, Romney had cited 'Brigham Young, John and Samuel Adams, and the seventeenth-century Puritan descendent Roger Williams'; and Professor Lepore takes him to task because 'Romney's Founding Fathers [aren't] the usual ones'.[82] Instead, she argues, '[h]istorians of religious liberty have typically referred' to 'four foundational texts': the Constitution's two provisions dealing with religion, plus two documents from Virginia: Madison's 'Memorial' against a proposed tax to support religion and Jefferson's statute for religious freedom.[83] The historian of religious liberty on whom she calls to represent the usual approach is Martha Nussbaum, the Ernst Freund Distinguished Professor of Law and Ethics at the University of Chicago.[84]

In her brief foray into originalism, Professor Lepore does not dig deeply into archival material, nor does she analyze the strengths of competing interpretations. Rather, she relies on someone from her own peer group, which led her to a version of the framers' thinking that is likely to be compatible with her own views. Here was a chance to be 'picky' and 'demanding', but, instead, she rapidly defaulted to one of the conventional accounts. She did not ask why two distinguished Virginians were the best representatives of American thinking when, for example, an eminent Massachusetts contemporary of Madison and Jefferson could defend that state's embrace of Protestantism because it was 'a religion, which, by its benign and energetic influences, might cooperate with human institutions, to promote and secure the happiness of its citizens'.[85]

People disagreed vehemently then, as we do now, on the proper relationship of church and state. To understand the constitutional history would seem to require us to figure out how they settled that fundamental preference diversity when they came together to create the Bill of Rights. One answer, following Professors Lepore and Nussbaum, is that Jefferson and Madison won. The new country rejected the views prevailing in New England and chose a strict separation of church and state. That answer has been popular in academic circles since late in the nineteenth-century, when, as Columbia University legal historian Philip Hamburger has shown, liberal secularism and 'traditional fears about the anti-Christian character of Catholicism and its union of church and state' combined to make 'the separation of church and state... an almost irresistible dogma of Americanism'.[86] It is at this point that Madison's 'Memorial' and Jefferson's statute—both of which addressed local Virginia church–state controversies rather than national issues—were elevated by scholars and judges to canonical status in constitutional interpretation. Then, as I have argued, the religious school-aid cases in the 1940s and 1950s provided further impetus for 'Madison's and Jefferson's "strict separationist" writings [to] provide an appealing intellectual and constitutional pedigree for a Court anxious to protect critical democratic institutions, especially the schools, from the sectarian threat that could be unleashed by a breach in the wall of separation'.[87]

Is a wall-of-separation approach to the First Amendment merely an after-the-fact secular gloss on the Constitution's religion clauses, or is it the original meaning that Professor Lepore believes jurists need to uncover? That is a terrific question, and it is unlikely to be answered simply by citing one side of the debate, whether it comes from a University of Chicago professor or the Tea Party-endorsed book, *The Constitution Made Easy*, by an author whom Professor Lepore describes (not necessarily favorably) as having 'studied at Biola University (a Christian college offering a biblically centered education)'.[88] These complex issues invite us to ask how a new nation created by states with conflicting church–state views were able to agree—and to do so quickly, easily and with hardly any debate—on the religion clauses of the First Amendment. Professor Lepore is right: jurists and legislators (and a surprisingly large segment of the public[89]) want to understand this historical event. Since she has held out modern academic historians for their skepticism and their insights into the study of conflict,[90] this would be an ideal opportunity to apply those tools to a case where conflict was unaccountably absent, and skepticism could profitably be applied to all of the conventional accounts, whether they come from Christian colleges or secular universities.

The future of diversity in academia

Toolbox diversity appears to be growing, albeit slowly, in scholarly circles, as interdisciplinary centers, institutes and programs have been increasingly popular on university campuses. It is not clear that the professional incentives for scholars at research universities are sufficiently aligned with the need for toolbox diversity for it to grow as rapidly as it could, however. In responding to a humanities scholar's question, 'Is it *ever* a good [idea] to go to conferences that are . . . very interdisciplinary', the *Chronicle of Higher Education*'s advice columnist focused on the fact that, for tenure, 'you must be eligible within one or, at most, two fields. Academia still rewards specialization.'[91] In the meantime, policy-makers needing scholarly advice may have to bear the burden of seeking out diverse perspectives by consulting multiple scholars in a variety of disciplines.

Perhaps the more difficult arena for increasing the diversity of thinking at elite research universities will be in the realm of fundamental preferences. There are few higher education values held more fervently than the commitment to academic freedom: the American Association of University Professors (AAUP) calls academic freedom 'the indispensable quality of institutions of higher education'. The rationale for academic freedom, the AAUP continues, is that 'institutions of higher education are conducted for the common good and not to further the interest of either the individual teacher or the institution as a whole. The common good depends upon the free search for truth and its free exposition.'[92] As a result of these important commitments to academic freedom, greater attention to fundamental preference diversity will come to universities, if at all, not as a result of public policy or administrative edict, but because scholars themselves think it is a good idea. I am optimistic that, over time, increasing numbers of researchers will seek to engage with a wider set of fundamental preferences about controversial issues because it will make those problems more complex and, therefore, more interesting.

In doing so, researchers will encounter views that are now overlooked or downplayed, perhaps merely to comprehend the nature of public opinion, and possibly with the goal of debunking those mistaken preferences. Rather than simply writing off, for example, the public's support for civic acknowledgments of religion, or the widespread appeal of constitutional originalism, as inconsistent with serious academic inquiry, increasing numbers of scholars may begin to appreciate that there can be intellectual value in considering the origins and continued political salience of ideas that seem to them to be both wrong and impressively popular with the public. In explaining why those ideas are wrong, scholars will need to refocus on why their own views are right, beyond the knowledge that so many of their peers agree with them.

There is certainly value in scholars' efforts to produce ever more nuanced arguments based on assumptions that are widely shared by other scholars, but it could be even more valuable—and potentially more interesting—for them to consider how to persuade people who do not share those premises. In doing so, academic researchers may find it useful to apply the tools of modern scholarship to, well, modern scholarship. If scholars believe that knowledge really is socially constructed, then they can learn a great deal by exploring how the culture of academia has influenced the direction, nature and conclusions of contemporary academic scholarship. That process should also encourage them to seek out more frequently the scholars who study and analyze—and maybe even represent—those portions of the political spectrum that are rarely visible among today's humanities scholars. Making additional room for thoughtful voices from underrepresented regions of the political spectrum could not only deepen and enrich scholarly conversations, but, if Professor Page's elegant equations are correct, that increase in fundamental preference diversity could make for a better society as well.

5
The Humanities and the Common Good

Consider, for a moment, the contrasting approaches to the value of the humanities evident in these two vignettes.

The story is told that Cambridge classicist A. S. F. Gow (or perhaps it was another classicist) was accosted on the street during the First World War by a woman wondering what he was doing there when able-bodied men were off fighting the enemy. 'What', she asked angrily, 'are you doing to defend our civilization?' To which the distinguished scholar, who actually couldn't serve in the military because of a bad heart, replied, 'Madam, I am that civilization.'[1]

A century later, at a meeting of Princeton PhDs discussing the future of the humanities, one alumnus spoke of his doctoral program in literature:

> We came to graduate school in the '60s and '70s to study great literature, and what we got was theory—theory that everything means whatever you want it to mean, theory that said that no work of literature is better than any other. Of course there's a crisis in the humanities. We told the world there was nothing there. And they believed us.[2]

* * *

Being the intellectual embodiment of civilization as we know it is perhaps too much to ask of any field of endeavor, but, at the same time, there is definitely something there when we reach out to the humanities. They have a great deal to tell us about the answers to 'What are we?' and 'Where do we come from?' as society continually reflects on the core question for policy-makers: 'Where are we going?'[3] In some eras, humanities scholars have been more willing to make a strong case for their contributions to the rest of society than they have in others. But we need the humanities whether they want to be needed or not. Society looks to both the STEM fields and the humanities to provide insights and information that can contribute to the common good. Therefore, it would be a valuable investment for society to provide the support needed to sustain the necessary research in the humanities, as it does for the STEM disciplines.

At the same time, the humanities appear to need, or at least would welcome, the support of society—mostly via the funding of research universities, where publishing scholarly research is an important part of a faculty member's job. It is certainly not essential for the needed scholarship to be performed by university employees, however. As we have seen in Professor Turner's history of humanistic study over the centuries, there have been numerous times when the women and men whom we would now call independent scholars were responsible for carrying the field forward.[4] Some of them remain largely hidden from view, such as the debt-ridden Elstobs and their contributions to the study of Anglo-Saxon, but others are quite visible through the continuing influence of their works. These include, among many others, John Locke's Enlightenment philosophy, John Stuart Mill's arguments for utilitarianism, and T.S. Eliot's poems and other writings. Moreover, the nineteenth century historians who set the Supreme Court on its course toward building a wall-of-separation between church and state earned their livings primarily outside academia, and James Madison's biographer, Irving Brant, whose work featured so prominently in the Court's subsequent expansion of that wall, was a newspaper editor.[5]

Humanities scholars have been, and will be, valuable resources for the resolution of important issues of public policy, but they do not need to be academics to do so. Yet, since so many humanities scholars are employed as university faculty members, and scholarship appears to be an essential (perhaps *the* essential) part of the position, especially in research universities, it would be sensible for society to find the insights it seeks there. But, if academic scholars do not provide what is needed, then my arguments for the financial support of the humanities will relate more directly to encouraging and sustaining the pursuit of scholarship outside the academy.

Although we do not need to obtain the humanities scholarship we need from institutions of higher education, universities seem willing, and even eager, to accept this role. Institutional mission statements regularly proclaim that university research should contribute to society. The mission of the University of Cambridge, for example, is 'to contribute to society through the pursuit of education, learning, and research at the highest international levels of excellence'.[6] Similarly, the University of California at Los Angeles 'advances knowledge [and] addresses pressing societal needs'.[7] Neither statement suggests that the contributions of research to society should be solely the responsibility of the STEM fields. These kinds of institutional pledges of allegiance to the good of society are unlikely to be controversial in the abstract: the critical question is how they relate to basic research, especially since the path from any particular scholarly inquiry in the humanities to a contribution to the public good is often far from clear.

The same question arises in the STEM fields, where there is often no clearly discernible link between a government grant-funded basic research project and some practical benefit to society. In the life sciences, for example, only a small fraction, well below 1 percent, of the proposals for grant-funded research eventually relate directly to a new treatment for human disease. In 2012, the National Institutes of Health (NIH) received over 63,000 grant applications, each of which argued that the proposed research would 'advance our understanding of biological systems, to improve the control of disease, and to enhance health'.[8] About 11,000 of the projects were awarded a total of about $16 billion.[9] Based on historical averages of patents issued to academic institutions and novel treatments approved by the FDA, the likely results of the $16 billion of grants funding 11,000 projects are: about 450 patents, and, sometime 15–20 years later, three or four new medicines.[10] The difficulty, now and probably forever, is that it is impossible to tell in advance, or even during the course of the research, which of the 63,000 grant proposals will ultimately lead, a generation later, to a small handful of new medicines.

Take, for example, a scientific project based on the biology of the mouse spleen. We can hope (and it may well be little more than hope) that scientists might someday transfer some of that learning into the human context, thus (remotely) possibly, many years later, develop an insight that might be helpful to researchers trying to create a new medicine, which itself would have little more than a one-in-one-thousand chance of ultimately healing the sick. So it will be with a great deal of research in the humanities. How can we connect contemporary public policy issues, with, for example, a bone dry, church-by-church ecclesiastical history of evangelical groups on the eighteenth-century American frontier? In each case, these researchers' efforts to illuminate more brilliantly the human—or murine—condition were simply the stuff of scholarship, with no immediate relevance outside the fairly narrow communities of mouse immunologists and church historians (although, as noted earlier, the nature of the grant-funding process in the sciences may have spurred the mouse immunologists to develop a better vocabulary for describing the potential future value of their research than the church historians have, at least so far).

Of course, I have cherry-picked these examples for reasons other than their manifest obscurity. The work at Cambridge with mouse spleens did not, at that time, have a sufficiently visible pathway toward future practical use to be worth the modest cost of filing a patent.[11] But it has led to two dozen new medicines, including some of the most important cancer treatments discovered in over a generation. Meanwhile, the early history of Virginia's frontier Baptists has been translated by the Supreme Court into one of the principal building blocks of modern American religious freedom law.[12] The path from insular and obscure to important and pragmatic was neither predictable nor hurried. In both cases, it took decades before the basic research blossomed in unexpected ways that ultimately contributed to addressing issues of great practical relevance for modern society.

Arguing for public support for research in the humanities is, therefore, quite similar to the same task in the STEM fields. What we know today is that we can point to numerous examples of scholarship that only became profoundly important many decades later. The University of Cambridge's lead story of its research impact for the 2014 Research Excellence Framework evaluation was a recently approved drug called Lemtrada for the treatment of multiple sclerosis. The announcement accurately described a 'longstanding programme of research', which began over 30 years earlier.[13] It was, in fact, one of the continuing contributions of that obscure work with mouse spleens. Seeking a return on an investment in research in virtually any field will require us to be far more patient than probably seems reasonable, especially during difficult economic times. In both STEM and humanities research, we need to continue to foster that basic, blue sky, likely-to-stay-obscure work so that, in due course, scientists, physicians, historians, philosophers, judges and legislators can someday, in an unforeseeable future, mine those discoveries for insights that will make us wonder why no one saw their value in the first place.

In the meantime, humanities scholars who are closer to what physician-scientists call bench-to-bedside translational research—the ones whose work most obviously relates to matters of public concern—would do well to highlight their debts to the predecessors on whose intellectual shoulders they stand. As anyone who has worked to raise funds for scientific R&D knows (and this is what a career in the business of biotechnology is mostly about), it is important to be able to have some victories to declare—to show how prior research investments have, in fact, paid off. Translational researchers in the humanities, therefore, would benefit themselves and their scholarly colleagues not only by giving full credit to the intellectual foundations of their scholarship, but also by thinking about what will make their work as valuable as possible in contributing to the commonweal. They are the standard-bearers for their colleagues who may be engaged in projects of less immediate relevance to society.

A member of an American Political Science Association task force aimed at promoting more 'effective engagement' with the public, Dartmouth Professor Brendan Nyhan, has noted, 'We've written hundreds of books on lobbying and Congress, yet our strategy on lobbing is deeply flawed.' Among other things, the task force recommended 'developing a training program to teach political scientists how to communicate, and establishing awards for scholars who are effective at outreach'.[14] That is, scholars should learn how to be more effective when they describe their research to the public, and how it relates to issues of importance for society. This sounds like good advice for any academic field, although it is not something for which scholars appear to be rewarded at the moment.

Take, for example, the art historians aggrieved by President Obama's job jibe. While the vast majority of art history departments in the United States rate teaching and research as essential considerations for tenure, only 2 percent require faculty to 'make... the humanities and/or humanities scholarship accessible to the general public'.[15] The art historians are actually at the upper end of the humanities scale on this issue. Among surveyed departments in various humanities disciplines, the proportion of departments describing the 'public humanities' as essential to tenure is as follows: English, 0 percent; Languages and Literatures other than English, 2 percent; History, 0 percent; Religion, 3 percent; Musicology, 3 percent; Classical Studies, 0 percent; and Philosophy, 1 percent.[16]

In light of these survey data, it is not surprising that the humanities defense literature tends to focus on professors' roles in teaching their students,[17] the one area where they are professionally obliged to do something other than talk to each other. Their scholarship, the result of enormous amounts of time, effort and sometimes expense, is published largely by and for other scholars, and there are few professional incentives for sharing it more broadly. The same survey of US humanities programs provided subgroup data for faculty at 'primarily research' institutions, that is, the major universities where a great deal of scholarship takes place. At those universities, humanities departments uniformly ranked publications above teaching; in English, for example, publications are essential for tenure at 96 percent of departments, compared to teaching, which is essential only for 55 percent.[18] Meanwhile, making humanities scholarship accessible to the public is described as completely 'unimportant' or, at most, 'marginally important' at 66 percent of the English departments, a number that rises to 95 percent in Philosophy.[19] With few professional incentives for communicating scholarly research to the public—and with the word 'popularizer' rarely used as a compliment in academic discourse—it is not surprising that politicians, trustees and others involved in higher education policy may genuinely wonder about the value of all the time that humanities professors spend producing scholarly books and articles.[20]

My goal is not necessarily to turn every humanities scholar into an op-ed writing public intellectual, although such efforts may be valuable for both the humanities and society. Not every important idea in the humanities is susceptible of being discussed in several hundred well-chosen words appearing in an op-ed piece or blog posting aimed at the general public. In fact, some of the most influential scholarly work has been just that—the product of long study, deep research, and careful thinking, as published in the peer-reviewed journals and monographs in which humanities scholars regularly present their work. There are multiple ways for scholarship to influence people's views and behaviors: one way is through direct outreach by scholars seeking to engage the interest of the public. Another is for scholars to produce books and articles (in the standard scholarly outlets) that can help powerful policy-makers make better decisions. There is clearly room for active researchers to pay additional attention to how their insights could be shared more broadly with the public, but the latter aspect of impact—the influence of scholarship on political elites, and, through the decisions of those elites, to the rest of us—has been the focus of this book.

At the same time, it would be helpful for humanities scholars, even those at the most fundamental end of research, to think about how their work might contribute to the common good in some way. Humanities scholars are powerful thinkers and dedicated researchers, many of whom have exceptional communication skills. If the standard defenses of the humanities are true, this is to be expected; and, if, as many advocates for the humanities argue, the study of the humanities prepares students to be good citizens,[21] then it would seem that the women and men who have devoted their professional lives to the humanities would be especially able and anxious to consider the contributions that they could make to the common good. It would be helpful to the rest of us if they could focus those skills on explaining how the scholarly conversations in which they participate might illuminate the human condition in a way that connects with the concerns of civil society.

* * *

A quarter of a century ago, when the potential for profound medical and economic benefits from biomedical research consisted primarily of a growing accumulation of hopes and aspirations, nearly a hundred scientists, physicians and entrepreneurs convened in France to discuss their latest findings.[22] They shared a dedication to a particularly exciting field where new biological tools had been designed to activate the immune system to target cancer cells for destruction. These tools were being rapidly translated from laboratory testing to initial human clinical trials. This streamlined bench-to-bedside pathway for developing new medical treatments was becoming one of the most exciting possibilities of biotechnology research.

Leading scientists made the pilgrimage from medical schools across the United States, from California and the huge land grant universities in the Midwest to the Ivy League and the National Institutes of Health in the East; they came as well from Canada and from academic centers throughout Europe—Cambridge, Paris, Rome and other places where ancient halls of learning stood side-by-side new, high-tech laboratories.

The meeting took place in a region best known for humanist and physician Francois Rabelais, and for its famous red wine (produced, incidentally, by the process of fermentation, much as many modern biotech drugs are made today). Several days of lively scientific exchange concluded with a festive dinner in a huge cavern carved into the rock of the Loire Valley. The great room was set for a multicourse banquet and illuminated by flaming torches that flickered against the stone walls.

During the dinner, there was a formal ceremony for several of the leaders of the scientific congress to be inducted as honorary *chevaliers* of the local wine society. One-by-one they were called to a raised dais until about a dozen stood facing the assembly. They were waiting to be examined by *La Confrérie des Bons Entonneurs Rabelaisiens*, a group of men garbed in academic-style habits: *Les Entonneurs* wore long red robes edged with gold and trimmed with fur, and each had a large, inscribed golden medallion on a chain around his neck. Copious amounts of wine were consumed in this medieval fraternity initiation, but mere exhibitions of drinking prowess would not be sufficient. Before being tapped as *chevaliers*, the inductees needed to demonstrate their intellectual fitness for the role. The *Entonneurs'* leader, speaking in French with universally comprehensible hand gestures that provided simultaneous translation, posed the question: if you were stranded on a desert island, and could only bring with you two of these three things, which would be left behind—wine, women or philosophy?

In short order, *la philosophie* was jettisoned, and the *chevaliers* received their rewards. With a trumpet fanfare in the background, they were dubbed with a long wooden sword, had red robes draped on their shoulders, and gold medallions were placed around their necks. This grand ceremony would not be the last time in the history of scientific research that philosophy—and its confrères within the humanities—would be abandoned in the rush for more immediate gratification. My goal in this book has been to find a little more room for them in higher education's ship of state in hopes that we will not end up being stranded somewhere science alone cannot help us.

Notes

Preface

1. Philip Kreager, *Humanities Graduates and the British Economy: The Hidden Impact* (Oxford: Oxford University, July 2013), http://torch.ox.ac.uk/sites/torch/files/publications/Humanities%20Graduates%20and%20the%20British%20Economy%20-%20University%20of%20Oxford.pdf, 1.
2. Quoted in David Matthews, 'A How-Not-To Guide to Defending Humanities,' *Times Higher Education Supplement*, no. 2124 (October 24, 2013): 11.
3. Helen Small, *The Value of the Humanities* (Oxford: Oxford University Press, 2013), 61. Professor Small's book is an unusually thoughtful analysis of the various arguments that appear in the humanities defense literature.
4. Abram L. Harris, 'John Stuart Mill: Servant of the East India Company,' *The Canadian Journal of Economics and Political Science* 30, no. 2 (May, 1964): 185–202; Peter Smith and Geoffrey Summerfield, eds., *Matthew Arnold and the Education of the New Order* (Cambridge: Cambridge University Press, 1969); Ellyn Sanna, 'Biography of T.S. Eliot,' in *T.S. Eliot*, ed. Harold Bloom (Broomall, PA: Chelsea House, 2003), 3.
5. Small, *Value of the Humanities*, 61–62.
6. Ibid., 62.
7. Nigel Biggar, 'What Are Universities For?' *Standpoint Magazine*, July/August 2010, http://www.standpointmag.com/uk/print/3156. Turner points out that seventeenth- and eighteenth-century scholars in England, whether they were professors or not, needed to find patrons to cover the cost of publishing. Locke lived with a rich friend, the 'Lord Chief Justice paid for... the Anglo-Saxon type to print [a] grammar,' and 'Samuel Johnson financed his edition of Shakespeare by subscription.' Turner concludes, 'Absent modern research universities, scholars needed subsidy': James Turner, *Philology: The Forgotten Origins of the Modern Humanities* (Princeton, NJ: Princeton University Press, 2014), 87–88.
8. Quoted in Matthews, 'How-Not-To Guide,' 11. This strikes me as an instrumental argument opposed to instrumental arguments.
9. Louis Menand has written about the humanities in America: 'There are fewer students majoring in humanities fields than was once the case, but undergraduates continue to take courses in literature, art, music, and philosophy; despite an uncertain job market, people continue to apply to doctoral programs in those fields; and a great deal of scholarship continues to get published. The humanities disciplines may go through a period of reorganization, but they aren't likely to become extinct.' Professor Menand's observation that 'despite an uncertain job market, people continue to apply to doctoral programs in [humanities] fields' is something

of an understatement. That the numbers of postgraduate students in the humanities have typically been unchanged—or have increased—during very poor job markets is not only one of the best arguments for the intrinsic value of the humanities, but also a significant challenge to the rational choice methodologies that have often been employed by social scientists: Louis Menand, *The Marketplace of Ideas: Reform and Resistance in the American University* (New York: W.W. Norton & Co., 2010), 62–63.

10. Citing Professor Collini, Professor Small notes, 'What many, I'm guessing, most, academics object to is not . . . the idea that they should be socially beneficial; rather, the peculiarly reductive variant of political economy that dictates the terms of assessment, and that fundamentally mistakes the nature and purpose of writing in the humanities, the arts, and the pure sciences.' Nevertheless, she continues, 'There is . . . a hardcore anti-instrumentalist position . . . that goes further and claims that social benefit is not the brief of universities, and that the pursuit of knowledge and engagement in research must be understood as mattering for its own sake and its own sake alone': Small, *The Value of the Humanities*, 62–63.
11. Judith Butler, 'Ordinary, Incredulous,' in *The Humanities and Public Life*, ed. Peter Brooks (New York: Fordham University Press, 2014), 16.
12. Ibid., 16.
13. Stefan Collini, *What Are Universities For?* (London: Penguin Books, 2012).
14. David Willetts, 'A Mistaken Conception That the University System Is Under Attack,' *Times Higher Education*, March 1, 2012, http://www.timeshighereducation.co.uk/news/a-mistaken-conception-that-the-university-system-is-under-attack/419209.article.
15. Jonathan Bate, ed., 'Introduction,' in *The Public Value of the Humanities* (London: Bloomsbury Publishing, 2010), 3.
16. Dan Berrett, 'Humanities, for Sake of Humanity,' *Inside Higher Ed*, March 30, 2011, http://www.insidehighered.com/news/2011/03/30/scholars_seek_to_craft_argument_for_urgency_of_the_humanities_in_higher_education.
17. Turner, *Philology*, 83–84. In describing how private chaplaincies provided a way to subsidize scholarship in seventeenth- and eighteenth-century Britain, William Gibson points out that 'Bishop William Nicolson appointed two noted Anglo-Saxon scholars as his chaplains so they could complete their research: Thomas Benson and William Elstob . . . . Nicolson was particularly fortunate in appointing Elstob because his sister, also a noted Anglo-Saxon scholar, came with her brother to study in the bishop's household': William Gibson, *A Social History of the Domestic Chaplain, 1530–1840* (London: Leicester University Press, 1997), 60. Gibson also notes that there 'had been a similar fashion for literary chaplains in the 1590s, when Lord Mountjoy, the Earl of Essex, Lord Evers and Sir William Brooke . . . all appointed poets and scholars as their chaplains.' Ibid., 209, note 102.
18. William Clark, *Academic Charisma and the Origins of the Research University* (Chicago: University of Chicago Press, 2007), 46. Here, the author is speaking specifically about early modern German universities, where the

professors lacking academic chairs not only had to collect the fees, but often had to rent a room from a senior professor just to have a place to teach. Clark, *Academic Charisma*, 154.

19. Various reviewers have thoughtfully pointed to a variety of other areas where the humanities may have a direct influence on real world decision-making, from the influence of the study of art on architecture and design to the formation of energy and environmental policies. There are excellent suggestions, and I encourage other writers to explore those relationships more deeply. My focus, which will concentrate on healthcare and civil liberties, is based in part on my familiarity with those fields, and in part on my sense that they may be unusual in the degree to which crucial decisions are made by very small, unelected bodies who have explicitly relied on humanities scholarship.
20. Bernard Williams, 'What Hope for the Humanities?' in *Bernard Williams, Essay and Reviews 1959–2002* (Princeton, NJ: Princeton University Press, 2014), 270. For a methodological approach to defining the humanities over long periods of time and several continents, see Rens Bod, *A New History of the Humanities: The Search for Principles and Patterns from Antiquity to the Present* (Oxford: Oxford University Press, 2014).
21. He continues, 'Any understanding of social reality must be based in understanding its history, and you cannot read its history without insight into its cultural products and those of other times.' Williams, 'What Hope for the Humanities?' 270.

1 The Ups and Downs of the Humanities

1. 'Commencement Number 25!' *The Princeton Tiger*, 1935, reproduced in Don Oberdorfer, *Princeton University: The First 250 Years* (Princeton, NJ: Princeton University Press, 1995), 124.
2. 'Trend Away from the Humanities,' *The Princeton Alumni Weekly* 36, no. 16 (January 31, 1936): 369. The article indicates that, between the academic years 1924–1925 and 1935–1936, the humanities (English, Modern Languages, Philosophy, Architecture, Art and Classics) dropped by 24 percent, the Social Sciences (Politics, Economics and History) were up 44 percent, but with none of the growth in history, and the Natural Sciences (Engineering, Biology, Geology, Chemistry, Psychology, Physics, Mathematics and Astronomy) went up 82 percent. In the Natural Sciences, the greatest growth was in Engineering and Biology, with declines in Physics and Mathematics. These patterns of nearly a century ago are similar in a number of ways to more recent trends.
3. David Silbey, 'A Crisis in the Humanities?' *The Edge of the American West* (blog), *The Chronicle of Higher Education*, June 10, 2013, http://chronicle.com/blognetwork/edgeofthewest/2013/06/10/the-humanities-crisis/. See, in particular, the data on humanities degrees compiled by Ben Schmidt, and compare with any chart showing the ups and downs of the US stock market.

4. Jennifer Levitz and Douglas Belkin, 'Humanities Fall from Favor: Far Fewer Harvard Students Express Interest in Field with Weak Job Prospects,' *The Wall Street Journal*, June 6, 2013, http://online.wsj.com/news/articles/SB10001424127887324069104578527642373232184;
Jasper Copping, 'A Level Students Shun Humanities at University,' *The Telegraph*, August 14, 2011, http://www.telegraph.co.uk/educationnews/8699717/A-level-students-shun-humanities-at-university.htm.
5. Michael Bérubé, 'The Futility of the Humanities,' *Qui Parle: Critical Humanities and Social Sciences* 20, no. 1 (Fall/Winter 2011): 99. Michael Bérubé has pointed out that a close look at the evidence for declining enrollments in the humanities shows that there was a precipitous drop—from 17.4 percent of American undergraduates in 1967—to a more stable 'hovering around 8 percent for the past twenty years', and he concludes that any crisis is, at most, old news. While his observation is correct, it may overlook the effect of that extraordinary peak of interest in 1967. Charts of enrollment patterns need to be scaled to show numbers that high, which tends to obscure the fact that a drop from over 8 percent to under 7 percent of all undergraduate degrees, which looks like just a wiggle on the charts, can represent a reduction of nearly 20,000 humanities students. *Fast Facts*, for example, shows 1.6 million bachelor's degrees granted in 2009–2010 in the United States. That reduction is enough to be felt by departments and observed by trustees, especially when those declines are not evenly distributed. Some departments, such as foreign languages and classics, in not especially well-endowed private colleges, or state universities in impecunious states, may find the number of concentrators to be perilously low. *Fast Facts*, 'Degrees Conferred by Sex and Race,' *The National Center for Education Statistics*, http://nces.ed.gov/fastfacts/display.asp?id=72. William Chace notes, for example, that 'from 1970/71 to 2003/04' foreign languages dropped from 2.5 percent to 1.3 percent of undergraduates. William M. Chace, 'The Decline of the English Department: How It Happened and What Could Be Done to Reverse It,' *The American Scholar*, September 1, 2009, http://theamericanscholar.org/the-decline-of-the-english-department/#.U_4xIGK9KK0.

Perhaps exacerbating the periodic feeling of crisis is that the number of humanities doctorates granted each year by US universities has grown from about 1,500 in 1960 to over 5,500 in 2012. As a result, the various humanities disciplines tend to produce substantially more PhD recipients seeking employment as college or university faculty members than are able to find positions doing so. The data about doctorates come from a special tabulation by Mark Fiegener, PhD, analyzed by Michael Breidenbach, PhD, and are taken from Survey of Earned Doctorates (SED) by the National Center for Science and Engineering Statistics in partnership with the National Science Foundation, National Institutes of Health, US Department of Education, US Department of Agriculture, National Endowment for the Humanities, and National Aeronautics and Space Administration. Since 1957, the SED has published a census of all individuals who earned a research doctorate from an accredited US institution of higher learning each academic year. For the purposes of the SED, 'Humanities' include 'foreign languages and literature', 'history', 'letters' and 'other humanities'. 'Letters' include American literature (the United States and Canada), classics, comparative literature, creative writing, English language, English literature (British and Commonwealth), folklore, rhetoric and composition, speech and rhetorical studies, letters general and letters other. 'Other humanities' include American/US studies, archaeology, art history/criticism/conservation, Bible/biblical studies, drama/theatre arts, ethics, film/cinema/video studies, Jewish/Judaic studies and history, music, musicology/ethnomusicology, music performance, music theory and composition, music other, philosophy, religion/religious studies, humanities general and humanities other.

For a very detailed survey of statistical data from humanities departments in the United States, see Susan White, Raymond Chu, and Roman Czujko, *The 2012–13 Survey of Humanities Departments at Four-Year Institutions* (College Park, MD: Statistical Research Center, American Institute of Physics, 2014). The 'first attempt to assess the worldwide state of the humanities' is Poul Holm, Arne Jarrick, and Dominic Scott, *Humanities World Report 2015* (Basingstoke, UK: Palgrave Macmillan, 2015), 1.

6. '2013–2014 PayScale College Salary Report,' www.payscale.com/college-salary-report-2014/majors-that-pay-you-back. For a somewhat contrary view, see Jordan Weisman, 'The Best Argument for Studying English? The Employment Numbers,' *The Atlantic*, June 25, 2013, http://www.theatlantic.com/business/archive/2013/06/the-best-argument-for-studying-english-the-employment-numbers/277162/
7. Ami Sedghi, 'Graduate Employment: By Skill, Subject and Graduation,' *The Guardian*, March 6, 2012, http://www.theguardian.com/news/datablog/2012/mar/06/graduate.employment-low-skill-jobs. It is not as clear that short-term enrollment trends show as much movement away from the humanities in the UK as in the United States, although overall patterns may be similar. According to Brian Ramsden, citing UCAS statistics, the total number of undergraduate applications increased by 57 percent between 1996 and 2010. While classical studies, English studies, French studies and religious studies fall below the average, philosophy experienced one of the largest increases: Brian Ramsden, *Institutional Diversity in UK Higher Education* (Oxford: HEPI, 2012).
8. Scott Jaschik, 'Obama vs. Art History,' *Inside Higher Ed*, January 31, 2014, https://www.insidehighered.com/news/2014/01/31/obama-becomes-latest-politician-criticize-liberal-arts-discipline.
9. Tracy Mueller, 'The Famous Obama Apology Note and the Truth about Art History,' *UT Know*, February 20, 2014, http://www.utexas.edu/know/2014/02/20/obama-art-history-apology-letter/.
10. Ibid. (emphasis added).
11. Leslie Larson, 'Marco Rubio Disses Obama's "Pathetic" Apology to Art History Majors,' *New York Daily News*, February 19, 2014, http://www.

nydailynews.com/news/politics/marco-rubio-slams-obama-art-history-apology-article-1.1619563.

12. '2013–2014 PayScale College Salary Report.' The largest enrollment increases at Princeton following the Great Depression were in economics and biology, as noted above, and the same phenomenon occurred at Dartmouth College following the 2008 recession: David Blanchflower, 'David Blanchflower on Degree Trends that Follow Money,' *Times Higher Education*, August 28, 2014, http://www.timeshighereducation.co.uk/features/david-blanchflower-on-degree-trends-that-follow-the-money/2015329.fullarticle. The social sciences, especially economics, may prove to be attractive choices for students who are disinclined to focus on the sciences, but who believe that the employment projects for students concentrating in economics (#15 on the Payscale.com chart) may be better than for humanities majors. See also the enrollment trends shown in Harvard's Humanities Working Group: James Simpson and Sean Kelly, *The Teaching of the Arts and Humanities at Harvard College: Mapping the Future* (Cambridge, MA: Harvard University, May 31, 2013), http://artsandhumanities.fas.harvard.edu/files/humanities/files/mapping_the_future_31_may_2013.pdf.
13. Robert N. Charette, 'Is It Fair to Steer Students into STEM Disciplines Facing a Glut of Workers?' *IEEE Spectrum*, November 21, 2013, http://spectrum.ieee.org/riskfactor/at-work/tech-careers/stem-crisis-as-myth-gets-yet-another-workout; Michael Anft, 'The STEM Crisis: Reality or Myth?' *The Chronicle of Higher Education*, November 11, 2013, http://chronicle.com/article/The-STEM-Crisis-Reality-or/142879/.
14. Ry Rivard, 'Gauging Graduates' Well-Being,' *Inside Higher Ed*, May 6, 2014, https://www.insidehigher-ed.com/news/2014/05/06/gallup-surveys-graduates-gauge-whether-and-why-college-good-well-being. Compare a McKinsey survey of recent graduates that concluded, 'Liberal-arts and performing-arts graduates tend to be lower paid, deeper in debt, less happily employed, and slightly more likely to wish they'd done things differently', compared to those who studied business or the STEM fields: *Voice of the Graduate* (New York: McKinsey & Company, May 2013), http://mckinseyonsociety.com/downloads/reports/Education/UXC001%20Voice%20of%20the%20Graduate%20v7.pdf, 5.
15. Philip Kreager, *Humanities Graduates and the British Economy: The Hidden Impact* (Oxford: Oxford University, July 2013), http://torch.ox.ac.uk/sites/torch/files/publications/Humanities%20Graduates%20and%20the%20British%20Economy%20-%20University%20of%20Oxford.pdf, 1.
16. Paul Jump, 'Chemists: Public Backs STEM Spending Formula,' *Times Higher Education*, October 14, 2010, http://www.timeshighereducation.co.uk/news/chemists-public-backs-stem-spending-formula/413851.article. The Royal Society of Chemistry commissioned the poll; 85 percent of the responders called medicine a high priority, compared to 8 percent for classics and 10 percent for philosophy.
17. Ruth Levitt, Claire Celia, Stephanie Diepeveen, Siobhán Ní Chonaill, Lila Rabinovich, Jan Tiessen, *Assessing the Impact of Arts and*

Humanities Research at Cambridge (Santa Monica, CA: RAND Corporation, 2010), http://www.rand.org/content/dam/rand/pubs/technical_reports/2010/RAND_TR816.pdf, 1 (emphasis added), quoting University of Cambridge, 'Research into the Impacts of Arts and Humanities Research at the University of Cambridge: Invitation to Tender Documents,' 2009, §1.1. See also Alan Hughes, Michael Kitson, Jocelyn Probert, Royce Turner, Anna Bullock, Isobel Milner, *Cultural Connections: The Role of the Arts and Humanities in Competitiveness and Local Development* (Cambridge: Centre for Business Research, University of Cambridge, March 2014), http://www.researchgate.net/profile/Michael_Kitson/publication/262818416_Cultural_Connections_The_Role_of_the_Arts_and_Humanities_in_Competitiveness_and_Local_Development/links/0c960538f12a0ca4d1000000?ev=pub_ext_doc_dl&origin=publication_detail&inViewer=true.

18. Ibid., xiii.
19. James Turner, *Philology: The Forgotten Origins of the Modern Humanities* (Princeton, NJ: Princeton University Press, 2014), 71.
20. Martha Nussbaum, *Not for Profit: Why Democracy Needs the Humanities* (Princeton, NJ: Princeton University Press, 2010); Peter Brooks and Hilary Jewett, ed., *The Humanities and Public Life* (New York: Fordham University Press, 2014); Jonathan Bate, ed., *The Public Value of the Humanities* (London: Bloomsbury Publishing, 2010); Eleonora Belfiore and Anna Upchurch, eds., *Humanities in the Twenty-First Century* (Basingstoke, UK: Palgrave Macmillan, 2013); and Michael Bérubé and Cary Nelson, ed., *Higher Education Under Fire: Politics, Economics, and the Crisis of the Humanities* (New York: Routledge, 1995); Mark William Roche, *Why Choose the Liberal Arts?* (South Bend, IN: University of Notre Dame Press, 2010). Regarding moral values, see Anthony T. Kronman, *Education's End: Why Our Colleges and Universities Have Given Up on the Meaning of Life* (New Haven, CT: Yale University Press, 2007); Harry R. Lewis, *Excellence Without a Soul: Does Liberal Education Have a Future?* (New York: Public Affairs, 2007); John Henry Newman, *The Idea of a University* (Notre Dame, IN: University of Notre Dame Press, 1982); Stanley Fish, *Save the World on Your Own Time* (New York: Oxford University Press, 2012); Stanley Fish, 'Will the Humanities Save Us?' *Opinionator* (blog), *New York Times*, January 6, 2008, http://fish.blogs.nytimes.com/2008/01/01/will-the-humanities-save-us?_php=true&_type=blogs&-R=0.
21. Alan Ryan, 'Not Just How, But Why: Insight and Independent Thinking Are Truly Vocational Skills, Argues Alan Ryan,' *Times Higher Education*, October 14, 2010, http://www.timeshighereducation.co.uk/comment/columnists/not-just-how-but-why/413855.article. Ryan instead writes,

> the best defense comes from [Matthew] Arnold . . . , who expected the cultivated mind to allow a "stream of fresh and free thought" to enliven our stock opinions. That, if anything, is the benefit both to individuals and society at large; and it suggests that humanities, social sciences, and physical sciences are all in the same boat—taught well, they liberate us; taught badly, they induce mental cramp.

See also Alan Ryan, *Liberal Anxieties and Liberal Education* (New York: Hill and Wang, 1998).

22. Louis Menand, *The Marketplace of Ideas: Reform and Resistance in the American Research University* (New York: W. W. Norton & Company, Inc., 2010), 61–62.
23. 'Real world' is an unfortunate term, but one in wide circulation, especially in contradistinction to academia. I urge readers from academia not to take offense at the possible implication that life inside universities is somehow unreal, or at the fact that the term has sometimes been used as a way of criticizing academia or some particular aspect of academic scholarship. I use it here as a shorthand term for the considerably more cumbersome 'those aspects of society that are not directly connected to the realm of higher education and scholarship'. The Oxford English Dictionary records that the distinction between academic theory and the 'real world' has been cited by academics at least for decades. One reference is to the statement, 'The modified algorithm has been tested on 5 real-world problems': Lt. Commander W. S. Shields, 'Note—A Note on the Criss-Cross Algorithm,' *Management Science* 23, no. 1 (1976): 103.
24. Arundeep S. Pradhan, 'Defending the University Tech Transfer System,' *Businessweek*, February 19, 2010, http://www.businessweek.com/smallbiz/content/feb2010/sb20100219_307735.htm.
25. Association of University Technology Managers, 'AUTM US Licensing Activity Survey FY 2012 Highlights,' 2012, http://www.autm.net/AM/Template.cfm?Section=FY2012_Licensing_Activity_Survey&Template=/CM/ContentDisplay.cfm&ContentID=11435, 4.
26. Lisa W. Foderaro, 'Budget-Cutting Colleges Bid Some Languages Adieu,' *New York Times*, December 3, 2010, http://www.nytimes.com/2010/12/05/education/05languages.html?pagewanted=all; John Morgan, 'What Would Lindsay Say? Keele's Plan to Shut Philosophy and Ethics Units Is a "Disaster," Say Scholars,' *Times Higher Education*, March 24, 2011, http://www.timeshighereducation.co.uk/news/what-would-lindsay-say/415593.article.
27. Lord Browne, *Securing a Sustainable Future for Higher Education: An Independent Review of Higher Education Funding and Student Finance* (October 12, 2010), www.independent.gov.uk/browne-report; Hannah Richardson, 'Humanities to Lose English Universities Teaching Grant,' *BBC News*, October 26, 2010, www.bbc.com/news/education-11627843. This particular recommendation has not been adopted as of 2014. It did, however, generate a flurry of defenses of the humanities in the UK: see, e.g., Stefan Collini, 'Browne's Gamble,' *London Review of Books* 32, no. 21 (November 4, 2010): 23–25.
28. Lara V. Marks, *The Lock and Key of Medicine: Monoclonal Antibodies and Their Transformation of Healthcare* (New Haven, CT: Yale University Press, 2015); Mark Jones, 'The Invention of Recombinant DNA Technology,' *LSF Magazine* (Summer 2013), http://zrnage.com/magazine-invention_of_recombinant_dna_technology.htm.

29. See Chapter 2. *The Pharmaceutical Price Regulation Scheme: An OFT Market Study* (London: Office of Fair Trading, 2007), 4. NICE actively seeks to export its expertise around the world: Kalipso Chalkidou, 'The (Possible) Impact on Comparative Effectiveness Research on Pharmaceutical Industry Decision Making,' *Clinical Pharmacology & Therapeutics* 87 (March 2010): 264–266.
30. For an analysis of economic growth associated with the life sciences, and, in particular, showing that net job growth in the life sciences is strongest in the 'drugs and pharmaceuticals segment,' see Ian Hathaway and Robert E. Litan, 'Entrepreneurship and Job Creation in the US Life Sciences Sector,' *Economic Studies at Brookings* (June 2014).
31. For different approaches, compare Nussbaum, *Not For Profit*, and the essays in Bradley C. S. Watson, ed., *Civic Education and Culture* (Wilmington, DE: ISI Books, 2005).
32. Wilfred M. McClay, 'The Burden of the Humanities,' *Wilson Quarterly* 32, no. 3 (Summer 2008): 34–43.
33. Michael Dirda, 'Freelance,' *Times Literary Supplement* (July 18, 2014): 16.
34. Jill Lepore, *The Whites of Their Eyes: The Tea Party's Revolution and the Battle over American History* (Princeton, NJ: Princeton University Press, 2010), 124.
35. José L. Duarte, Jarret T. Crawford, Charlotta Stern, Jonathan Haidt, Lee Jussim, Philip E. Tetlock, 'Political Diversity Will Improve Social Psychological Science' (unpublished manuscript), 2.
36. Howard Kurtz, 'College Faculties a Most Liberal Lot, Study Finds,' *The Washington Post*, March 29, 2005, http://www.washingtonpost.com/wp-dyn/articles/A8427-2005Mar28.html; Stanley Rothman, S. Robert Lichter, and Neil Nevitte, 'Politics and Professional Advancement Among College Faculty,' *The Forum* 3, no. 1 (2005): 1–16.
37. Menand, *The Marketplace of Ideas*, 138, 140, 133n9. Menand writes, citing a study by sociologists Neil Gross and Solon Simmons, 'What is striking about these results is not the finding that professors tend to be mainstream liberals. It is the finding that they are so *overwhelmingly* mainstream liberals': Ibid., 136.
38. The dominant strains of humanities scholarship, with a primary focus on the past, have over time often been linked with the support of a conservative status quo. In his 1987 essay, 'What Hope for the Humanities,' Bernard Williams noted the concern that 'an emphasis on the Humanities, certainly as against some of the social sciences, is conventionally often seen as itself conservative.' Bernard Williams, 'What Hope for the Humanities?' in *Bernard Williams, Essay and Reviews 1959–2002* (Princeton, NJ: Princeton University Press, 2014), 272.
39. Jamal Greene, Nathaniel Persily and Stephen Ansolabehere, 'Profiling Originalism,' *Columbia Law Review* 37, no. 3 (2011): 111. It could be argued that Professor Lepore did not mean to eliminate the study of originalism from academic inquiry, but to place it in a category with astrology as a subject that might be studied by scholars of religion and folklore as a form of popular religion (which, I would add, would

be a good idea). My point is that both large segments of the public and powerful intellectual elites, such as Supreme Court justices, have shown evidence of taking originalism seriously in ways that are typically addressed in the fields of history, law and political science, as well.

40. See Leonard Todd, *Carolina Clay: The Life and Legend of the Slave Potter Dave* (New York: W. W. Norton, 2008). For the paintings, see http://www.jonathangreenstudios.com/Artists.

2 The Humanities and the Future of the Life Sciences

1. Quoted in Frederick Rudolph, *The American College and University: A History* (Athens, GA: University of Georgia Press, 1962), 226. It did not take long for commentators to worry that higher education was not supporting economic growth. The 1828 Yale Reports noted, 'From different quarters, we have heard the suggestion, that our colleges must be new-modelled; that they are not adapted to the spirit... of the age; that they [must be] better accommodated to the business character of the nation.' 'Report of the Faculty,' in 'Reports on the Course of Instruction in Yale College (1828),' reprinted in David B. Potts, *Liberal Education for a Land of Colleges: Yale's Reports of 1828* (New York: Palgrave Macmillan, 2010).
2. Association of University Technology Managers, 'AUTM US Licensing Activity Survey Highlights,' 2012, http://www.autm.net/AM/Template.cfm?Section=FY2012_Licensing_Activity_Survey&Template=/CM/ContentDisplay.cfm&ContentID=11435; Association of University Technology Managers, 'Highlights of AUTM's US Licensing Activity Survey FY2013,' 2013, http://www.autm.net/AM/Template.cfm?Section=FY_2013_Licensing_Activity_Survey&Template=/CM/ContentDisplay.cfm&ContentID=13870. When fees and cashed-in equity are added to the royalties, the total reaches $2.6 billion.
3. Middlesex University in the UK closed its Philosophy department. The State University of New York at Albany eliminated concentrations in classics, French, Italian and Russian; and, on campuses experiencing reductions in enrollment, trustees are scrutinizing just how many (or how few) students are showing enthusiasm for comparative literature and religion. Governing boards and policy-makers witnessing declining interest in the humanities from potential students on the one hand, and counting grants, licensing revenues and job growth from the STEM fields on the other, undoubtedly imagine that they would be making a perfectly rational choice if they elect to cut back on their support for the humanities in favor of investing instead in the academic engines that are driving both technological and economic growth. See, for example, the letter from many scholars 'deplor[ing] Middlesex University's recent decision to close its philosophy programmes'. 'Philosophical View: Middlesex, Think Again,' *Times Higher Education Supplement*, May 6, 2010, http://www.timeshighereducation.co.uk/411499.

article. The Middlesex department was able to relocate to Kingston University. Frederika Whitehead, 'Middlesex Philosophers Celebrate Survival,' *The Guardian*, June 10, 2010, http://www.theguardian.com/education/2010/jun/10/middlesex-philosophers-celebrate-survival. As for Albany, see Scott Jaschik, 'Disappearing Languages at Albany,' *Inside Higher Ed*, October 4, 2010, http://www.insidehighered.com/layout/set/print/news/2010/10/04/albany.

4. 'The Scientific Century: Securing Our Future Prosperity,' *The Royal Society*, March 9, 2010, https://royalsociety.org/policy/publications/2010/scientific-century/.
5. Ibid., 4. The British Academy has spoken up in strong terms for the value, including the economic value, of the humanities. Among other things, the title of that report is interesting because it alludes to an economic instrumentalism that has not always been popular with humanities scholars, as discussed in the previous chapter. One point made by the British Academy (#99 of 174 such points) is, 'Health policy-makers and managers often have to make ethical decisions about the allocation of health care.... Ethical review and philosophical analysis is now seen as indispensable part of health care.' Much of this chapter discusses how this '[e]thical review and philosophical analysis' relates directly to the economic growth associated with the life sciences. *'That Full Complement of Riches': The Contributions of the Arts, Humanities and Social Sciences to the Nation's Wealth* (London: The British Academy, 2004), 35.
6. Birch Bayh, Joseph P. Allen, and Howard W. Bremer, 'Universities, Inventors, and the Bayh-Dole Act,' *Life Sciences Law and Industry* 3, no. 24 (December 18, 2009): 3.
7. National Institutes of Health, *Report to Congress* (2001).
8. Bayh, Allen, and Bremer, 'Universities,' 3.
9. K. Drivers, Z. Lei, and B. Wright, 'A Preliminary View of UC Data on Disclosures, Licensing, and Patenting' (Washington, DC: National Academy of Sciences, May 27, 2009), http://sites.nationalacademies.org/cs/groups/pgasite/documents/webpage/pga_058895.pdf. Drivers, Lei and Wright observe that 75 percent of invention disclosures in the University of California system over five years were in the life sciences. Most of this data comes from the Association of University Technology Managers (AUTM). AUTM has stopped publishing industry-specific data, but data from the late 1990s consistently show that the life sciences make up nearly 70 percent of all spin-off companies and about 85 percent of income received by licensors. It is not a coincidence that these indications of financial and medical success are found primarily in reports from technology managers or in an article by former Senator Birch Bayh (who co-sponsored the Bayh-Dole Act), which laid the legal foundation for university licensing efforts. The point here is not to defend any particular set of data about the economic impact of academic research in the life sciences. It is, rather, to observe that these are the data that motivate policy-makers to increase funding in the STEM fields so as to boost the

economy. See Ben Butkus, 'AUTM's 2006 survey Finds University Technology Transfer is Strong, Though Spinouts Wane,' *GenomeWeb*, December 10, 2007, https://www.genomeweb.com/biotechtransferweek/autm's-2006-survey-finds-university-tech-transfer-strong-though-spinouts-wane.

10. Ashley J. Stevens, Jonathan J. Jensen, Katrine Wyller, Patrick C. Kilgore, Sabarni Chatterjee, and Mark L. Rohrbaugh, 'The Role of Public-Sector Research in the Discovery of Drugs and Vaccines,' *The New England Journal of Medicine* 364, no. 6 (2011): 535–541.
11. *MRC Delivery Plan 2011/12 to 2014/15* (Swindon: Medical Research Council, 2010), 2.
12. He also notes that the 'US and China are increasing investment in science, calculating that it will help to generate growth.' Harpal Kumar, 'Years of Crucial Investment Could Fall by the Wayside,' *The Times*, September 8, 2010, 16.
13. Joseph J. Seneca, and Will Irving, *The Economic Benefits of the New Jersey Stem Cell Research Initiative* (Rutgers University: Edward J. Bloustein School of Planning and Public Policy, September 2005), 1–54; Joseph J. Seneca, and Will Irving, *Updated Economic Benefits of the New Jersey Stem Cell Capital Project and Research Bond Acts* (Rutgers University: Edward J. Bloustein School of Planning and Public Policy, October 2007), 1–23. Unless otherwise indicated, this chapter relies on the original 2005 report.
14. For a summary of the 'bidding war between states' to attract stem cell research, see Hevesi and Bleiwas.

    > Voters in California recently approved a referendum to spend $3 billion in state funding over ten years to create the California Institute for Regenerative Medicine, eclipsing efforts by other states (including New York) to attract elements of the biotech industry and stem cell research. New Jersey announced plans to invest $380 million in the Stem Cell Institute of New Jersey. Connecticut has also dedicated approximately $20 million in budget surpluses to stem cell research, and substantial state and private investments have been proposed in Illinois, Indiana, Massachusetts and Pennsylvania. These programs have escalated an ongoing bidding war between states to attract and retain biotech companies and stem cell researchers.

    Alan G. Hevesi and Kenneth B. Bleiwas, *The Economic Impact of the Biotechnology and Pharmaceutical Industries in New York* (Office of the State Comptroller: New York, Report 11–2005, February 2005), 2.
15. The efforts continue. For developments in the UK, see All-Party Parliamentary Group, 'Harnessing Stem Cells for Patients and Economic Growth' (Meeting, The House of Commons, July 15, 2014), http://www.amrc.org.uk/sites/default/files/doc_lib/Harnessing%20stem%20cells%20for%20patients%20and%20economic%20growth%20-%20note%20of%20meeting.pdf.

16. Laurence Baker, and Bruce Deal, *Economic Impact Analysis* (California Stem Cell Research and Cures Initiative, September 14, 2004), 2. For a discussion of some alternate scenarios, not all of which yield such promising economic outcomes, see Michael T. Longaker, Laurence C. Baker, and Henry T. Greely, 'Proposition 71 and CIRM – assessing the return on investment,' *Nature Biotechnology* 25, no. 5 (May 2007): 513–521.
17. Ibid., 72.
18. It is certainly the case that during the 1960s, 1970s and 1980s, the period examined during the Toole study, NIH funding and industry funding increased in tandem. Whether there is a direct causative effect is less clear, especially since Toole's data suggest an unlikely (in my opinion) 'U-shaped' response in which industry responds positively to increases in public spending in the first and second years after the public increase, and in the seventh and eighth years, but not in years three through six. Andrew A. Toole, 'Does Public Scientific Research Complement Private Investment in Research and Development in the Pharmaceutical Industry?' *Journal of Law and Economics* 50 (2007): 81–96; Health Economics Research Group, 'Annotated Bibliography' in *Medical Research: What's It Worth? Estimating the Economic Benefits from Medical Research in the UK* (London: UK Evaluation Forum, 2008) (hereafter, the 'HERG Report').
19. Numerous studies have discussed the high cost and low likelihood of new medicines. For my views about the process of creating important new medicines, see Donald L. Drakeman, 'Benchmarking Biotech and Pharmaceutical Product Development,' *Nature Biotechnology* 32, no. 7 (2014): 621–625.
20. New drugs are sometimes the product of entirely internal R&D efforts at large pharmaceutical companies. A significant majority of the innovative medicines reaching FDA approval in the last decade have instead been derived from the biotech industry, often employing technology licensed from universities: Ibid., 623.
21. Robert Kneller, 'The Importance of New Companies for Drug Discovery: Origins of a Decade of New Drugs,' *Nature Reviews Drug Discovery* 9 (2010): 870.
22. Katherine Ku, director of the Office of Technology Licensing at Stanford University said that 'Less than 1 percent of the Stanford patent disclosures have generated $1 million or more in cumulative royalties.' Stephen A. Merrill, and Anne-Marie Mazza, eds., *Managing University Intellectual Property in the Public Interest* (Washington, DC: The National Academy Press, 2011), 23.
23. A 2014 report showed that over 80 percent of worldwide investors in venture capital are in North America and Europe. Overall, over half of those investors are pension plans, endowment funds and foundations. *Preqin Special Report: Venture Capital* (Preqin, November 2014), 9.
24. Some university-sponsored funds specifically focus on home-grown technology, as can be seen in the UK's Imperial Innovations. But most venture investing by university endowments goes to venture firms that have no

special link to the university's scientific output; they are purely financial investments.

25. The existence of a robust IPO market for biotechnology companies will not fundamentally change the arguments of this chapter, for the reasons discussed below.
26. An analysis of over 1,000 venture capital investments in the life sciences between 2000 and 2010 showed that nearly 60 percent lost money. The ones that turn a profit—because of an exit opportunity for the venture capitalists—will not necessarily develop a successful new medicine. Bruce L. Booth, and Bijan Salehizadeh, 'In Defense of Life Sciences Venture Investing,' *Nature Biotechnology* 29 (July 2011): 580.
27. If the opportunity for biotechnology IPOs returns, the IPO investors will need to share these same beliefs about the possibility of profitable products, since they will be investing either in the expectation that the company will become profitable or (more likely) be acquired by a large pharmaceutical company.
28. Justin Chakma, et al., 'Asia's Ascent-Global Trends in Biomedical R&D Expenditures,' *New England Journal of Medicine* 370 (January 2, 2014): 1–6.
29. *MRC Delivery Plan*, 2.
30. Jim Gilbert, Preston Henske, and Ashish Singh, 'Rebuilding Big Pharma's Business Model,' *In Vivo: The Business & Medicine Report* 21, no. 10 (November 2003): 73.
31. J. A. DiMasi, R. W. Hansen, and H. G. Grabowski, 'The Price of Innovation: New Estimates of Drug Development Costs,' *Journal of Health Economics* 22 (2003): 151–185; Bernard Muños, 'Lessons From 60 Years of Pharmaceutical Innovation,' *Nature Reviews Drug Discovery* 8 (2009): 959–968.
32. Robert F. Service, 'Surviving the Blockbuster Syndrome,' *Science* 303 (March 19, 2004): 1797.
33. Michael Hay, David W. Thomas, John L. Craighead, Celia Economides, and Jesse Rosenthal, 'Clinical Development Success Rates for Investigational Drugs,' *Nature Biotechnology* 32, no. 1 (January 2014): 40.
34. Biotechnology companies are defined as any drug-development company founded since 1975. Drakeman, 'Benchmarking Biotech and Pharmaceutical Product Development,' 621, 624.
35. 'Remarks Made by the President, Prime Minister Tony Blair of England (via satellite), Dr. Francis Collins, Director of the National Human Genome Research Institute, and Dr. Craig Venter, President and Chief Scientific Officer, Celera Genomics Corporation, on the Completion of the First Survey of the Entire Human Genome Project,' *National Human Genome Research Institute*, June 26, 2000, http://www.genome.gov/10001356.
36. The target for many of the modern biomedical cancer products is the protein for which the gene provides the genetic information.
37. Some of the pharmaceutical industry's financial capacity to seek additional uses of new medicines comes from the monopoly pricing of patented products that can put those products out of reach for some

patients (or even some countries). Years later, when the patent expires, generic versions will be a great deal less expensive, and considerably more is likely to be known about the product. Nevertheless, for some of the products—especially the biologically based ones, such as monoclonal antibodies—the manufacturing costs alone can be much higher than the amounts the same patients have paid for all expenses associated with prior, lower tech, treatments.

38. 'Moore's Law and Intel Innovation,' *Intel,* http://www.intel.com/content/www/us/en/history/museum-gordon-moore-law.html.
39. 'Fun Facts: Exactly How Small (and Cool) is 22 Nanometers?' *Intel,* http://www.intel.com/content/dam/www/public/us/en/documents/corporate-information/history-moores-law-fun-facts-factsheet.pdf.
40. HERG Report, 83.
41. Longaker, Baker and Greely state that

> new stem cell therapies will not necessarily reduce spending; indeed, they may drive spending up.... [I]f the costs of the new therapies were sufficiently high, there may not be any net healthcare savings. New therapies that significantly lengthen life could also elevate costs simply by increasing the amount of baseline health spending, though presumably also producing the benefit of longer life. Perhaps the most important possibility, however, is that stem cell research will make possible treatments that augment the set of therapies used for conditions, rather than replacing or obviating the need for other therapies. The history of healthcare innovation includes many instances where the development and improvement of treatments expanded the medical arsenal, rather than replaced older treatments. This increases health spending over time.

Longaker, Baker, and Greely, 'Proposition 71,' 518.

42. 'Expenditures on research that prolong life without increasing expenditures are almost sure to be worthwhile...but expenditures that significantly increase costs could easily generate more expenditures than gains given the distortions in the care market (the prevalence of third-party payers and the annuitization of benefits).' Kevin M. Murphy and Robert H. Topel, 'The Economic Value of Medical Research,' in *Measuring the Gains from Medical Research: An Economic Approach,* ed. Kevin M. Murphy and Robert H. Topel (Chicago: University of Chicago Press, 2003): 71.
43. Alexander S. Zider and Donald L. Drakeman, 'The Future of Monoclonal Antibody Technology,' *MAbs* 2, no. 4 (2010): 361–364. Since I have started several biotech companies focused on monoclonal antibodies, I may be inclined to emphasize this technology disproportionately to other important new biomedical technologies. The points I am making by discussing this technology could also be made using other technologies as examples.
44. *Antibody Drugs: Technologies and Global Markets* (Wellesley, MA: BCC Research, January 2015), http://www.bccresearch.com/market-research/biotechnology/antibody-drugs-market-bio016j.html; Alex Philippidis,

'Top 20 Best-Selling Drugs of 2012,' *Genetic Engineering & Biotechnology News,* March 5, 2013, http://www.genengnews.com/insight-and-intelligence/top-20-best-selling-drugs-of-2012/77899775/?page=2.

45. Michael D. Rawlins, and Anthony J. Culyer, 'National Institute for Clinical Excellence and Its Value Judgments,' *British Medical Journal* 329, no. 7459 (2004): 224–227.
46. *Social Value Judgements: Principles for the Development of NICE Guidance,* 2nd edition (National Institute for Health and Clinical Excellence, 2008), 8.
47. Ibid., 9.
48. Ibid., 10. NICE cites, and relies heavily on, the work of two Harvard professors, Norman Daniels and James Sabin. Norman Daniels, and James E. Sabin, *Setting Limits Fairly: Learning to Share Resources for Health* (New York: Oxford University Press, 2008).
49. *Social Value Judgements,* 9–10; Daniels, and Sabin, *Setting Limits,* 2.
50. Hope, Reynolds and Griffiths describe the Oxfordshire Health Authority. Tony Hope, John Reynolds, and Siân Griffiths, 'Rationing Decisions: Integrating Cost-Effectiveness with other Values,' in *Medicine and Social Justice: Essays on the Distribution of Health Care,* eds. Rosamond Rhodes, Margaret P. Battin, and Anita Silvers (New York: Oxford University Press, 2002), 151.
51. *Social Value Judgements,* 10.
52. Micah 6:8.
53. Compare Samuel Fleischacker, *A Short History of Distributive Justice* (Cambridge, MA: Harvard University Press, 2004); Siegfried Van Duffel, and Dennis Yap, 'Distributive Justice before the Eighteenth Century: The Right of Necessity,' *History of Political Thought* 32, no. 3 (2011): 449–464; and John Roemer, *Theories of Distributive Justice* (Cambridge, MA: Harvard University Press, 1996), 1.
54. Julian Lamont, and Christi Favor, 'Distributive Justice,' *Stanford Encyclopedia of Philosophy,* January 2, 2013, http://plato.stanford.edu/entries/justice-distributive.
55. Ibid.
56. Brigitte Bechtold, 'More Than *A Room* and *Three Guineas*: Understanding Virginia Woolf's Social Thought,' *Journal of International Women's Studies* 1, no. 2 (May 2000): 1–11. See also Ed Block, Jr., 'Experience, Existence, and Mystery: Biblical Ideas of Justice in Postcolonial Fiction,' in *Post Colonial Literature and the Biblical Call for Justice,* ed. Susan V. Gallagher (Jackson, MS: University Press of Mississippi, 1994).
57. Daniels, and Sabin, *Setting Limits,* 2. For a good summary of many—often conflicting—views on how principles of justice relate to healthcare, see the 34 essays from physicians, philosophers, lawyers and public health professionals in Rosamond Rhodes, Margaret P. Battin, and Anita Silvers, eds., *Medicine and Social Justice.*
58. Bernard H. Baumrin predicts that 'competition to expand health-care services to meet health-care expectations will be the main social battlefield

of the 21st century.' Bernard H. Baumrin, 'Why There is No Right to Health Care,' in *Medicine and Social Justice*, 83.

59. 'Cancer Drugs Fund,' *Cancer Research UK*, September 2014, http://www.cancerresearchuk.org/about-cancer/cancers-in-general/cancer-questions/cancer-drugs-fund; 'The Cancer Drugs Fund,' *NHS England*, 2014, www.england.nhs.uk/ourwork/pe/cdf/; Daniel, and Sabin, *Setting Limits*, 6; and C. Ham and S. Pickard, 'Tragic Choices in Health Care: Lessons from the Child B Case,' *British Medical Journal* 319, no. 7219 (November 1999): 1258–1261.
60. Sunder Katwala, 'The NHS: Even More Cherished than Monarchy and the Army,' *New Statesman*, January 14, 2013, http://www.newstateman.com/politics/2013/01/nhs-even-more-cherished-monarchy-and-army.
61. 'Principle 6,' *The NHS Constitution* (NHS, March 26, 2013), 4.
62. By far the most popular subject from any university is the degree in PPE (philosophy, politics and economics) from the University of Oxford, which is held by over 40 members. Greg Hurst, Emily Gosden, Chris Davalle, and Matthew Lyons, eds., *The Times Guide to the House of Commons* (London: HarperCollins, 2010).
63. John Morgan, 'The Appliance of Extra Science is No Economic Panacea,' *Times Higher Education*, August 26, 2010, http://www.timeshighereducation.co.uk/413171.article.
64. Ruth Levitt, Claire Celia, Stephanie Diepeveen, Siobhan Ni Chronall, Lilla Ratinovich, and Jan Tiessen, *Assessing the Impact of Arts and Humanities Research at the University of Cambridge* (RAND Technical Report, 2010), 13–16.
65. *The Pharmaceutical Price Regulation Scheme: An OFT Market Study* (London: Office of Fair Trading, 2007), 4.
66. Beyond these near-term economic concerns, some economists have argued that 'health—as measured by life expectancy and adult survival rates—has been shown to be just as important as educational attainment, in the development of human capital and hence economic productivity'. Rifat Atun, and Susan Fitzpatrick, *Advancing Economic Growth: Investing in Health* (London: Chatham House, 2005), 9. See also Robert W. Fogel, 'Economic Growth, Population Theory, and Physiology: The Bearing of Long-Term Processes on the Making of Economic Policy.' *The American Economic Review* 84, no. 3 (1994): 369–395.
67. Organization for Economic Co-operation and Development, 'Pharmaceutical Expenditure.' In *Health at a Glance 2011: OECD Indicators* (Paris: OECD Publications, 2011), 155.
68. 'Current Federal Law and Policy.' In *Monitoring Stem Cell Research* (Washington, DC: The President's Council of Bioethics, January 2004), Chapter 2.
69. Megan Kearl, 'Dickey-Wicker Amendment,' *Embryo Project Encyclopedia*, September 25, 2013, http://embryo.asu.edu/handle/10776/2050.
70. Barack Obama, 'Removing Barriers to Responsible Scientific Research Involving Human Stem Cells.' The White House, Executive Order 13505,

March 9, 2009, http://www.whitehouse.gov/the_press_office/Removing-Barriers-to-Responsible-Scientific-Research-Involving-Human-Stem-Cells/.

71. Sherley v. Sebelius, 644 F.3d 388 (2011).
72. E. Ray Dorsey, Jason de Roulet, Joel P. Thompson, Jason I. Reminick, Ashley Thai, Zachary White-Stellato; Christopher A. Beck, Benjamin P. George, Hamilton Moses, 'Funding of US Biomedical Research, 2003–2008.' *Journal of the American Medical Association* 303 (January 13, 2010): 137–143.

3 The Humanities and the Law

1. Quoted in Paul Kane, 'Kagan Sidesteps Empathy Question, Says "It's Law All the Way Down,"' *Washington Post*, June 29, 2010, http://www.washingtonpost.com/wp-dyn/content/article/2010/06/29/AR2010062903935.html.
2. Justice Kagan's phrase, 'law all the way down', strongly evokes the 'turtles all the way down' legend describing what holds the world in place (the popularization of which is variously attributed to William James and Clifford Geertz). The 'turtles' version had appeared in a Supreme Court opinion by Justice Scalia three years earlier, and is described there as follows:

   > The allusion is to a classic story told in different forms and attributed to various authors. See, e.g., Clifford Geertz, Thick Description: Toward an Interpretation Theory of Culture, in The Interpretation of Cultures 28–29 (1973). In our favored version, an Eastern guru affirms that the earth is supported on the back of a tiger. When asked what supports the tiger, he says it stands upon an elephant; and when asked what supports the elephant he says it is a giant turtle. When asked, finally, what supports the giant turtle, he is briefly taken aback, but quickly replies, 'Ah, after that it is turtles all the way down.'

   Rapanos v. United States, 547 US 715 (2006), at 36, n. 14. It may be worth thinking about whether Justice Kagan was arguing for an infinite regression or simply trying to capture a memorable phrase that allowed her to avoid the issue of the role of empathy in judicial decision-making. As discussed later in the chapter, some justices ascribing to an originalist approach to interpretation look for an (arguably) objectively determined historical meaning or event at the base of constitutional interpretation, whereas those preferring an approach based on 'evolving conceptions' of liberty or dignity may fall closer to the infinite regression analogy.
3. This section of the Fourteenth Amendment reads: 'nor shall any deprive any person of life, liberty, or property, without due process of law; nor deny to any person within its jurisdiction the equal protection of the laws'.
4. As discussed in earlier chapters, my definition of the humanities is considerably broader than the fields commonly grouped in the administrative divisions labeled 'humanities' or 'social sciences' by modern universities.

5. The 1856 Republican platform asserted that 'it is both the right and the operative duty of congress to prohibit in the territories those twin relics of barbarism—polygamy and slavery'. Kirk H. Porter and Donald B. Johnson, eds. *National Party Platforms 1840–1960* (Champaign, IL: University of Illinois Press, 1966), 27, quoted in Magrath, 'Chief Justice Waite,' 507–543.
6. For a detailed discussion of this case, see Sarah Barringer Gordon, *The Mormon Question: Polygamy and Constitutional Conflict in Nineteenth Century America* (Chapel Hill: University of North Carolina Press, 2002).
7. Reynolds v. United States, 98 US 145 (1879).
8. Permoli v. Municipality No. 1 of the City New Orleans, 44 US 589 (1845).
9. C. Peter Magrath, 'Chief Justice Waite and the Twin Relic: Reynolds v. United States,' *Vanderbilt Law Review* 18, no. 2 (March 1965): 507. See also C. Peter Magrath, *Morrison R. Waite: The Triumph of Character* (New York: Macmillan Company, 1963).
10. See George Bancroft, *History of the United States from the Discovery of the Continent*, 10 vols. (Boston: Little Brown, 1834–1875); George Bancroft, *History of the Formation of the Constitution of the United States* (New York: Appleton, 1882). For biographical information, see M. A. DeWolfe Howe, *The Life and Letters of George Bancroft* (New York: Charles Scribner & Sons, 1908); Russell B. Nye, *George Bancroft: Brahmin Rebel* (New York: Alfred A. Knopf, 1945).
11. Quoted in Magrath, 'Chief Justice Waite,' 527.
12. The first historian to pick up on Bancroft's influence on the Court's opinion appears to be Bruce R. Trimble. Bruce R. Trimble, *Chief Justice Waite: Defender of the Public Interest* (Princeton: Princeton University Press, 1938). A more detailed discussion is found in Magrath, 'Chief Justice Waite.'
13. This document has become one of the most influential presidential statements in American constitutional history, but it was unknown or ignored for over half a century before it came to Justice Waite's attention. Daniel Dreisbach has written that 'the letter was not reprinted in a forum accessible to a wide audience' until it entered Professor Washington's edition of Jefferson's papers, and it was not included 'in the formal record before the Court, including lower court rulings and the parties' legal briefs.' Daniel L. Dreisbach, *Thomas Jefferson and the Wall of Separation between Church and State* (New York: New York University Press, 2002), 96, 98.
14. See Donald L. Drakeman, *Church, State, and Original Intent* (Cambridge: Cambridge University Press, 2010), 21–73.
15. *Reynolds*, 98 US at 164.
16. *Reynolds*, 98 US. See also Dreisbach, *Thomas Jefferson and the Wall of Separation.*
17. See Thomas Jefferson, 'A Bill for Establishing Religious Freedom,' 1779 and 1786, in *The Sacred Rights of Conscience: Selected Readings on Religious Liberty and Church-State Relations in the American Founding*, ed. Daniel

L. Dreisbach and Mark David Hall (Indianapolis, IN: Liberty Fund, 2009), 250.

18. Waite cited the Appendix to Semple's *Virginia Baptists*, which included Madison's 'Memorial and Remonstrance.' Waite wrote that the General Assessment bill was defeated, but that Jefferson's bill for establishing religious freedom passed. He cited both Jefferson's collected works and Howison's *History of Virginia*. *Reynolds*, 98 US at 162.
19. Robert R. Howison, *History of Virginia from Its Discovery and Settlement by Europeans to the Present Time* (Richmond, VA: Drinker and Morris, 1848), 2:333.
20. Jefferson, 'A Bill for Establishing Religious Freedom,' 250.
21. *Reynolds*, 98 US at 166, citing '2 Kent Com. 81, note (e).' Waite is quoting Kent, who is, in turn, quoting Francis Lieber, *Manual of Political Ethics* (Philadelphia: J. B. Lippincott Company, 1911). Kent writes,

    > Lieber, in his Political Ethics, Vol. ii, p. 9, says that polygamy leads to the patriarchal principle, and which, when applied to large communities, fetters the people in stationary despotism, while that principle cannot exist long [Waite's opinion reverses the order of the two preceding words] in connection with monogamy. The remark is equally striking and profound.

    In the text, Kent observes, 'Polygamy may be regarded as exclusively the feature of Asiatic manners, and of half-civilized life, and to be incompatible with civilization, refinement and domestic felicity.' William Kent, *Commentaries on American Law*, 7th edition (New York: William Kent, 1851), 2:45(h). Magrath notes that Waite read Kent's commentaries as an undergraduate at Yale. Magrath, *Triumph*, 31. For more on Lieber, see James Farr, 'Francis Lieber and the Interpretation of American Political Science,' *The Journal of Politics* 52, no. 4 (November 1990): 1027–1049.
22. Farr, 'Francis Lieber,' 1033.
23. Magrath, *Morrison R. Waite*, 31.
24. Employment Division v. Smith, 494 US 872 (1990).
25. For example, Congress tried to reverse the effect of the Court's decision in the modern *Smith* case via the Religious Freedom Restoration Act ('RFRA'). The Court then held RFRA to be unconstitutional as applied to actions of state governments in City of Boerne v. Flores, 521 US 507 (1997).
26. Magrath, 'Chief Justice Waite,' 523–524. Magrath notes that Waite often 'shifted his vote so that he could control the assignment of an important opinion.' Ibid., 510.
27. 'Transcript of a Letter,' transcribed by Ernest J. Enrich (Washington, DC: Manuscript Division, Library of Congress, December 2, 2003).
28. Trimble, *Chief Justice Waite*, 288.
29. Legal scholar Philip Kurland describes law office history as being 'written the way brief writers write briefs by picking and choosing statements and events favorable to the client's case.' Philip B. Kurland, 'The Origins of the Religion Clauses of the Constitution,' *William and Mary Law*

Review 27 (1985–1986): 839, 842. Leonard Levy says the following of court history: 'Two centuries of Court history should bring us to understand what really is a notorious fact: the Court has flunked history.' Leonard W. Levy, *Original Intent and the Framers Constitution* (New York: Macmillan Company, 1988), 300.

30. See, for example, Vincent Phillip Muñoz, *God and the Founders: Madison, Washington, and Jefferson* (Cambridge: Cambridge University Press, 2009).
31. For more along these lines, see Drakeman, *Church, State, and Original Intent*, 21–73.
32. Everson v. Board of Education, 330 US 1 (1947), *reh. denied*, 330 US 855 (1947).
33. Irving Brant, *James Madison: The Virginia Revolutionist* (Indianapolis, IN: Bobbs-Merrill, 1941), 250. For more on Brant's influence on Justice Rutledge's opinion, see Drakeman, *Church, State, and Original Intent*, 74–148.
34. *Everson*, 330 US at 37 and 39.
35. Ibid., 40–41.
36. Black's footnote reads, 'See e.g. Macaulay, History of England (1849) I, cc. 2, 4; The Cambridge Modern History (1908) V, cc. V, IX, XI; Beard, Rise of American Civilization (1937) I, 60; Cobb, Religious Liberty in America (1902) c. II; Sweet, The Story of Religion in America (1939) c. II; Sweet, Religion in Colonial America (194) 320–322.' *Everson*, 330 US at 30, n. 5.
37. James Madison, 'Monopolies, Perpetuities, Corporations Ecclesiastical Endowments,' in Elizabeth Fleet, 'Madison's "Detached Memorandum,"' *William and Mary Quarterly* 3, no. 4 (1946): 534, 552, 555, cited in *Everson*, 330 US at 34, n. 12.
38. *Everson*, 330 US at 18.
39. Quoted in Del Dickson, ed., *The Supreme Court in Conference (1940–1985): The Private Discussions behind Nearly 300 Supreme Court Decisions* (New York: Oxford University Press, 2001), 402.
40. *Everson*, 330 US at 15.
41. Charles Beard, *The Republic* (New York: Viking Press, 1943), 165.
42. Roger Newman, *Hugo Black: A Biography* (New York: Fordham University Press, 1997), 363.
43. A. E. Dick Howard, 'The Wall of Separation: The Supreme Court as Uncertain Stonemason,' in *Religion and the State: Essays in Honor of Leo Pfeffer*, ed. James E. Wood, Jr. (Waco, TX: Baylor University Press, 1985), 88.
44. Johnathan O'Neill, *Originalism in American Law and Politics: A Constitutional History* (Baltimore, MD: Johns Hopkins University Press, 2007); Grant Huscroft and Bradley W. Miller, ed., *The Challenge of Originalism: Theories of Constitutional Interpretation* (Cambridge: Cambridge University Press, 2011).
45. Wallace v. Jaffree, 472 US 38 (1985), at 92.
46. *Wallace*, 472 US at 92–93.

47. Ibid., 113.
48. Ibid., 104.
49. Ibid., 113–114.
50. Ibid.
51. Town of Greece v. Galloway, 572 US ____ (2014).
52. Brown v. Board of Education, 347 US 483 (1954).
53. Plessy v. Ferguson, 163 US 537 (1896).
54. Ibid. at 540.
55. Ibid. at 544.
56. Ibid. The opinion, by Justice Brown, went on to describe a Massachusetts case discussing racial segregation in schools. Roberts v. City of Boston, 5 Cush. 19 (Mass. S. Ct. 1848–1849).
57. See, for example, Alexander M. Bickel, 'The Original Understanding and the Segregation Decision,' *Harvard Law Review* 69, no. 1 (1955), an article that began as a memorandum for Justice Frankfurter when Bickel was a Supreme Court clerk. Compare Michael McConnell, 'Originalism and the Desegregation Decisions,' *Virginia Law Review* 81 (1995), 947–1140. Jack Balkin notes that 'the general consensus has been that most of the framers and ratifiers of the Fourteenth Amendment did not expect that it would outlaw segregation of the public schools.... [E]ven the galleries of Congress were segregated.' Jack M. Balkin, ed., *What Brown v. Board of Education Should Have Said* (New York: New York University Press, 2001), 53.
58. Dickson, *Supreme Court in Conference*, 659.
59. Ibid., 658.
60. *Brown*, 347 US at 494.
61. Lucas A. Powe, Jr., *The Warren Court and American Politics* (Cambridge: Harvard University Press, 2000), 29.
62. Brown v. Board of Education, 345 US 972 (1953), quoted in Richard Kluger, *Simple Justice: The History of Brown v. Board of Education and Black America's Struggle for Equality* (New York: Random House, Inc., 2004), 619. Some historians have suggested that this request for re-argument may have largely been a delaying tactic to provide the Court with more time. See Richard Kluger, 'At Loggerheads,' in *Simple Justice: The History of Brown v. Board of Education and Black America's Struggle for Equality* (New York: Random House, Inc., 2004), 585–619; Morton J. Horwitz, *The Warren Court and the Pursuit of Justice* (New York: Hill and Wang, 1998).
63. Kluger, *Simple Justice*, 489.
64. Ibid., 489–490.
65. Ibid., 490.
66. Chief Justice Warren specifically cites 'Butts and Cremin, A History of Education in American Culture (1953)...Cubberley, Public Education in the United States (1934 ed.)...Knight, Public Education in the South (1922).... Beale, A History of Freedom of Teaching in American Schools (1941)....' *Brown*, 347 US at 489, n. 4, in Kluger, *Simple Justice*, 490.
67. Kluger, *Simple Justice*, 547.

68. *Brown*, 347 US at 492.
69. Ibid., 493.
70. Ibid., 494.
71. Ibid.
72. Ibid.
73. These materials were brought to the Court's attention in the appellants' brief (that is, the brief of the parties seeking desegregation), and were summarized in considerable detail in an appendix to the brief written by three social scientists and reprinted 50 years later in *American Psychologist*. The statement was signed by 32 social scientists. Kenneth B. Clark, Isidor Chein, and Stuart W. Cook, 'The Effects of Segregation and the Consequences of Desegregation: A (September 1952) Social Science Statement in the Brown v. Board of Education of Topeka Supreme Court Case,' *American Psychologist* 59, no. 6 (September 2004): 495–501.
74. Ibid.
75. James Reston, 'A Sociological Decision,' *New York Times*, May 18, 1954, quoted in Balkin, *What Brown v. Board of Education*, 53.
76. James Jackson Kilpatrick, *The Southern Case for School Segregation* (Springfield, OH: The Crowell-Collier Press, 1962), 105, quoted in Sanjay Mody, 'Brown Footnote Eleven in this Historical Context: Social Science and the Supreme Court's Quest for Legitimacy,' *Stanford Law Review* 54 (April 2002), 803n40.
77. Kluger, *Simple Justice*, 420.
78. Ibid., 420, 422.
79. *Brown*, 347 US at 494, quoted in Kluger, *Simple Justice*, 425.
80. Kluger, *Simple Justice*, 421–422.
81. Balkin, *What Brown v. Board of Education*.
82. Kluger, *Simple Justice*, 315–345.
83. Michael Heise, 'Brown v. Board of Education, Footnote 11, and Multidisciplinarity,' *Cornell Law Review* 90 (2005): 279, 295.
84. Dickson, *Supreme Court in Conference*, 648. See also Mody, 'Brown Footnote Eleven.'
85. Dickson, *Supreme Court in Conference*, 657. These materials are from the justices' private notes of their colleagues' comments, and they may not read as smoothly as written opinions.
86. Heise, 'Brown v. Board of Education, Footnote 11,' 296. See also Martha Minow, *In Brown's Wake: Legacies of America's Educational Landmark* (New York: Oxford University Press, 2010), 138–168.
87. See William J. Brennan, Jr., 'Speech to the Text and Teaching Symposium' (Georgetown University, Washington, DC, October 12, 1985), http://www.Fed-soc.org/resources/id.49/default.asp; Edwin Meese III, 'Speech of Attorney General Edwin Meese III to the American Bar Association' (Washington, DC, July 9, 1985), http://www.Fed-soc.org/resources/id.49/default.asp.
88. Meese, 'Speech.'
89. Brennan, 'Speech.'

90. Ibid.
91. Ibid.
92. Ibid.
93. Neomi Rao, 'A Backdoor to Policy Making: The Use of Philosophers by the Supreme Court,' *University of Chicago Law Review* 65 (1998): 1371–1401; Thom Brooks, 'Does Philosophy Deserve a Place at the Supreme Court?' *Rutgers Law Record* 27 (2003): 1–17. Brooks, a philosopher, thinks philosophers should play a role in judicial decision-making; Rao, now a law professor, does not. See also Richard H. Fallon, Jr., 'Non-Legal Theory in Judicial Decision-Making,' *Harvard Journal of Law and Public Policy* 17 (1994): 87–99.
94. See Ronald Dworkin, 'Assisted Suicide: The Philosophers Brief,' *New York Review of Books* (March 27, 1997): 41. See also, Brooks, 'Does Philosophy Deserve a Place,' 13.
95. Vacco v. Quill, 117 S. Ct. 2293 (1997); Washington v. Glucksberg, 521 US 702 (1997).
96. *Washington*, 521 US.
97. Ibid.
98. Ibid., citing Ronald Dworkin, *Life's Dominion: An Argument about Abortion, Euthanasia and Individual Freedom* (New York: Alfred A. Knopf, 1993).
99. See, for example, Justice Stevens reference to John Donne's 'No man is an island' in the assisted suicide case, *Washington*, 521 US.
100. This data is from a poll conducted in October 2010. *Role of Government Survey* (Washington Post-Kaiser Family Foundation-Harvard University, September 22–October 3, 2010), 33.
101. Donald L. Drakeman, 'What's the Point of Originalism?' *Harvard Journal of Law and Public Policy* 37 (2014): 1135. The poll was described in the article as follows: 'The Originalism 2012 survey was conducted over the Internet by YouGov as part of a 1003-person YouGov Omnibus survey of the general population conducted July 20–23, 2012. YouGov calculates the margin of error to be ± 3.4%.' Ibid., 1133.
102. Marsh v. Chambers, 463 US 783 (1983). The record of the conference discussions is found in Dickson, *Supreme Court in Conference*, 395–397.
103. For much more along these lines, see Drakeman, 'What's the Point of Originalism?'
104. District of Columbia v. Heller, 554 US 570 (2008). For a similarly detailed historical disagreement, see Printz v. United States, 521 US 898 (1997), where justices Scalia and Souter battled over the Federalist Papers.
105. *District of Columbia*, 554 US.
106. See Joyce Lee Malcolm, 'The Supreme Court and the Uses of History: District of Columbia v. Heller,' *UCLA Law Review* 56 (2008–2009): 1378. For Justice Scalia's scholarly contributions to originalism, see Antonin Scalia, *A Matter of Interpretation: Federal Courts and the Law* (Princeton, NJ: Princeton University Press, 1998); Antonin Scalia, 'Originalism: The Lesser Evil,' *University of Cincinnati Law Review* 57 (1988–1989): 849.

107. District of Columbia, 554 US at 56–57, quoting *Parker v. District of Columbia*, 478 F.3d 370, 400 (2007).
108. *District of Columbia*, 554 US at 1.
109. Ibid. at 1.
110. Ibid. at 4.
111. Ibid.
112. Ibid. at 14.
113. Ibid. at 44.
114. Bowers v. Hardwick, 478 US 186 (1986).
115. Lawrence v. Texas, 539 US 558 (2003).
116. See Dudgeon v. United Kingdom, 45 Eur. Ct. H. R. (1991), especially the opinion of Judge Walsh: 'This raises the age-old philosophical question of what is the purpose of law.'
117. National Coalition for Gay and Lesbian Equality v. The Minister of Justice, 1 SA 6 (Con. Ct. 1999), excerpted in Vikram David Amar and Mark V. Tushnet, ed., *Global Perspectives on Constitutional Law* (New York: Oxford University Press, 2009), 120–121.
118. Amar and Tushnet, *Global Perspectives*, 128, describing 'S. v. Banana, 1998 (2) ZLR 5333 (H).'
119. Amar and Tushnet, *Global Perspectives*, 129. There is an interesting debate about the role of originalism outside the United States between Jamal Greene and David Fontana. Greene notes that originalism is not prevalent in Canada and Australia, while Fontana counters that 'countries whose courts . . . make originalist arguments tend to come from revolutionary constitutional moments; the post-colonial constitutions of Africa and Latin America, for instance, foster many originalist arguments'. Jamal Greene, 'On the Origins of Originalism,' *Texas Law Review* 88 (2009): 1–80; David Fontana, 'Response: Comparative Originalism,' *Texas Law Review* 78 (2009): 189–199.
120. For a discussion of 'alternatives to American-style concrete review,' see the discussion of various approaches to 'abstract' or advisory opinions in Michael C. Dorf, 'Abstract and Concrete Review,' in *Global Perspectives on Constitutional Law*, ed. Vikram David Amar and Mark V. Tushnet (New York: Oxford University Press, 2009), 3–14.
121. For an argument that the Congress, as well as the Supreme Court, should follow an originalist understanding of the Constitution (and, therefore, will likely need to seek out the guidance of historians and other scholars), see José Joel Alicea, 'Originalism and the Legislature,' *Loyola Law Review* 56 (Summer 2010): 513–534.
122. The fuller quotation is: 'Merely corroborative detail, intend to give artistic verisimilitude to an otherwise bald and unconvincing narrative.' Whether the 'bald and unconvincing' part is accurate in controversial cases is a matter of heavily debated public opinion. W. S. Gilbert, 'The Mikado.'
123. Arizona Christian School Tuition Organization v. Winn 563 US ____ (2011).

4 Toolboxes, Preferences and the Humanities

1. I am assuming that most readers of this book will live in democracies committed to advancing the welfare of their citizens. As Professor Angus Deaton, among others, has observed,

    > Unfortunately, governments do not always act to improve the health or wellbeing of their citizens.... [M]any countries around the world are not democratic, and more broadly, many governments are not bound to act in the interest of their populations, whether by circumstance—for example the need to persuade citizens to let them raise revenue—or by effective constitutional rules or constraints.

    Angus Deaton, *The Great Escape: Health, Wealth, and the Origins of Inequality* (Princeton, NJ: Princeton University Press, 2013), 121.
2. Christopher L. Eisgruber, *Constitutional Self-Government* (Cambridge, MA: Harvard University Press, 2007), 126–127.
3. Ibid.
4. Scott E. Page, *The Difference: How the Power of Diversity Creates Better Groups, Firms, Schools, and Societies* (Princeton, NJ: Princeton University Press, 2007), 55–69.
5. Ibid., 9.
6. Ibid., 348.
7. Ibid.
8. Ibid., 348–349.
9. Ibid., 283.
10. Ibid.
11. According to Cancer Research UK, 'The Cancer Drugs Fund is money the government has now set aside to pay for cancer drugs that haven't been approved by [NICE] and aren't available within the NHS in England.' 'Cancer Drugs Fund,' *Cancer Research UK,* http://www.cancerresearchuk.org/about-cancer/cancers-in-general/cancer-questions/cancer-drugs-fund.
12. Joseph J. Seneca, and Will Irving, *The Economic Benefits of the New Jersey Stem Cell Research Initiative* (Rutgers University: Edward J. Bloustein School of Planning and Public Policy, September 2005), 1–54, http://policy.rutgers.edu/news/press/stemcell.pdf. See, also, Joseph J. Seneca, and Will Irving, *Updated Economic Benefits of the New Jersey Stem Cell Capital Project and Research Bond Acts* (Rutgers University: Edward J. Bloustein School of Planning and Public Policy, October 2007), 1–23, http://www.policy.rutgers.edu/reports/other/stemcelloct07.pdf; Laurence Baker, and Bruce Deal, *Economic Impact Analysis: Proposition 71 California Stem Cell Research and Cures Initiative* (Analysis Group, September 14, 2004), 2.
13. The California report cites 'Schmidt, E., et al., "Biotech Pipeline Monitor," SG Cowen Analyst Report, March 2004, p. 8.' Baker and Deal, *Economic Impact Analysis*, 81n140. The New Jersey report relies on the California report. Seneca, and Irving, *Economic Benefits*, 40.
14. Seneca, and Irving, *Economic Benefits,* 28–30.

15. See *Social Value Judgements: Principles for the Development of NICE Guidance* (National Institute for Health and Clinical Excellence: December 2005), and its references to, for example, Norman Daniels, and James E. Sabin, *Setting Limits Fairly: Can We Learn to Share Medical Resources?* (New York: Oxford University Press, 2002).
16. Regarding the value of quality's adjusted life-years (QALY), see Michael D. Rawlins, and Anthony J. Culyer, 'National Institute for Clinical Excellence and its Value Judgments,' *British Medical Journal* 329, no. 7459 (July 24, 2004): 225: 'NICE and its advisory bodies have taken the view that . . . [NICE] would need special reasons for accepting technologies with ratios over £25,000–£35,000/QALY as cost effective.'
17. Daniels, and Sabin, *Setting Limits Fairly*, 119n2.
18. Neil Gross, *Why Are Professors Liberal and Why Do Conservatives Care?* (Cambridge, MA: Harvard University Press, 2013), 21.
19. Ibid., 216. For largely similar conclusions, see Robert Maranto, Richard E. Redding, and Frederick M. Hess, *The Politically Correct University: Problems, Scope, and Reforms* (Washington, DC: AEI Press, 2009).
20. Gross, *Why Are Professors Liberal,* 144, 152, citing Paul Lazarfeld, and Wagner Thielens, Jr., *The Academic Mind: Social Scientists in a Time of Crisis* (New York: Free Press, 1958), and Everett Carl Ladd, and Seymour Martin Lipset, *The Divided Academy: Professors and Politics* (New York: W. W. Norton & Co., 1976).
21. Jeremy Black, 'The Problems of Being a Conservative Academic: Jeremy Black Considers the Challenges Faced by a Conservative Professor in the UK,' *The Social Affairs Unit*, 2007, http://www.socialaffairsunit.org.uk/blog/archives/001562.php. In contrasting United States and United Kingdom conservatives, he continues,

    > All of those elements are present among British conservatives, but at a much lower level. American Conservatives in Britain are seen as extremist and right-wing and would not be welcome to David Cameron's brand of conservatism. Rather British conservatives are far more concerned about the rights of the individual in relation to the state—about personal freedom, privacy, the ability to work within a free market, the re-statement of what are seen as the traditional values of Victorian society—the importance of the family, self-help, thrift and responsibility (rather than rights).
    >
    > (Ibid.)

    A study comparing political views of United States and United Kingdom academics reported that, 'College teachers in the US are more liberal on seven [of nine] issues and conservative in none. . . . College teachers in the UK are also more liberal on five issues, and more conservative in none.' Sean M. Christy, 'Essays on the Economics of Signaling Goodness,' *PhD Dissertation* (Binghamton, NY: Binghamton University, 2006), 35. In this economic study of the 'signaling theory of charitable behavior,' individuals 'may imitate members of their group so as [to] better fit in . . . . Therefore one's opinion on a public policy question can be determined not solely by that individual's self-interest, but also by the self-interest of his group.' Ibid., 8–9. Leading economists have argued that 'good public policy positions are those that were beneficial to community survival in the hunter-gatherer stage of human evolution,' such as 'sharing and redistribution of food resources.' Ibid., 10. Therefore, the '"good" policy positions [are those in favor of] more public expenditures on that issue.' Ibid. It is possible that conservatives interested in 'self-help, thrift and responsibility,' as Professor Black describes in the UK, or perhaps 'small government conservatives' in the United States, might argue that a person who starts a charitable food bank for the homeless might signal some degree of 'goodness' even if she does not necessarily advocate greater government spending on homelessness programs.

22. Clem Brooks, 'Nations, Classes, and the Politics of Professors: A Comparative Perspective,' in *Professors and Their Politics*, ed. Neil Gross, and Solon Simmons (Baltimore, MD: Johns Hopkins University Press, 2014), 94. The countries studied are Australia, Britain, Denmark, Germany, New Zealand, Norway, Portugal, Russia, Spain and the United States. Brooks notes that the United States and Britain are at the low end of support for civil liberties, even if those levels are higher than found in the general public: 'The American professoriate's score . . . places at third from the bottom in the ranking of civil liberties attitudes, ahead of only British and Russian faculty.' Ibid. This study is limited by the fact that the data is derived from the International Social Survey Program. The question relating to the 'policy domain' of civil liberties is: 'There are many ways people or organizations can protest against a government action they strongly oppose.' The choices were: 'Organizing public meetings to protest against the government? Organizing protest marches and demonstrations? Organizing a nationwide strike of all workers against the government?' Ibid., 107, note 5.
23. Ibid., 106.
24. Neil Gross, and Solon Simmons, 'The Social and Political Views of American College and University Professors' in *Professors and Their Politics* ed. Neil Gross and Solon Simmons (Baltimore, MD: Johns Hopkins University Press, 2014), 42.
25. Ibid., 26. Conservatives in the social sciences are likely to be concentrated in Economics, where leading Princeton economist, Alan Blinder, has expressed concern that 'ideological predispositions infect economists' conclusions far too much [and] economics has drifted to the right (along with the American body politic).' Alan S. Blinder, 'replies,' in '"What's the Matter with Economics?": An Exchange,' *New York Review of Books* 62, no. 1 (January 8, 2015).
26. Gross, and Simmons, 'Social and Political Views,' 26–29; Jeffrey M. Jones, 'Liberal Self-Identification Edges Up to New High in 2012,' *Gallup*, http://www.gallup.com/poll/166787/liberal-self-identification-edges-new-high-2013.aspx. Throughout this chapter, I will be mixing and matching data from different surveys in a manner that social scientists will undoubtedly see as methodologically suspect. My goal is to show large differences, not minor gradations, and the data shown should be adequate

for the purposes. Carefully controlled studies would make the observations methodologically stronger, but I doubt they would change the outcomes. As James Ceaser and Robert Maranto point out, 'Some facts are so obvious that not even a behavioral political scientist would demand proof. One of these is that the vast majority of card-carrying political scientists in America today are on the left of the political spectrum.' James W. Ceaser, and Robert Maranto, 'Why Political Science Is Left But Not Quite PC: Causes of Disunion and Diversity,' in *The Politically Correct University: Problems, Scope, and Reforms*, ed. Robert Maranto, Richard E. Redding, and Frederick M. Hess (Washington, DC: AEI Press, 2009), 209.

27. Stanley Rothman, and S. Robert Lichter, 'The Vanishing Conservative—Is There a Glass Ceiling?' in *Politically Correct University*, ed. Robert Maranto, Richard E. Redding, and Frederick M. Hess (Washington, DC: AEI Press, 2009), 60–76.
28. Ibid., 68.
29. Ibid.
30. Ibid., 69.
31. Lawrence H. Summers, quoted in Robert Maranto, Richard E. Redding, and Frederick M. Hess, 'The PC Academy Debate: Questions Not Asked,' in *Politically Correct University*, ed. Robert Maranto, Richard E. Redding, and Frederick M. Hess (Washington, DC: AEI Press, 2009), 4. As Daniel Stern and Charlotta Stern have concluded in a study of 'The Ideological Profile of Professors,' 'few professors in the social sciences and humanities today are not on the left, and... there has been a decline since the 1960s in professors who are not on the left, as indicated by Republican voting, self-identified conservative leanings or policy views'. Daniel Stern, and Charlotta Stern, 'By the Numbers: The Ideological Profile of Professors' in *Politically Correct University*, ed. Robert Maranto, Richard E. Redding, and Frederick M. Hess(Washington, DC: AEI Press, 2009), 15.
32. See, Gross, *Why Are Professors Liberal*, 220–252. See also, Robert P. George, 'Liberalism, Liberation, and the Liberal Arts,' in *Conscience and its Enemies: Confronting the Dogmas of Liberal Secularism* (Wilmington, DE: ISI Books, 2013): 27–41; and the reports issued by the National Association of Scholars on 'The Vanishing West: 1964–2010,' 'Recasting History: Are Race, Class, and Gender Dominating American History?,' and 'What Does Bowdoin Teach? How a Contemporary Liberal Arts College Shapes Students,' all available at www.nas.org. See, also, Emory University English professor Mark Bauerlein's comments about the subjects covered in literature courses: 'Nobody who has paid attention to the deterioration of the humanities should be surprised at this evolution from principled objection to the canon in the 1980s to informal disregard in the 2010s. The process has unfolded through a deceptive dialectic of hard radicalism and soft liberalism among the professorate.' Mark Bauerlein, 'Humanities: Doomed to Lose?,' *The New Criterion*, November 2014, http://www.newscriterion.com/articieprint.cfm/

Humanities-doomed-to-lose-7989. The intellectual forefather for many of these efforts is William F. Buckley, *God and Man at Yale* (Chicago, IL: Regnery, 1951).

33. Hiring patterns may contribute to a concentration of similar views at the top universities. See Robert B. Townsend, 'New Study Highlights Prominence of Elite PhD Programs in History,' *Perspectives on History*, October 2005, http://www.historians.org/publications-and-directories/perspectives-on-history/October-2005/new-study-highlights-prominence-of-elite-phd-programs-in-history. This study shows that over 70 percent of faculty members at the 'Top 25 Research Universities' and the 'Top 25 Liberal Arts Colleges' received their PhD degree from a 'Graduate Program Ranked in Top 20.' Ibid.
34. One analysis has noted that, 'even controlling for publication achievement, social liberals tend to work at more prestigious institutions than do social conservatives.' Stanley Rothman, April Kelly-Woessner, and Matthew Woessner, *The Still Divided Academy: How Competing Vision of Power, Politics, and Diversity Complicate the Mission of Higher Education* (Lanham, MD: Rowman & Littlefield Publishers, Inc., 2011), 94.
35. Beyond the general unavailability of right-of-center scholars at top universities, there may also be a tendency for the conservative scholars themselves to be discounted by their fellow scholars. Professor Gross observes, for example, 'On the left, among those willing to acknowledge that the academic profession is more liberal than conservative, two explanations dominate. The first holds that liberals are smarter than conservatives.' The second relates to fundamental preferences: 'What do liberals value? Social justice and truth. What do conservatives value? Preserving their distorted vision of the American way of life and making money.' Gross, *Why Are Professors Liberal*, 9. It is not clear how widespread these views may be, but, with conservatives in extremely short supply among humanities faculties at research universities, these kinds of explanations for their absence are unlikely to inspire liberal academics to seek greater engagement either with their few right-leaning colleagues (if any), or conservative scholars at less prestigious institutions. Based on the current state of the social science literature, however, Gross concludes that these dismissive views of conservative intelligence are largely unsupported by the data: 'None of these arguments holds much water. There is a statistical association between verbal intelligence and political liberalism. But it is not as strong an association as liberals would like to believe.' Ibid., 9. Nevertheless, Professor Satoshi Kanazawa, of the London School of Economics and Political Science has written, '[B]oth in the relatively more conservative capitalist United States and in the relatively more liberal socialist United Kingdom, more intelligent individuals are more like to be liberal than less intelligent individuals.' Satoshi Kanazawa, 'Why Liberals and Atheists Are More Intelligent,' *Social Psychology Quarterly* 73, no. 1 (2010): 33–57, 52.
36. Christopher L. Eisgruber, and Lawrence G. Sager, *Religious Freedom and the Constitution* (Cambridge, MA: Harvard University Press, 2007).

37. Ibid., 2.
38. Ibid.
39. Ibid., 4.
40. Ibid., 21 (emphasis added).
41. Ibid., 64.
42. Ibid., 21.
43. Ibid., 120.
44. Ibid., 19.
45. Ibid., 127.
46. Ibid., 164.
47. Ibid.
48. Ibid., 127.
49. Freedom From Religion Foundation v. Obama, 705 F. Supp. 2d 1039, 1049 (W. D. Wis., 2010).
50. 36 US Code §119. This law was based on a very similar 1952 statute. Ibid.
51. *Freedom*, 705 F. Supp. 2d 1039 at 19.
52. *Freedom*, 705 F. Supp. 2d 1039.
53. Freedom From Religion Foundation v. Obama 641F.3d 803 (7th Circ. 2011).
54. *Freedom*, 641 F. 3d 803 (7th Circ. 2011) at 6.
55. *Freedom*, 705 F. Supp. 2d 1039 at 19.
56. *Freedom*, 641 F. 3d 803 at 6 (emphasis added).
57. Eisgruber, and Sager, *Religious Freedom*, 127.
58. Ibid., 144.
59. For a thoughtful discussion of 'the incoherence of the idea of social meaning,' see Richard Ekins, 'Equal Protection and Social Meaning,' *American Journal of Jurisprudence* 57, no. 1 (2012): 35.
60. Ibid., 21, 74–75.
61. Neil Gross, and Solon Simmons, 'How Religious Are America's College and University Professors?' *SSRC* (February 6, 2007): 7.
62. Ibid.
63. Professors Eisgruber and Sager appear to have begun their collaboration when they were professors at New York University's law school. A recent study of 'political bias in legal scholarship' discovered that, in an initial sampling of constitutional law tenured professors at top-ranked law schools, only one of 21 had made more contributions to Republican than Democratic candidates. After analyzing data from these professors' scholarly publications, the authors conclude that 'constitutional rights scholars are less ideologically diverse than other legal scholars'. Adam S. Chilton, and Eric A. Posner, 'An Empirical Study of Political Bias in Legal Scholarship' (University of Chicago Coase-Sandor Institute for Law & Economics Research Paper No. 696, August 11, 2014), http://ssrn.com/abstract=2478908.
64. Jeffrey M. Jones, 'Few Americans Oppose National Day of Prayer,' *Gallup*, May 5, 2010, http://www.gallup.com/poll/127721/few-americans-oppose-national-day-payers.aspx.

65. Rebecca Riffkin, 'In US, Support for Daily Prayer in Schools Dips Slightly,' *Gallup*, September 25, 2014, http://www.gallup.com/poll/177401/support-daily-prayer-schools-dips-slightly.aspx. A 2005 survey showed that 'three in four Americans supported a constitutional amendment to allow voluntary prayer in schools'. Ibid.
66. The questions employed in this poll do not directly address the public's perception of social meaning. A reasonable interpretation of the data showing a majority of the public in support of public prayer would be either (a) that the public does not share the view expressed by Professors Eisgruber and Sager that the social meaning of such a public endorsement of religion is to disparage non-believers, or (b) that the public agrees that the social meaning is to disparage non-believers, but does not share the authors' premise that believers and non-believers should be treated equally.
67. Eisgruber, *Constitutional Self-Government*, 126–127.
68. Jill Lepore, *The Whites of Their Eyes: The Tea Party's Revolution and the Battle Over American History* (Princeton, NJ: Princeton University Press, 2011), 7.
69. Ibid., 14.
70. Ibid., 15.
71. Ibid.
72. Ibid., 19.
73. Ibid., 67.
74. Ibid., 69.
75. Ibid., 12. Later Lepore notes that the

> scholarship academic historians have written since the 1960s...was not without substantial shortcomings. Critics...had charged scholars...not only with an inability to write for general readers and an unwillingness to examine the relationship between past and present, but also with a failure to provide a narrative synthesis....Those criticisms were warranted. They were also criticisms academic historians had made of themselves. Scholars criticize and argue-and must, and can-because scholars share a common set of ideas about how to argue, and what counts as evidence.
>
> (Ibid., 95)

76. Ibid., 69.
77. Ibid., 112.
78. Ibid., 118, 123.
79. Ibid., 124.
80. Ibid., 46.
81. Ibid., 122.
82. Ibid., 121.
83. Ibid.
84. Professor Lepore specifically cites the book by Martha Nussbaum, *Liberty of Conscience: In Defense of America's Tradition of Religious Equality* (New York: Basic Books, 2008).

85. Theophilus Parsons, Jr., *Memoir of Theophilus Parsons, Chief Justice of the Supreme Judicial Court of Massachusetts* (Boston: Ticknor and Fields, 1859), 405–406.
86. Philip Hamburger, *Separation of Church and State* (Cambridge, MA: Harvard University Press, 2002), 202, 270–271.
87. Donald L. Drakeman, *Church, State, and Original Intent* (Cambridge: Cambridge University Press, 2010), 80.
88. Lepore, *Whites of Their Eyes*, 167.
89. A 2012 survey asked American voters not only whether they would prefer originalism to a more modern interpretation (about half usually do) but how many thought the framers' views were at least relevant to the Supreme Court's interpretation of the Constitution: over 90 percent said yes. Donald L. Drakeman, 'What's the Point of Originalism?,' *Harvard Journal of Law and Public Policy* 37 (2014): 1124–1150.
90. Lepore, *Whites of Their Eyes*, 12.
91. 'Should You Attend that Interdisciplinary Conference?,' *The Chronicle of Higher Education*, December 16, 2014 (italics added), https://chroniclevitae.com/news/835-should-you-attend-that-interdisciplinary-conference?cid=at&utm.source=at&utm_medium=en.
92. 'Academic Freedom,' *American Association of University Professors*, www.aaup.org, quoting the 1940 AAUP 'State of Principles on Academic Freedom and Tenure.'

5 The Humanities and the Common Good

1. Paul Johnson, 'Dirty Rotten Scholars,' *The Spectator*, February 26, 2011, http://www.spectator.co.uk/print/essays/6725758/dirty-rotten-scholars.html.
2. This is my best paraphrasing from memory of a comment made by Brian Abel Ragen, an Emeritus Professor of English at Southern Illinois University, Edwardsville, during the comments portion of a panel discussion on 'The Role of the Humanities in Higher Education,' which was part of a multi-day conference, 'Many Minds, Many Stripes: A Princeton University Conference for Graduate Alumni,' October 17–19, 2013.
3. Bernard Williams, 'What Hope for the Humanities?' in *Bernard Williams, Essay and Reviews 1959–2002* (Princeton, NJ: Princeton University Press, 2014), 270.
4. James Turner, *Philology: The Forgotten Origins of the Modern Humanities* (Princeton, NJ: Princeton University Press, 2014).
5. See Chapter 3.
6. 'University of Cambridge Mission Statement,' http://www.cam.ac.uk/about-the-university/how-the-university-and-colleges-work/the-universitys-mission-and-core-values.
7. 'University of California at Los Angeles, Mission Statement,' http://www.ucla.edu/about/mission-and-values.
8. Anthony M. Coelho, 'NIH Announces Updated Criteria for Evaluating Research Grant Applications,' *National Institutes of Health*, October 12,

2004, https://csde.washington.edu/research/funding/archive/nih_criteria.shtml.

9. While this represents an overall success rate of about 18 percent, the new grants eligible to be paid were closer to 10 percent. Sally Rockey, 'FY2012 By the Numbers: Success Rates, Applications, Investigators, and Awards,' *National Institutes of Health*, January 2, 2013, http://nexus.od.nih.gov/all/2013/01/02/fy2012-by-the-numbers-success-rates-applications-investigators-and-awards/.
10. There are many assumptions involved in estimating the output from these grants. The number of patents was derived by dividing the number of patents in the relevant fields awarded to academic institutions between 1990 and 2010 by the number of NIH grant-funded projects during the same period. The expected number of products was estimated based on data relating to the number of innovative drugs whose origins were traced to academic research between 1998 and 2007. Robert Kneller, 'The Importance of New Companies for Drug Discovery: Origins of a Decade of New Drugs,' *Nature Reviews Drug Discovery* 9 (November 2010): 869–870.
11. For the original article, see G. Köehler, and C. Milstein, 'Continuous Cultures of Fused Cells Secreting Antibody of Predefined Specificity,' *Nature* 256 (August 7, 1975): 495–497. See also Lara V. Marks, *The Lock and Key of Medicine: Monclonal Antibodies and the Transformation of Healthcare since the 1970s* (New Haven, CT: Yale University Press, 2015), Chapter 1.
12. See Donald L. Drakeman, 'The Church Historians Who Made the First Amendment What It Is Today,' *Religion in American Culture* 17, no. 1 (Winter 2007): 27–56.
13. 'Research Excellence Framework Confirms Cambridge's Global Strength and Depth in Research,' *University of Cambridge*, http://www.cam.ac.uk/research/news/research-excellence-framework-confirms-cambridges-global-strength-and-depth-in-research.
14. Beth McMartrie, 'Political Scientists Propose New Ways to Engage Policy Makers and the Public,' *The Chronicle of Higher Education*, August 29, 2014, http://chronicle.com/article/political-scientists-propose/148523/?cid=at&utm_source=at&utm_medium=en.
15. Susan White, Raymond Chu, and Roman Czujko, *The 2012–13 Survey of Humanities Departments at Four-Year Institutions* (College Park, MD: Statistical Research Center, American Institute of Physics, 2014), 49.
16. Ibid., 149–197.
17. A notable exception here is Jonathan Bate, ed., *The Public Value of the Humanities* (London: Bloomsbury Publishing, 2010).
18. White, Chu, and Czujko, *Survey of Humanities Departments*, 65.
19. Ibid., 149–197.
20. Professors may counter that scholarly research is an essential foundation for effective teaching. The data are generally mixed to negative on this point, although it is a difficult relationship to measure. In a review of review articles on the subject, the authors concluded that 'most analyses come to the conclusion [that] while research productivity does not

preclude quality teaching, the two are unrelated at the individual faculty level'. Michael J. Prince, Richard M. Felder, and Rebecca Brent, 'Does Faculty Research Improve Undergraduate Teaching? An Analysis of Existing and Potential Strategies,' *Journal of Engineering Education* 96, no. 4 (2007): 284. Irrespective of whether research has a bearing on teaching, William Clark notes that research has been the 'essential modern academic capital' since at least the late eighteenth century, thanks largely to the efforts of Minister Münchhausen in Göttingen. William Clark, *Academic Charisma and the Origins of the Research University* (Chicago: University of Chicago Press, 2007), 247.

21. Martha Nussbaum, *Not for Profit: Why Democracy Needs the Humanities* (Princeton, NJ: Princeton University Press, 2010). Former university president Nannerl O. Keohane quotes Nussbaum as follows: 'Democracies need complete citizens who can think for themselves, criticize tradition, and understand the significance of another person's sufferings.' Nannerl O. Keohane, 'The Liberal Arts as Guideposts in the 21st Century,' *The Chronicle of Higher Education*, January 29, 2012, http://chronicle.com/article/The-Liberal-Arts-as-Guideposts/130475/. Where Nussbaum and Keohane emphasize the need to criticize tradition, the National Humanities Alliance focuses on America's tradition of 'world leadership': 'Advancement in the humanities is critical to our nation's well-being and continued status as a world leader.' National Humanities Alliance, *Now More than Ever: Why America Needs the Humanities in the 21st Century* (November 2008): 1. See also John Fonte, 'Is the Purpose of Civic Education to Transmit or Transform the American Regime?' in *Civic Education and Culture*, ed. Bradley C. S. Watson (Wilmington, DE: Intercollegiate Studies Institute Press, 2005), 73–111; James W. Ceaser, *Liberal Democracy and Political Science* (Baltimore, MD: Johns Hopkins University Press, 1990).
22. This is my best recollection of a portion of the proceedings of the Second International Conference on Bispecific Antibodies and Targeted Cellular Cytotoxicity, which took place in 1990 in Seillac, France.

Bibliography

'Academic Freedom.' American Association of University Professors. www.aaup.org.

Alicea, José Joel. 'Originalism and the Legislature.' *Loyola Law Review* 56 (Summer 2010): 513–534.

All-Party Parliamentary Group. 'Harnessing Stem Cells for Patients and Economic Growth.' Meeting, The House of Commons, July 15, 2014. http://www.amrc.org.uk/sites/default/files/doc_lib/Harnessing%http:20stem%http:20cells%http:20for%http:20patients%http:20and%http:20economic%http:20growth%http:20-%http:20note%http:20of%http:20meeting.pdf.

Amar, Vikram David, and Mark V. Tushnet, eds. *Global Perspectives on Constitutional Law*. New York: Oxford University Press, 2009.

Anft, Michael. 'The STEM Crisis: Reality or Myth?' *The Chronicle of Higher Education*, November 11, 2013. http://chronicle.com/article/The-STEM-Crisis-Reality-or/142879/.

Association of University Technology Managers. 'AUTM US Licensing Activity Survey Highlights.' 2012. http://www.autm.net/AM/Template.cfm?Section=FY2012_Licensing_Activity_Survey&Template=/CM/ContentDisplay.cfm&ContentID=11435.

——. 'Highlights of AUTM's US Licensing Activity Survey FY2013.' 2013. http://www.autm.net/AM/Template.cfm?Section=FY_2013_Licensing_Activity_Survey&Template=/CM/ContentDisplay.cfm&ContentID=13870.

Atun, Rifat, and Susan Fitzpatrick. *Advancing Economic Growth: Investing in Health*. London: Chatham House, 2005.

Baker, Laurence, and Bruce Deal. *Economic Impact Analysis: Proposition 71 California Stem Cell Research and Cures Initiative*. Analysis Group, September 14, 2004.

Balkin, Jack M., ed. *What Brown v. Board of Education Should Have Said*. New York: New York University Press, 2001.

Bancroft, George. *History of the Formation of the Constitution of the United States*. New York: Appleton, 1882.

——. *History of the United States from the Discovery of the Continent*, 10 vols. Boston: Little Brown, 1834–1875.

Bate, Jonathan, ed. *The Public Value of the Humanities*. London: Bloomsbury Publishing, 2010.

Bauerlein, Mark. 'Humanities: Doomed to Lose?' *The New Criterion*, November 2014. http://www.newscriterion.com/articieprint.cfm/Humanities-doomed-to-lose-7989.

Baumrin, Bernard H. 'Why There Is No Right to Health Care.' In *Medicine and Social Justice*, edited by Rosamond Rhodes, Margaret P. Battin, and Anita Silvers, 78–83. Oxford: Oxford University Press, 2002.

Bayh, Birch, Joseph P. Allen, and Howard W. Bremer. 'Universities, Inventors, and the Bayh-Dole Act.' *Life Sciences Law and Industry* 3, no. 24 (December 18, 2009): 1–5.

Beard, Charles. *The Republic*. New York: Viking Press, 1943.

Bechtold, Brigitte. 'More Than *A Room* and *Three Guineas*: Understanding Virginia Woolf's Social Thought.' *Journal of International Women's Studies* 1, no. 2 (May 2000): 1–11.

Belfiore, Eleonora, and Anna Upchurch, eds. *Humanities in the Twenty-First Century*. Basingstoke, UK: Palgrave Macmillan, 2013.

Berrett, Dan. 'Humanities, for Sake of Humanity.' *Inside Higher Ed*, March 30, 2011. http://www.insidehighered.com/news/2011/03/30/scholars_seek_to_craft_argument_for_urgency_of_the_humanities_in_higher_education.

Bérubé, Michael. 'The Futility of the Humanities.' *Qui Parle: Critical Humanities and Social Sciences* 20, no. 1 (Fall/Winter 2011): 95–107.

——, and Cary Nelson, eds. *Higher Education Under Fire: Politics, Economics, and the Crisis of the Humanities*. New York: Routledge, 1995.

Bickel, Alexander M. 'The Original Understanding and the Segregation Decision.' *Harvard Law Review* 69, no. 1 (1955): 1–65.

Biggar, Nigel. 'What Are Universities For?' *Standpoint Magazine*, July/August 2010. http://www.standpointmag.com/uk/print/3156.

Black, Jeremy. 'The Problems of Being a Conservative Academic: Jeremy Black Considers the Challenges Faced by a Conservative Professor in the UK.' *The Social Affairs Unit*, 2007. http://www.socialaffairsunit.org.uk/blog/archieves/001562.php.

Blanchflower, David. 'David Blanchflower on Degree Trends that Follow Money.' *Times Higher Education*, August 28, 2014. http://www.timeshighereducation.co.uk/features/david-blanchflower-on-degree-trends-that-follow-the-money/2015329.fullarticle.

Blinder, Alan S. '"What's the Matter with Economics?": An Exchange.' *New York Review of Books* 62, no. 1 (January 8, 2015): 55–57.

Block, Jr., ed. 'Experience, Existence, and Mystery: Biblical Ideas of Justice in Postcolonial Fiction.' In *Post Colonial Literature and the Biblical Call for Justice*, edited by Susan V. Gallagher, 34–47. Jackson, MS: University Press of Mississippi, 1994.

Brant, Irving. *James Madison: The Virginia Revolutionist*. Indianapolis, IN: Bobbs-Merrill, 1941.

Brennan, Jr., William J. 'Speech to the Text and Teaching Symposium.' Georgetown University, Washington, DC, October 12, 1985. http://www.Fed-soc.org/resources/id.49/default.asp.

Brooks, Clem. 'Nations, Classes, and the Politics of Professors: A Comparative Perspective.' In *Professors and Their Politics*, edited by Neil Gross and Solon Simmons, 82–107. Baltimore, MD: Johns Hopkins University Press, 2014.

Brooks, Peter, and Hilary Jewett, eds. *The Humanities and Public Life*. New York: Fordham University Press, 2014.

Brooks, Thom. 'Does Philosophy Deserve a Place at the Supreme Court?' *Rutgers Law Record* 27 (2003): 1–17.

Bod, Rens. *A New History of the Humanities: The Search for Principles and Patterns from Antiquity to the Present*. Oxford: Oxford University Press, 2014.

Booth, Bruce L., and Bijan Salehizadeh. 'In Defense of Life Sciences Venture Investing.' *Nature Biotechnology* 29 (July 2011): 579–583.

Browne, Lord. *Securing a Sustainable Future for Higher Education: An Independent Review of Higher Education Funding and Student Finance*. October 12, 2010. www.independent.gov.uk/browne-report.

Buckley, William F. *God and Man at Yale*. Chicago, IL: Regnery, 1951.

Butkus, Ben. 'AUTM's 2006 Survey Finds University Technology Transfer Is Strong, Though Spinouts Wane.' *GenomeWeb*, December 10, 2007. https://www.genomeweb.com/biotechtransferweek/autm's-2006-survey-finds-university-tech-transfer-strong-though-spinouts-wane.

Butler, Judith. 'Ordinary, Incredulous.' In *The Humanities and Public Life*, edited by Peter Brooks, 15–40. New York: Fordham University Press, 2014.

'Cancer Drugs Fund.' *Cancer Research UK*, September 2014. http://www.cancerresearchuk.org/about-cancer/cancers-in-general/cancer-questions/cancer-drugs-fund.

'The Cancer Drugs Fund.' *NHS England*, 2014. www.england.nhs.uk/ourwork/pe/cdf/.

Ceaser, James W. *Liberal Democracy and Political Science*. Baltimore, MD: Johns Hopkins University Press, 1990.

Chace, William M. 'The Decline of the English Department: How It Happened and What Could Be Done to Reverse It.' *The American Scholar*, September 1, 2009. http://theamericanscholar.org/the-decline-of-the-english-department/#.U_4xIGK9KK0.

Chakma, Justin, Gordon H. Sun, Jeffrey D. Steinberg, Stephen M. Sammut, and Reshma Jagsi. 'Asia's Ascent-Global Trends in Biomedical R&D Expenditures.' *New England Journal of Medicine* 370 (January 2, 2014): 1–6.

Chalkidou, Kalipso. 'The (Possible) Impact on Comparative Effectiveness Research on Pharmaceutical Industry Decision Making.' *Clinical Pharmacology & Therapeutics* 87 (March 2010): 264–266.

Charette, Robert N. 'Is It Fair to Steer Students into STEM Disciplines Facing a Glut of Workers?' *IEEE Spectrum*, November 21, 2013. http://spectrum.ieee.org/riskfactor/at-work/tech-careers/stem-crisis-as-myth-gets-yet-another-workout.

Chilton, Adam S., and Eric A. Posner. 'An Empirical Study of Political Bias in Legal Scholarship.' University of Chicago Coase-Sandor Institute for Law & Economics Research Paper No. 696, August 11, 2014. http://ssrn.com/abstract=2478908.

Christy, Sean M. 'Essays on the Economics of Signaling Goodness.' PhD Diss., Binghampton, NY: Binghamtpon University, 2006.

Clark, Kenneth B., Isidor Chein, and Stuart W. Cook. 'The Effects of Segregation and the Consequences of Desegregation: A (September 1952) Social Science Statement in the Brown v. Board of Education of Topeka Supreme Court Case.' *American Psychologist* 59, no. 6 (September 2004): 495–501.

Clark, William. *Academic Charisma and the Origins of the Research University.* Chicago: University of Chicago Press, 2007.

Coelho, Anthony M. 'NIH Announces Updated Criteria for Evaluating Research Grant Applications.' *National Institutes of Health*, October 12, 2004. https://csde.washington.edu/research/funding/archive/nih_criteria.shtml.

Collini, Stefan. 'Browne's Gamble.' *London Review of Books* 32, no. 21 (November 4, 2010): 23–25.

——. *What Are Universities For?* London: Penguin Books, 2012.

Daniels, Norman, and James E. Sabin. *Setting Limits Fairly: Learning to Share Resources for Health.* New York: Oxford University Press, 2008.

Deaton, Angus. *The Great Escape: Health, Wealth, and the Origins of Inequality.* Princeton, NJ: Princeton University Press, 2013.

Dewan, Shalini S., Honey Dave, and Lakshmi Prasanna. *Antibody Drugs: Technologies and Global Markets.* Wellesley, MA: BCC Research, January 2015. http://www.bccresearch.com/market-research/biotechnology/antibody-drugs-market-bio016j.html.

Dickson, Del, ed. *The Supreme Court in Conference (1940–1985): The Private Discussions Behind Nearly 300 Supreme Court Decisions.* New York: Oxford University Press, 2001.

DiMasi, J. A., R. W. Hansen, and H. G. Grabowski. 'The Price of Innovation: New Estimates of Drug Development Costs.' *Journal of Health Economics* 22 (2003): 151–185.

Dirda, Michael. 'Freelance.' *Times Literary Supplement*, July 18, 2014. http://www.the-tls.co.uk/tls/reviews/arts_and_commentary/article1434651.ece.

Dorf, Michael C. 'Abstract and Concrete Review.' In *Global Perspectives on Constitutional Law*, edited by Vikram David Amar and Mark V. Tushnet, 3–14. New York: Oxford University Press, 2009.

Dorsey, E. Ray, Jason de Roulet, Joel P. Thompson, Jason I. Reminick, Ashley Thai, Zachary White-Stellato, Christopher A. Beck, Benjamin P. George, and Hamilton Moses. 'Funding of U.S. Biomedical Research, 2003–2008.' *Journal of the American Medical Association* 303 (January 13, 2010): 137–143.

Drakeman, Donald L. 'Benchmarking Biotech and Pharmaceutical Product Development.' *Nature Biotechnology* 32, no. 7 (2014): 621–625.

——. 'The Church Historians Who Made the First Amendment What It Is Today.' *Religion in American Culture* 17, no. 1 (Winter 2007): 27–56.

——. *Church, State, and Original Intent.* Cambridge: Cambridge University Press, 2010.

——. 'What's the Point of Originalism?' *Harvard Journal of Law and Public Policy* 37 (2014): 1124–1150.

Dreisbach, Daniel L. *Thomas Jefferson and the Wall of Separation Between Church and State.* New York: New York University Press, 2002.

Drivers, K., Z. Lei, and B. Wright. 'A Preliminary View of UC Data on Disclosures, Licensing, and Patenting.' Washington, DC: National Academy of Sciences, May 27, 2009. http://sites.nationalacademies.org/cs/groups/pgasite/documents/webpage/pga_058895.pdf.

Duarte, José L., Jarret T. Crawford, Jonathan Haidt, Lee Jussim, Philip E. Tetlock, and Jonathan Haidt. 'Political Diversity Will Improve Social Psychological Science.' Unpublished manuscript.

Dworkin, Ronald. 'Assisted Suicide: The Philosophers Brief.' *New York Review of Books* (March 27, 1997).

——. *Life's Dominion: An Argument About Abortion, Euthanasia and Individual Freedom.* New York: Alfred A. Knopf, 1993.

Eisgruber, Christopher L. *Constitutional Self-Government.* Cambridge, MA: Harvard University Press, 2007.

Eisgruber, Christopher L. and Lawrence G. Sager. *Religious Freedom and the Constitution.* Cambridge, MA: Harvard University Press, 2007.

Ekins, Richard. 'Equal Protection and Social Meaning.' *American Journal of Jurisprudence* 57, no. 1 (2012): 21–48.

Fallon, Jr., Richard H. 'Non-Legal Theory in Judicial Decision Making.' *Harvard Journal of Law and Public Policy* 17 (1994): 87–99.

Farr, James. 'Francis Lieber and the Interpretation of American Political Science.' *The Journal of Politics* 52, no. 4 (November 1990): 1027–1049.

Fast Facts. 'Degrees Conferred by Sex and Race.' *The National Center for Education Statistics.* http://nces.ed.gov/fastfacts/display.asp?id=72.

Fish, Stanley. *Save the World on Your Own Time.* New York: Oxford University Press, 2012.

——. 'Will the Humanities Save Us?' *Opinionator* (blog). *New York Times,* January 6, 2008. http://fish.blogs.nytimes.com/2008/01/01/will-the-humanities-save-us?_php=true&_type=blogs&-R=0.

Fleischacker, Samuel. *A Short History of Distributive Justice.* Cambridge, MA: Harvard University Press, 2004.

Foderaro, Lisa W. 'Budget-Cutting Colleges Bid Some Languages Adieu.' *New York Times,* December 3, 2010. http://www.nytimes.com/2010/12/05/education/05languages.html?pagewanted=all.

Fogel, Robert W. 'Economic Growth, Population Theory, and Physiology: The Bearing of Long-Term Processes on the Making of Economic Policy.' *The American Economic Review* 84, no. 3 (1994): 369–395.

Fontana, David. 'Response: Comparative Originalism.' *Texas Law Review* 78 (2009): 189–199.

Fonte, John. 'Is the Purpose of Civic Education to Transmit or Transform the American Regime?' In *Civic Education and Culture,* edited by Bradley C. S. Watson, 73–112. Wilmington, DE: Intercollegiate Studies Institute Press, 2005.

George, Robert P. *Conscience and Its Enemies: Confronting the Dogmas of Liberal Secularism.* Wilmington, DE: ISI Books, 2013.

Gibson, William. *A Social History of the Domestic Chaplain, 1530–1840.* London: Leicester University Press, 1997.

Gilbert, Jim, Preston Henske, and Ashish Singh. 'Rebuilding Big Pharma's Business Model.' *In Vivo: The Business & Medicine Report* 21, no. 10 (November 2003): 73–82.

Gordon, Sarah Barringer. *The Mormon Question: Polygamy and Constitutional Conflict in Nineteenth Century America*. Chapel Hill: University of North Carolina Press, 2002.

Greene, Jamal. 'On the Origins of Originalism.' *Texas Law Review* 88 (2009): 1–80.

Greene, Jamal, Nathaniel Persily, and Stephen Ansolabehere. 'Profiling Originalism.' *Columbia Law Review* 37, no. 3 (2011): 356–419.

Gross, Neil. *Why Are Professors Liberal and Why Do Conservatives Care?* Cambridge, MA: Harvard University Press, 2013.

Gross, Neil, and Solon Simmons. 'How Religious Are America's College and University Professors?' *SSRC*, February 6, 2007.

——. 'The Social and Political Views of American College and University Professors.' In *Professors and Their Politics*, edited by Neil Gross and Solon Simmons, 19–52. Baltimore, MD: Johns Hopkins University Press, 2014.

Hamburger, Philip. *Separation of Church and State*. Cambridge, MA: Harvard University Press, 2002.

Ham, C., and S. Pickard. 'Tragic Choices in Health Care: Lessons from the Child B Case.' *British Medical Journal* 319, no. 7219 (November 1999): 1258–1261.

Harris, Abram L. 'John Stuart Mill: Servant of the East India Company.' *The Canadian Journal of Economics and Political Science* 30, no. 2 (May 1964): 185–202.

Hathaway, Ian, and Robert E. Litan. 'Entrepreneurship and Job Creation in the US Life Sciences Sector.' *Economic Studies at Brookings* (June 2014): 1–10.

Hay, Michael, David W. Thomas, John L. Craighead, Celia Economides, and Jesse Rosenthal. 'Clinical Development Success Rates for Investigational Drugs.' *Nature Biotechnology* 32, no. 1 (January 2014): 40–51.

Health Economics Research Group. 'Annotated Bibliography.' In *Medical Research: What's It Worth? Estimating the Economic Benefits from Medical Research in the UK*. London: UK Evaluation Forum, 2008.

Heise, Michael. 'Brown v. Board of Education, Footnote 11, and Multidisciplinarity.' *Cornell Law Review* 90 (2005): 279–319.

Hevesi, Alan G., and Kenneth B. Bleiwas. *The Economic Impact of the Biotechnology and Pharmaceutical Industries in New York*. New York: Office of the State Comptroller, Report 11–2005, February 2005.

Holm, Poul, Arne Jarrick, and Dominic Scott. *Humanities World Report 2015*. Basingstoke, UK: Palgrave Macmillan, 2015.

Hope, Tony, John Reynolds, and Siân Griffiths. 'Rationing Decisions: Integrating Cost-Effectiveness with Other Values.' In *Medicine and Social Justice: Essays on the Distribution of Health Care*, edited by Rosamond Rhodes, Margaret P. Battin, and Anita Silvers, 144–155. New York: Oxford University Press, 2002.

Horwitz, Morton J. *The Warren Court and the Pursuit of Justice*. New York: Hill and Wang, 1998.

Howard, A. E. Dick. 'The Wall of Separation: The Supreme Court as Uncertain Stonemason.' In *Religion and the State: Essays in Honor of Leo Pfeffer*, edited by James E. Wood, Jr., 85–144. Waco, TX: Baylor University Press, 1985.

Howe, M. A. DeWolfe. *The Life and Letters of George Bancroft*. New York: Charles Scribner & Sons, 1908.

Howison, Robert R. *History of Virginia from Its Discovery and Settlement by Europeans to the Present Time*, 2 vols. Richmond, VA: Drinker and Morris, 1848.

Hughes, Alan, Michael Kitson, Jocelyn Probert, Royce Turner, Anna Bullock, and Isobel Milner. *Cultural Connections: The Role of the Arts and Humanities in Competitiveness and Local Development*. Cambridge: Centre for Business Research, University of Cambridge, March 2014. http://www.researchgate.net/profile/Michael_Kitson/publication/262818416_Cultural_Connections_The_Role_of_the_Arts_and_Humanities_in_Competitiveness_and_Local_Development/links/0c960538f12a0ca4d1000000?ev=pub_ext_doc_dl&origin=publication_detail&inViewer=true.

Hurst, Greg, Emily Gosden, Chris Davalle, and Matthew Lyons, eds. *The Times Guide to the House of Commons*. London: HarperCollins, 2010.

Huscroft, Grant, and Bradley W. Miller, eds. *The Challenge of Originalism: Theories of Constitutional Interpretation*. Cambridge: Cambridge University Press, 2011.

Intel Corporation. 'Fun Facts: Exactly How Small (and Cool) Is 22 Nanometers?' *Intel*. http://www.intel.com/content/dam/www/public/us/en/documents/corporate-information/history-moores-law-fun-facts-factsheet.pdf.

——. 'Moore's Law and Intel Innovation.' *Intel*. http://www.intel.com/content/www/us/en/history/museum-gordon-moore-law.html.

Jaschik, Scott. 'Disappearing Languages at Albany.' *Inside Higher Ed*, October 4, 2010. http://www.insidehighered.com/layout/set/print/news/2010/10/04/albany.

——. 'Obama vs. Art History.' *Inside Higher Ed*, January 31, 2014. https://www.insidehighered.com/news/2014/01/31/obama-becomes-latest-politician-criticize-liberal-arts-discipline.

Jefferson, Thomas. 'A Bill for Establishing Religious Freedom, 1779 and 1786.' In *The Sacred Rights of Conscience: Selected Readings on Religious Liberty and Church-State Relations in the American Founding*, edited by Daniel L. Dreisbach and Mark David Hall, 250. Indianapolis, IN: Liberty Fund, 2009.

Johnson, Paul. 'Dirty Rotten Scholars.' *The Spectator*, February 26, 2011. http://www.spectator.co.uk/print/essays/6725758/dirty-rotten-scholars.html.

Jones, Jeffrey M. 'Few Americans Oppose National Day of Prayer.' *Gallup*, May 5, 2010. http://www.gallup.com/poll/127721/few-americans-oppose-national-day-payers.aspx.

——. 'Liberal Self-Identification Edges Up to New High in 2012.' *Gallup*. http://www.gallup.com/poll/166787/liberal-self-identification-edges-new-high-2013.aspx.

Jones, Mark. 'The Invention of Recombinant DNA Technology.' *LSF Magazine*, Summer 2013. http://zrnage.com/magazine-invention_of_recombinant_dna_technology.htm.

Jump, Paul. 'Chemists: Public Backs STEM Spending Formula.' *Times Higher Education*, October 14, 2010. http://www.timeshighereducation.co.uk/news/chemists-public-backs-stem-spending-formula/413851.article.

Kanazawa, Satoshi. 'Why Liberals and Atheists Are More Intelligent.' *Social Psychology Quarterly* 73, no. 1 (2010): 33–57.

Kane, Paul. 'Kagan Sidesteps Empathy Question, Says "It's Law All the Way Down."' *Washington Post*, June 29, 2010. http://www.washingtonpost.com/wp-dyn/content/article/2010/06/29/AR2010062903935.html.

Katwala, Sunder. 'The NHS: Even More Cherished than Monarchy and the Army.' *New Statesman*, January 14, 2013. http://www.newstateman.com/politics/2013/01/nhs-even-more-cherished-monarchy-and-army.

Kearl, Megan. 'Dickey-Wicker Amendment.' *Embryo Project Encyclopedia*, September 25, 2013. http://embryo.asu.edu/handle/10776/2050.

Kent, William. *Commentaries on American Law*, 7th edition. New York: William Kent, 1851.

Keohane, Nannerl O. 'The Liberal Arts as Guideposts in the 21st Century.' *The Chronicle of Higher Education*, January 29, 2012. http://chronicle.com/article/The-Liberal-Arts-as-Guideposts/130475/.

Kilpatrick, James Jackson. *The Southern Case for School Segregation*. Springfield, OH: The Crowell-Collier Press, 1962.

Kluger, Richard. *Simple Justice: The History of Brown v. Board of Education and Black America's Struggle for Equality*. New York: Random House, Inc., 2004.

Kneller, Robert. 'The Importance of New Companies for Drug Discovery: Origins of a Decade of New Drugs.' *Nature Reviews Drug Discovery* 9 (November 2010): 869–870.

Köehler, G., and C. Milstein. 'Continuous Cultures of Fused Cells Secreting Antibody of Predefined Specificity.' *Nature* 256 (August 7, 1975): 495–497.

Kreager, Philip. *Humanities Graduates and the British Economy: The Hidden Impact*. Oxford: Oxford University, July 2013. http://torch.ox.ac.uk/sites/torch/files/publications/Humanities%20Graduates%20and%20the%20British%20Economy%20-%20University%20of%20Oxford.pdf.

Kronman, Anthony T. *Education's End: Why Our Colleges and Universities Have Given Up on the Meaning of Life*. New Haven, CT: Yale University Press, 2007.

Kumar, Harpal. 'Years of Crucial Investment Could Fall by the Wayside.' *The Times*, September 8, 2010.

Kurland, Philip B. 'The Origins of the Religion Clauses of the Constitution.' *William and Mary Law Review* 27 (1985–1986): 839–861.

Kurtz, Howard. 'College Faculties a Most Liberal Lot, Study Finds.' *The Washington Post*, March 29, 2005. http://www.washingtonpost.com/wp-dyn/articles/A8427-2005Mar28.html.

Ladd, Everett Carl, and Seymour Martin Lipset. *The Divided Academy: Professors and Politics*. New York: W. W. Norton & Co., 1976.

Lamont, Julian, and Christi Favor. 'Distributive Justice.' *Stanford Encyclopedia of Philosophy*, January 2, 2013. http://plato.stanford.edu/entries/justice-distributive.

Langford, Paul. *'That Full Complement of Riches': The Contributions of the Arts, Humanities and Social Sciences to the Nation's Wealth*. London: The British Academy, 2004.

Larson, Leslie. 'Marco Rubio Disses Obama's "Pathetic" Apology to Art History Majors.' *New York Daily News*, February 19, 2014. http://www.nydailynews.com/news/politics/marco-rubio-slams-obama-art-history-apology-article-1.1619563.

Lazarfeld, Paul, and Wagner Thielens, Jr. *The Academic Mind: Social Scientists in a Time of Crisis*. New York: Free Press, 1958.

Lepore, Jill. *The Whites of Their Eyes: The Tea Party's Revolution and the Battle over American History*. Princeton, NJ: Princeton University Press, 2010.

Levitt, Ruth, Claire Celia, Stephanie Diepeveen, Siobhan Ni Chronall, Lilla Ratinovich, and Jan Tiessen. *Assessing the Impact of Arts and Humanities Research at Cambridge*. Santa Monica, CA: RAND Corporation, 2010. http://www.rand.org/content/dam/rand/pubs/technical_reports/2010/RAND_TR816.pdf.

——. *Assessing the Impact of Arts and Humanities Research at the University of Cambridge*. RAND Technical Report, 2010.

Levy, Leonard W. *Original Intent and the Framers Constitution*. New York: Macmillan Company, 1988.

Lewis, Harry R. *Excellence Without a Soul: Does Liberal Education Have a Future?* New York: Public Affairs, 2007.

Lieber, Francis. *Manual of Political Ethics*. Philadelphia: J. B. Lippincott Company, 1911.

Longaker, Michael T., Laurence C. Baker and Henry T. Greely. 'Proposition 71 and CIRM – Assessing the Return on Investment.' *Nature Biotechnology* 25, no. 5 (May 2007): 513–521.

Madison, James. 'Monopolies, Perpetuities, Corporations Ecclesiastical Endowments.' In Elizabeth Fleet, 'Madison's "Detached Memorandum,"' *William and Mary Quarterly* 3, no. 4 (1946): 535–536.

Magrath, C. Peter. 'Chief Justice Waite and the "Twin Relic": Reynolds v. United States.' *Vanderbilt Law Review* 18, no. 2 (March 1965): 507–543.

——. *Morrison R. Waite: The Triumph of Character*. New York: Macmillan Company, 1963.

Malcolm, Joyce Lee. 'The Supreme Court and the Uses of History: *District of Columbia v. Heller*.' *UCLA Law Review* 56 (2008–2009): 1378–1397.

Matthews, David. 'A How-Not-To Guide to Defending Humanities.' *Times Higher Education Supplement* no. 2124 (October 24, 2013): 11. http://www.timeshighereducation.co.uk/tablet/71E628B5/2008395.shared.

Maranto, Robert, Richard E. Redding, and Frederick M. Hess, eds. *The Politically Correct University: Problems, Scope, and Reforms.* Washington, DC: AEI Press, 2009.

Marks, Lara V. *The Lock and Key of Medicine: Monoclonal Antibodies and Their Transformation of Healthcare.* New Haven, CT: Yale University Press, 2015.

Martin. Taylor. 'The Scientific Century: Securing Our Future Prosperity.' *The Royal Society*, March 9, 2010. https://royalsociety.org/policy/publications/2010/scientific-century/.

McClay, Wilfred M. 'The Burden of the Humanities.' *Wilson Quarterly* 32, no. 3 (Summer 2008): 34–43.

McConnell, Michael. 'Originalism and the Desegregation Decisions.' *Virginia Law Review* 81 (1995): 947–1140.

McMartrie, Beth. 'Political Scientists Propose New Ways to Engage Policy Makers and the Public.' *The Chronicle of Higher Education*, August 29, 2014. http://chronicle.com/article/political-scientists-propose/148523/?cid=at&utm_source=at&utm_medium=en.

Meese III, Edwin. 'Speech of Attorney General Edwin Meese III to the American Bar Association.' Washington, DC, July 9, 1985. http://www.Fed-soc.org/resources/id.49/default.asp.

Menand, Louis. *The Marketplace of Ideas: Reform and Resistance in the American Research University.* New York: W. W. Norton & Company, Inc., 2010.

Merrill, Stephen A., and Anne-Marie Mazza, eds. *Managing University Intellectual Property in the Public Interest.* Washington, DC: The National Academy Press, 2011.

Minow, Martha. *In Brown's Wake: Legacies of America's Educational Landmark.* New York: Oxford University Press, 2010.

Morgan, John. 'The Appliance of Extra Science Is No Economic Panacea.' *Times Higher Education* (August 26, 2010): 6. http://www.timeshighereducation.co.uk/413171.article.

——. 'What Would Lindsay Say? Keele's Plan to Shut Philosophy and Ethics Units Is a "Disaster," Say Scholars.' *Times Higher Education*, March 24, 2011. http://www.timeshighereducation.co.uk/news/what-would-lindsay-say/415593.article.

MRC Delivery Plan 2011/12 to 2014/15. Swindon: Medical Research Council, 2010.

Mueller, Tracy. 'The Famous Obama Apology Note and the Truth About Art History.' *UT Know*, February 20, 2014. http://www.utexas.edu/know/2014/02/20/obama-art-history-apology-letter/.

Muños, Bernard. 'Lessons from 60 Years of Pharmaceutical Innovation.' *Nature Reviews Drug Discovery* 8 (2009): 959–968.

Muñoz, Vincent Phillip. *God and the Founders: Madison, Washington, and Jefferson.* Cambridge: Cambridge University Press, 2009.

Murphy, Kevin M., and Robert H. Topel. 'The Economic Value of Medical Research.' In *Measuring the Gains from Medical Research: An Economic Approach*, edited by Kevin M. Murphy and Robert H. Topel, 41–73. Chicago: University of Chicago Press, 2003.

National Association of Scholars. 'The Vanishing West: 1964–2010'; 'Recasting History: Are Race, Class, and Gender Dominating American History?'; and 'What Does Bowdoin Teach? How a Contemporary Liberal Arts College Shapes Students.' www.nas.org.

National Humanities Alliance. *Now More than Ever: Why America Needs the Humanities in the 21st Century*. November 2008.

National Institutes of Health. *NIH Report to Congress: A Plan to Ensure Taxpayers' Interests Are Protected* (July 2001). http://www.nih.gov/news/070101wyden.htm.

National Institute for Health and Clinical Excellence. *Social Value Judgements: Principles for the Development of NICE Guidance*. 2nd edition. London: NICE, 2008.

Newman, John Henry. *The Idea of a University*. Notre Dame, IN: University of Notre Dame Press, 1982.

Newman, Roger. *Hugo Black: A Biography*. New York: Fordham University Press, 1997.

Nussbaum, Martha. *Liberty of Conscience: In Defense of America's Tradition of Religious Equality*. New York: Basic Books, 2008.

——. *Not for Profit: Why Democracy Needs the Humanities*. Princeton, NJ: Princeton University Press, 2010.

Nye, Russell B. *George Bancroft: Brahmin Rebel*. New York: Alfred A. Knopf, 1945.

Obama, Barack. 'Removing Barriers to Responsible Scientific Research Involving Human Stem Cells.' The White House, Executive Order 13505, March 9, 2009. http://www.whitehouse.gov/the_press_office/Removing-Barriers-to-Responsible-Scientific-Research-Involving-Human-Stem-Cells/.

Office of Fair Trading. *The Pharmaceutical Price Regulation Scheme: An OFT Market Study*. London: Office of Fair Trading, 2007.

O'Neill, Johnathan. *Originalism in American Law and Politics: A Constitutional History*. Baltimore, MD: Johns Hopkins University Press, 2007.

Organization for Economic Co-operation and Development. 'Pharmaceutical Expenditure.' In *Health at a Glance 2011: OECD Indicators*, edited by OECD Publishing, 154–155. Paris: OECD Publications, 2011.

Page, Scott E. *The Difference: How the Power of Diversity Creates Better Groups, Firms, Schools, and Societies*. Princeton, NJ: Princeton University Press, 2007.

Parsons, Jr., Theophilus. *Memoir of Theophilus Parsons, Chief Justice of the Supreme Judicial Court of Massachusetts*. Boston: Ticknor and Fields, 1859.

PayScale. '2013–2014 PayScale College Salary Report.' www.payscale.com/college-salary-report-2014/majors-that-pay-you-back.

Philippidis, Alex. 'Top 20 Best-Selling Drugs of 2012.' *Genetic Engineering & Biotechnology News*, March 5, 2013. http://www.genengnews.com/insight-and-intelligence/top-20-best-selling-drugs-of-2012/77899775/?page=2.

'Philosophical View: Middlesex, Think Again.' *Times Higher Education Supplement*, May 6, 2010. http://www.timeshighereducation.co.uk/411499.article.

Porter, Kirk H., and Donald B. Johnson, eds. *National Party Platforms 1840–1960*. Champaign, IL: University of Illinois Press, 1966.

Powe, Jr., Lucas A. *The Warren Court and American Politics*. Cambridge: Harvard University Press, 2000.

Pradhan, Arundeep S. 'Defending the University Tech Transfer System.' *Businessweek*, February 19, 2010. http://www.businessweek.com/smallbiz/content/feb2010/sb20100219_307735.htm.

Preqin Special Report: Venture Capital. Preqin, November 2014.

The President's Council of Bioethics. 'Current Federal Law and Policy.' In *Monitoring Stem Cell Research*. Washington, DC: January 2004.

Prince, Michael J., Richard M. Felder, and Rebecca Brent. 'Does Faculty Research Improve Undergraduate Teaching? An Analysis of Existing and Potential Strategies.' *Journal of Engineering Education* 96, no. 4 (2007): 283–294.

'Principle 6.' *The NHS Constitution*. NHS, March 26, 2013.

Ramsden, Brian. *Institutional Diversity in UK Higher Education*. Oxford: HEPI, 2012.

Rao, Neomi. 'A Backdoor to Policy Making: The Use of Philosophers by the Supreme Court.' *University of Chicago Law Review* 65 (1998): 1371–1401.

Rawlins, Michael D., and Anthony J. Culyer. 'National Institute for Clinical Excellence and Its Value Judgments.' *British Medical Journal* 329, no. 7459 (2004): 224–227.

'Remarks Made by the President, Prime Minister Tony Blair of England (via satellite), Dr. Francis Collins, Director of the National Human Genome Research Institute, and Dr. Craig Venter, President and Chief Scientific Officer, Celera Genomics Corporation, on the Completion of the First Survey of the Entire Human Genome Project.' *National Human Genome Research Institute*, June 26, 2000. http://www.genome.gov/10001356.

'Report of the Faculty.' In 'Reports on the Course of Instruction in Yale College (1828).' Reprinted in David B. Potts. *Liberal Education for a Land of Colleges: Yale's Reports of 1828*, 84–140. New York: Palgrave Macmillan, 2010.

Reston, James. 'A Sociological Decision.' *New York Times*, May 18, 1954.

Richardson, Hannah. 'Humanities to Lose English Universities Teaching Grant.' *BBC News*, October 26, 2010. www.bbc.com/news/education-11627843.

Riffkin, Rebecca. 'In US, Support for Daily Prayer in Schools Dips Slightly.' *Gallup*, September 25, 2014. http://www.gallup.com/poll/177401/support-daily-prayer-schools-dips-slightly.aspx.

Rivard, Ry. 'Gauging Graduates' Well-Being.' *Inside Higher Ed*, May 6, 2014. https://www.insidehigher-ed.com/news/2014/05/06/gallup-surveys-graduates-gauge-whether-and-why-college-good-well-being.

Roche, Mark William. *Why Choose the Liberal Arts?* South Bend, IN: University of Notre Dame Press, 2010.

Rockey, Sally. 'FY2012 by the Numbers: Success Rates, Applications, Investigators, and Awards.' *National Institutes of Health*, January 2, 2013. http://nexus.od.nih.gov/all/2013/01/02/fy2012-by-the-numbers-success-rates-applications-investigators-and-awards/.

Roemer, John. *Theories of Distributive Justice.* Cambridge, MA: Harvard University Press, 1996.

Rothman, Stanley, April Kelly-Woessner, and Matthew Woessner. *The Still Divided Academy: How Competing Vision of Power, Politics, and Diversity Complicate the Mission of Higher Education.* Lanham, MD: Rowman & Littlefield Publishers, Inc., 2011.

Rothman, Stanley S., Robert Lichter, and Neil Nevitte. 'Politics and Professional Advancement Among College Faculty.' *The Forum* 3, no. 1 (2005): 1–16.

Rudolph, Frederick. *The American College and University: A History.* Athens, GA: University of Georgia Press, 1962.

Ryan, Alan. *Liberal Anxieties and Liberal Education.* New York: Hill and Wang, 1998.

——. 'Not Just How, but Why: Insight and Independent Thinking Are Truly Vocational Skills, Argues Alan Ryan.' *Times Higher Education*, October 14, 2010. http://www.timeshighereducation.co.uk/comment/columnists/not-just-how-but-why/413855.article.

Sanna, Ellyn. 'Biography of T. S. Eliot.' In *T. S. Eliot*, edited by Harold Bloom, 3–44. Broomall, PA: Chelsea House, 2003.

Scalia, Antonin. *A Matter of Interpretation: Federal Courts and the Law.* Princeton, NJ: Princeton University Press, 1998.

——. 'Originalism: The Lesser Evil.' *University of Cincinnati Law Review* 57 (1988–1989): 894–865.

Sedghi, Ami. 'Graduate Employment: By Skill, Subject and Graduation.' *The Guardian*, March 6, 2012. http://www.theguardian.com/news/datablog/2012/mar/06/graduate.employment-low-skill-jobs.

Seneca, Joseph J., and Will Irving. *The Economic Benefits of the New Jersey Stem Cell Research Initiative.* Rutgers University: Edward J. Bloustein School of Planning and Public Policy, September 2005. http://policy.rutgers.edu/news/press/stemcell.pdf.

——. *Updated Economic Benefits of the New Jersey Stem Cell Capital Project and Research Bond Acts.* Rutgers University: Edward J. Bloustein School of Planning and Public Policy, October 2007. http://www.policy.rutgers.edu/reports/other/stemcelloct07.pdf.

Service, Robert F. 'Surviving the Blockbuster Syndrome.' *Science* 303 (March 19, 2004): 1796–1799.

Shields, Lt. Commander W. S. 'Note – A Note on the Criss-Cross Algorithm.' *Management Science* 23, no. 1 (1976): 426–445.

'Should You Attend that Interdisciplinary Conference?' *The Chronicle of Higher Education*, December 16, 2014. https://chroniclevitae.com/news/835-should-you-attend-that-interdisciplinary-conference?cid=at&utm.source=at&utm_medium=en.

Silbey, David. 'A Crisis in the Humanities?' *The Edge of the American West* (blog). *The Chronicle of Higher Education*, June 10, 2013. http://chronicle.com/blognetwork/edgeofthewest/2013/06/10/the-humanities-crisis/.

Simpson, James, and Sean Kelly. *The Teaching of the Arts and Humanities at Harvard College: Mapping the Future.* Cambridge, MA: Harvard University,

May 31, 2013. http://artsandhumanities.fas.harvard.edu/files/humanities/files/mapping_the_future_31_may_2013.pdf.
Small, Helen. *The Value of the Humanities*. Oxford: Oxford University Press, 2013.
Smith, Peter, and Geoffrey Summerfield, eds. *Matthew Arnold and the Education of the New Order.* Cambridge: Cambridge University Press, 1969.
Stevens, Ashley J., Jonathan J. Jensen, Katrine Wyller, Patrick C. Kilgore, Sabarni Chatterjee, and Mark L. Rohrbaugh. 'The Role of Public-Sector Research in the Discovery of Drugs and Vaccines.' *The New England Journal of Medicine* 364, no. 6 (2011): 535–541.
Todd, Leonard. *Carolina Clay: The Life and Legend of the Slave Potter Dave.* New York: W. W. Norton & Co., 2008.
Toole, Andrew A. 'Does Public Scientific Research Complement Private Investment in Research and Development in the Pharmaceutical Industry?' *Journal of Law and Economics* 50 (2007): 81–96.
Townsend, Robert B. 'New Study Highlights Prominence of Elite PhD Programs in History.' *Perspectives on History*, October 2005. http://www.historians.org/publications-and-directories/perspectives-on-history/October-2005/new-study-highlights-prominence-of-elite-phd-programs-in-history.
'Trend Away from the Humanities.' *The Princeton Alumni Weekly* 36, no. 16 (January 31, 1936): 369.
Trimble, Bruce R. *Chief Justice Waite: Defender of the Public Interest*. Princeton, NJ: Princeton University Press, 1938.
Turner, James. *Philology: The Forgotten Origins of the Modern Humanities*. Princeton, NJ: Princeton University Press, 2014.
'University of California at Los Angeles, Mission Statement.' http://www.ucla.edu/about/mission-and-values.
'University of Cambridge Mission Statement.' http://www.cam.ac.uk/about-the-university/how-the-university-and-colleges-work/the-universitys-mission-and-core-values.
University of Cambridge. 'Research Excellence Framework Confirms Cambridge's Global Strength and Depth in Research.' http://www.cam.ac.uk/research/news/research-excellence-framework-confirms-cambridges-global-strength-and-depth-in-research.
——. 'Research into the Impacts of Arts and Humanities Research at the University of Cambridge: Invitation to Tender Documents.' 2009.
Van Duffel, Siegfried, and Dennis Yap. 'Distributive Justice Before the Eighteenth Century: The Right of Necessity.' *History of Political Thought* 32, no. 3 (2011): 449–464.
Voice of the Graduate. New York: McKinsey & Company, May 2013. http://mckinseyonsociety.com/downloads/reports/Education/UXC001%20Voice%20of%20the%20Graduate%20v7.pdf.
Washington Post-Kaiser Family Foundation-Harvard University. *Role of Government Survey*. Menlo Park, CA: The Henry J. Kaiser Family Foundation (September 22–October 3, 2010): 1–21. http://www.washingtonpost.com/

wp-srv/special/politics/Post-Kaiser-Harvard-Role-of-Government-2010.pdf.

Watson, Bradley C. S., ed. *Civic Education and Culture*. Wilmington, DE: ISI Books, 2005.

Weisman, Jordan. 'The Best Argument for Studying English? The Employment Numbers.' *The Atlantic*, June 25, 2013. http://www.theatlantic.com/business/archive/2013/06/the-best-argument-for-studying-english-the-employment-numbers/277162/.

Whitehead, Frederika. 'Middlesex Philosophers Celebrate Survival.' *The Guardian*, June 10, 2010. http://www.theguardian.com/education/2010/jun/10/middlesex-philosophers-celebrate-survival.

White, Susan, Raymond Chu, and Roman Czujko. *The 2012–13 Survey of Humanities Departments at Four-Year Institutions*. College Park, MD: Statistical Research Center, American Institute of Physics, 2014.

Willetts, David. 'A Mistaken Conception that the University System Is Under Attack.' *Times Higher Education*, March 1, 2012. http://www.timeshighereducation.co.uk/news/a-mistaken-conception-that-the-university-system-is-under-attack/419209.article.

Williams, Bernard. *Essay and Reviews 1959–2002*. Princeton, NJ: Princeton University Press, 2014.

Zider, Alexander S., and Donald L. Drakeman. 'The Future of Monoclonal Antibody Technology.' *MAbs* 2, no. 4 (2010): 361–364.

Index

CPSIA information can be obtained at www.ICGtesting.com
Printed in the USA
LVOW10s0040130716

496088LV00027B/440/P

9 781137 497468